COLUMBIA CRITICAL GUIDES

Joseph Conrad

Heart of Darkness

EDITED BY NICOLAS TREDELL

Series editor: Richard Beynon

COLUMBIA UNIVERSITY PRESS ◆ NEW YORK

Columbia University Press
Publishers Since 1893
New York

First published in the Icon Critical Guides series in 1998 by Icon
Books Ltd.

Library of Congress Cataloging-in-Publication Data

Joseph Conrad : Heart of darkness / edited by Nicolas Tredell.
    p. cm. — (Columbia critical guides)
   Includes bibliographical references and index.
   ISBN 0–231–11922–4 (cloth : alk. paper). —
   ISBN 0–231–11923–2 (pbk. : alk. paper)
    1. Conrad, Joseph, 1857–1924. Heart of darkness.
  2. Psychological fiction, English—History and criticism.
  3. Africa—In literature. I. Tredell, Nicolas. II. Series.
PR6005.04H4768   2000
823'.912—dc21   99–41365

⊗

c 10 9 8 7 6 5 4 3 2 1
p 10 9 8 7 6 5 4 3 2 1

Contents

New Maps of Hell: Rereading 'Heart of Darkness' in the 1980s

Examines four of the most powerful new readings of 'Heart of Darkness' produced in the 1980s: Benita Parry's critique of its subversion and final reinforcement of imperialism; Peter Brooks's compelling analysis of its narrative complexities; Christopher L. Miller's balanced account of its place within Africanist discourse; and Nina Pelikan Straus's trenchant indictment of its sexism.

Metonymy, Neo-imperialism and a Biscuit-tin: Fresh Paths in 'Heart of Darkness' Criticism in the 1990s

Considers three crucial readings of 'Heart of Darkness' in the 1990s: Gail Fincham's examination of the function of metonymy in the novel's representation of colonialist and racist attitudes; Edward W. Said's investigation of its relation to the discourses of imperialism and neo-imperialism; and Valentine Cunningham's vivid tracing of the tortuous and surprising paths between the Congo and Reading Gaol.

A NOTE ON REFERENCES AND QUOTATIONS

Cross-references to the extracts in this Guide, and references to the 1995 Penguin edition of 'Heart of Darkness', edited by Robert Hampson, are given in brackets in the text of the Guide. Other page references are given in the endnotes. As 'Heart of Darkness' is, strictly speaking, a long short story or novella, its title is rendered in quotation marks throughout the Guide.

All quotations from 'Heart of Darkness' have been amended to accord with the Penguin edition. Non-indented quotations from Marlow should properly be in two sets of quotation marks, and while this Guide, like Peter Brooks (see p. 172, note 21), eliminates the first set for simplicity's sake, it remains significant that all Marlow's words are supposedly transmitted by the first narrator. In any quotation, a row of three dots indicates an editorial ellipsis within a sentence or paragraph, and a row of six dots indicates an editorial omission of one or more paragraphs, or of a paragraph break or section break.

INTRODUCTION

' HEART OF Darkness', first published in 1899, is one of the most potent texts of the twentieth century. This short work, hardly long enough to be called a novel, has produced a vast array of readings and has recently provoked intense controversy. But whether hailed as a masterpiece, or reviled as racist and sexist, it seems impossible to ignore. Its title and themes are likely to be invoked in discussions of the human condition, of good and evil, and of imperialism and its consequences; in any gathering of readers, or company of critics, it is likely to disturb and compel. This Guide aims to trace the critical history of 'Heart of Darkness' from the first reviews to the latest readings, and to select, from the huge range of available material, the most perceptive and relevant interpretations and evaluations. In this Introduction, 'Heart of Darkness' is set in the context of Conrad's life, and the criticism on which the Guide will focus is outlined.

It is useful to start by recalling Conrad's original name: Józef Teodor Konrad Nałęcz Korzeniowski. To do so is to highlight the otherness of this writer who identified himself so closely with England but who remained, in crucial respects, forever different. The boy who was later to become Joseph Conrad was born in 1857 at Berdyczów, in what is now the Ukraine; his father, Apollo, a romantic nationalist ardently opposed to Russian domination, was also a poet, playwright and translator. The Korzeniowskis moved to Warsaw in 1861, where a national resistance movement was centred, but Apollo's political activities soon led to his arrest and to his exile, with his wife and small son, to Vologda in northeast Russia. In 1863, the family were allowed to move to Cherikhov, but Conrad's mother died in 1865, when he was seven. Apollo, bitter and depressed, his lungs racked by consumption, was allowed to return from exile in 1867, and settled with his son at Lvov. The boy went to preparatory school, started to write plays, and read avidly. But his father was dying. Conrad later recalled the importance of reading as a refuge at this time: 'I don't know what would have become of me if I had not been a reading boy'.[1] In February 1869, father and son moved to Kraków, and on 23 May of that year Apollo died.

The young Józef, aged eleven, was then looked after by Thaddeus

Bobrowski, his wealthy uncle. In 1874, Thaddeus allowed his nephew, who had reached the age of sixteen, to fulfil a wish that had been developing for some time and become a sailor. He went to France to join the French merchant marine, and in 1875 sailed for the West Indies. But his personal and working life were unhappy; he fell heavily into debt; and in February 1878, he tried to kill himself. He had a miraculous escape; the bullet passed through his body but missed his heart. After this close encounter with death, he resolved to start a new life.

The first stage of this new life would be as a sailor in the British Merchant Navy; and here Conrad would have some success. He passed examinations to become a second mate in 1880, a first mate in 1884, and finally, in 1886, a Master. In that year, he also became a naturalised British subject, and apparently wrote his first short story, 'The Black Mate', before going on to begin a novel, *Almayer's Folly*, in 1889. But until that novel was published six years later, he was still, to all outward appearances, more seaman than writer. His voyages between December 1874 and January 1894 took him around the globe, to Sydney, Singapore, Bombay, the East Indies – and, very significantly for 'Heart of Darkness', to Africa.

By his own account, in the essay 'Geography and Some Explorers', Africa had long fascinated Conrad. Addicted as a boy to 'map-gazing',[2] he had aroused the derision of his schoolmates one day by 'putting [his] finger on a spot in the very middle of the then white heart of Africa' and declaring that 'some day I would go there'.[3] In 1890, at a time when Africa was the subject of intense newspaper interest because of Henry Morton Stanley's successful quest for Livingstone, Conrad at last made good his schoolboy boast, securing a post as steamboat captain with the company responsible for trading in the Belgian Congo. The boat to which he had been appointed was to take an exploring expedition, led by Alexandre Delcommune, from Kinshasa to Katanga. On 12 June 1890, Conrad landed in the Congo at Boma, moved on to Matadi, and then, on 28 June, set off on the 230-mile trek to Kinshasa, making brief entries in a diary as he travelled. The journey usually took about seventeen days, but Conrad's lasted thirty-five. This delay displeased the manager of the Kinshasa station, Camille Delcommune, the brother of the leader of the proposed Katanga expedition; he received Conrad coldly, and the feeling was mutual. In a letter to an aunt, Conrad called Delcommune 'a common ivory-dealer with base instincts'.[4] The boat Conrad had hoped to command was damaged, but on 13 August he and Camille Delcommune set off on the 1,000 mile journey up the Congo to Stanley Falls in what Conrad later recalled as 'a wretched little stern-wheel steamboat', the *Roi des Belges* (*King of the Belgians*); Conrad, as he himself put it, 'went as a supernumerary on board . . . in order to learn about the river'.[5]

In 'Geography and Some Explorers', he evokes a moment that sums up his complex feelings on at last reaching Stanley Falls. Alone on the deck of the steamer, 'smoking the pipe of peace after an anxious day' and with the 'subdued thundering mutter' of the Falls hanging 'in the heavy night air', he says to himself 'with awe, "This is the very spot of my boyish boast"'. But a 'great melancholy' then falls on him at the contrast between 'the idealized realities of a boy's daydreams' and 'the unholy recollection of a prosaic newspaper "stunt"' – Stanley's quest for Livingstone – and 'the distasteful knowledge of the vilest scramble for loot that ever disfigured the history of the human conscience and geographical exploration' – the European exploitation of the Belgian Congo.[6] It is this painful contradiction between dream and reality that seems to have formed the basis of 'Heart of Darkness'.

When the captain of the *Roi des Belges* steamer fell ill, Conrad took command for part of the journey back to Kinshasa. But he himself had suffered from fever and dysentery during the voyage, and after arriving in Kinshasa on 24 September, he acknowledged that he felt 'somewhat weak physically and not a little demoralized'.[7] He had no ship to command, and he could see no chance of promotion or a higher salary while Camille Delcommune was manager. Soon he was seriously ill. Much to his relief, the company released him from his three-year contract, and he returned to England in January 1891, going into hospital in London and then convalescing at Champel near Geneva. His attempt to fulfil his boyhood dream had been a painful, disillusioning experience.

It would be some years, however, before that experience fed into 'Heart of Darkness'. In the meantime, Conrad made the transition from seaman to writer, and from bachelor to husband. *Almayer's Folly* appeared in 1895, and he married Jessie George in March 1896. In the same year, *An Outcast of the Islands* came out, and *The Nigger of the 'Narcissus'* was published in 1897. It was also in 1897 that he began to write for *Blackwood's Magazine*, where the first version of 'Heart of Darkness' – or 'The Heart of Darkness', as it was initially called – would appear, in instalments, in 1899.

On 30 December 1898, William Blackwood, the magazine's proprietor and editor, had written to Conrad asking for a contribution for the February issue, which would be the thousandth number. Conrad quickly replied that he was already working on a story that was well advanced and should be finished in a few days. He called it 'a narrative after the manner of *youth* [*sic*] told by the same man [Marlow] dealing with his experiences on a river in Central Africa'; but he expressed reservations as to its suitability for the issue Blackwood had in mind. Affirming that he had 'no doubts as to the *workmanship*', he said that the '*idea* in it is not as obvious as in *youth* – or at least not so obviously presented' and that he did not 'know whether the *subject* will commend itself to you for that particular number'.[8] He then went on:

■ The title I am thinking of is 'The Heart of Darkness' but the narrative is not gloomy. The criminality of inefficiency and pure selfishness when tackling the civilizing work in Africa is a justifiable idea. The subject is of our time distinc[t]ly – though not topically treated. It is a story as much as my *Outpost of Progress* was but, so to speak, 'takes in' more – is a little wider – is less concentrated upon individuals.[9] □

Despite Conrad's doubts, the first part of 'Heart of Darkness' did appear in the thousandth issue of *Blackwood's Magazine*. Conrad found, as he went on with the story, that it expanded beyond his original conception – '[t]he thing has grown on me'[10] – and he continued to feel it might present difficulties of interpretation. Writing to his friend R. B. Cunninghame Graham on 8 February 1899, he avowed himself 'in the seventh heaven' because Graham liked the story so far; but he also warned of two more instalments to come 'in which the idea is so wrapped up in secondary notions that You – even You! – may miss it'.[11] He went on to tell Graham that '[y]ou must remember that I don't start with an abstract notion. I start with definite images and as their rendering is true some little effect is produced',[12] and then reiterated his apprehension about Graham's response to the forthcoming episodes, saying that '[s]o far the note struck chimes in with your convictions – mais après [but after?]? There is an après'. He thought, however, that if Graham looked 'a little into the episodes you will find in them the right intention though I fear nothing that is practically effective'.[13]

Conrad completed the tale, though telling John Galsworthy that the 'finishing of [it] took a lot out of me'.[14] Three years later, towards the end of 1902, Blackwood brought out a volume in which 'Youth', the title story, was accompanied by 'The End of the Tether' and by 'Heart of Darkness'. Earlier that year, Conrad had looked back on 'Heart of Darkness', along with 'Youth', as 'a thing intimately felt'[15] and had stressed its seriousness and substance. Writing to his French translator, H-D. Davray, on 10 April 1902, he called it 'a wild story of a journalist who becomes manager of a station in the interior and makes himself worshipped by a tribe of savages', and said '[t]hus described, the subject seems comic, but it isn't'.[16] In a letter to Blackwood himself on 31 May 1902, he spoke of his method as one in which 'the final incident' of a story functioned to make 'the whole story in all its descriptive detail . . . fall into place [and] acquire its value and significance', and he cited 'Heart of Darkness' as one example of this method:

■ [In] the last pages of ['Heart of Darkness'] the interview of the man and girl locks in – as it were – the whole 30000 words of narrative description into one suggestive view of a whole phase of life and makes of that story something quite on another plane than an anecdote of a man who went mad in the Centre of Africa.[17] □

Conrad's claim that 'Heart of Darkness' was 'quite on another plane than an anecdote of a man who went mad in the Centre of Africa' would be amply substantiated by twentieth-century critics. The first chapter of this Guide traces its critical reception from its first publication in book form in 1902 to the end of the 1950s. Even when it first appeared in book form, in the volume of which 'Youth' was the title story, certain reviewers, such as Edward Garnett and Hugh Clifford, sensed its importance, as we shall see. If 'Heart of Darkness' was then to be overshadowed by Conrad's longer fictions during the rest of his life, a sign of its imminent importance for the mid-twentieth century appeared in 1925, the year after his death, when T. S. Eliot used it as the epigraph to his poem 'The Hollow Men', a poem which quickly came to be seen as a classic modern expression of futility and despair. 'Heart of Darkness' suffered in the general posthumous decline in Conrad's reputation, but by the late 1930s a revival was under way, which resulted in the early 1940s in positive evaluations of Conrad by two leading Cambridge critics, M. C. Bradbrook and F. R. Leavis. Both of these praised 'Heart of Darkness' highly, although Leavis also mounted an influential critique of what he saw as Conrad's excessive use of abstract adjectives such as 'implacable' and 'inscrutable'. After the pioneering work of Bradbrook and Leavis, the next decade, the 1950s, was to see key interpretations of 'Heart of Darkness' by Raymond Williams, Thomas Moser, and, above all, Albert J. Guerard, all of which are discussed in the first chapter of this Guide.

In the 1960s 'Heart of Darkness' reached the height of its reputation, and the second chapter of this Guide looks at major readings by Lionel Trilling, who sees it as the quintessential modern text, Eloise Knapp Hay, who focuses on what she regards as its critique of imperialism, J. Hillis Miller, who analyses it as a potentially transformative recognition of nihilism, and Stanton de Voren Hoffman, who homes in on its humour and relates that relatively neglected aspect of Conrad's novel to its major themes.

The third chapter moves on to the 1970s, when the apparent consolidation of the novel's reputation – represented in this Guide by C. B. Cox's account – was shattered by Chinua Achebe's attack on the novel as racist. If Achebe's attack represented the challenge that post-colonial critics were starting to mount against established ways of reading and evaluating literature, another challenge came from what were then the guerrilla camps of post-structuralism and deconstruction; a critique of this kind is provided in this Guide by an extract from Perry Meisel's deconstructive reading of the novel as a textual process in which centres constantly shift and recede. But as far as Conrad was concerned, these new voices did not drown out the tones of more conventional scholarship and criticism; and chapter three of this Guide concludes with an extract from Ian Watt's informed and suggestive analysis of impressionism and symbolism in 'Heart of Darkness'.

In the new critical landscape of the 1980s, interpretations of 'Heart of Darkness' seemed to take on fresh energy. Chapter four of this Guide discusses Benita Parry's sustained critique of the novel as subverting but ultimately confirming imperialist ideology; Peter Brooks's intriguing analysis of its narrative compulsions; Christopher L. Miller's judicious exploration of its relation to Africanist discourse; and Nina Pelikan Straus's forceful indictment of its sexism.

The final chapter looks at powerful readings of the 1990s that demonstrate the novel's continued fertility: Gail Fincham's analysis of the novel's use of metonymy to portray a racist mentality; Edward W. Said's deeply engaged reading of the novel as both complicit with and critical of the discourses of imperialism and neo-imperialism; and Valentine Cunningham's vividly detailed account of the relations between the textual activity of the novel and the material realities outside the text.

'Heart of Darkness' is a tale that takes the reader on a compelling, intriguing, rewarding and disorientating journey. This Guide offers a journey through the critical history of that tale that is itself intended to be compelling, intriguing and rewarding, but which also aims, as the good seaman Conrad might have wished, to provide some orientation, to offer compass and chart, to give bearings and reckonings, to enable us to make journeys and provisional mappings of our own. It does not have the imperialist ambition of trying to dominate and subdue the infinitely complex territory of 'Heart of Darkness'; but it does seek to help its readers to know that territory better, in its detail, its uncanny likeness, and its difference.

CHAPTER ONE

Mistah Kurtz – he very much alive: The Rise of 'Heart of Darkness', 1899–1959

'HEART OF Darkness' was first published, as 'The Heart of Darkness', in *Blackwood's Magazine* in three episodes in February, March and April 1899. It was then revised to some extent, and collected in a volume with 'Youth' and 'The End of the Tether', which appeared in 1902. According to Norman Sherry, the early reviews focused on the story that gave the volume its title, *Youth*. *The Sketch* of 3 December 1902 mentioned only 'Youth' and the *Daily Telegraph* of 26 November 1902 praised 'Youth' highly. The *Daily Mail* of 26 November 1902, however, did refer to what it called 'The Haunt of Darkness' as the 'application of the methods of Mr. Henry James to Central Africa'[1] – a perceptive comment, in its way, highlighting the issues of narrative technique and psychological representation that would be taken up in Edward Garnett's important review, which will be considered later in this chapter. The tide turned more strongly in favour of 'Heart of Darkness' in Hugh Clifford's *Spectator* review of 29 November 1902. Clifford, a friend of Conrad's and a former governor of Malaya with much knowledge and experience of Asia and Africa, finds that 'Heart of Darkness' 'holds the central place' in the volume and that to him, 'it makes a stronger appeal than anything which its author has yet written, and appears . . . to represent Mr. Conrad at his very best'.[2] Clifford goes on:

■ ['Heart of Darkness'] is a sombre study of the Congo – the scene is obviously intended for the Congo, though no names are mentioned – in which, while the inefficiency of certain types of European 'administrators' is mercilessly gibbeted, the power of the wilderness, of contact with barbarism and elemental men and facts, to effect the demoralization of the white man is conveyed with marvellous force. The denationalization of the European, the 'going Fantee' [going native] of civilized man, has been treated often enough in fiction since Mr. Grant Allen wrote the story of the Rev. John Creedy [collected in Allen's *Twelve Tales* (1899)], and before, but never has the 'why of it' been appreciated by any author as Mr. Conrad here appreciates it, and never, beyond all question, has any writer till now succeeded in bringing the reason, and the ghastly unreason, of it all home to sheltered folk as does Mr. Conrad in this wonderful, this magnificent, this terrible study. Mr. Kurtz, the victim of this hideous obsession, the man whom the wilderness had 'found . . . out', on whom it had taken a terrible vengeance, to whom it had 'whispered . . . things about himself that he did not know, things of which he had no conception till he took counsel with this great solitude', and to whom 'the whisper had proved irresistibly fascinating' (p.95), makes his appearance very late in the story, and then only for a few moments. He is the climax, so to speak, up to which every word of the story has been leading, certainly, inevitably, from the very first; and this is how it comes to pass that when at last he is met with, the reader finds that he is utterly in accord with his surroundings, – in the innermost chamber of the Heart of Darkness.³ ☐

This appreciative review was followed by Edward Garnett's unsigned review in *The Academy and Literature* on 6 December 1902. Garnett was a man of letters – critic, biographer, playwright, novelist and essayist – who is best remembered as the publisher's reader, particularly for the firm of Cape, who encouraged writers such as D.H. Lawrence, E.M. Forster, and Conrad himself. In his review, Garnett asserts that 'Youth' and 'The End of the Tether' 'will be more popular' than 'Heart of Darkness', but he sees 'Heart of Darkness' as 'most amazing, a consummate piece of artistic *diablerie* [devil's work; sorcery]' which 'enriches English literature'⁴ and is 'the high-water mark of the author's talent'⁵ in 'the subtlety of its criticism of life'.⁶ He recognises that the novel might pose difficulties for readers, and he appeals to 'the intelligent reader' to read it 'very deliberately'⁷ and with 'close attention'. He stresses the way in which Conrad's 'method of presentation' enables him to capture the psychological truth of the 'infinite shades of the white man's uneasy, disconcerted, and fantastic relations with the exploited barbarism of Africa'. Garnett's review is a concise and judicious piece of advocacy that plays down the controversial political implications in the story – it has 'no intention . . . no *parti pris*, no prejudice one way or the other' – and which focuses on narrative technique and, above all, 'psychological' truth. In all these respects, Garnett sets an important precedent for much future criticism of 'Heart of Darkness'. This is what he has to say about the novel:

■ 'Heart of Darkness', to present its theme bluntly, is an impression, taken from life, of the conquest by the European whites of a certain portion of Africa, an impression in particular of the civilizing methods of a certain great European Trading Company face to face with the 'nigger'. We say this much because the English reader likes to know where he is going before he takes art seriously, and we add that he will find the human life, black and white, in 'Heart of Darkness' an uncommonly and uncannily serious affair. If the ordinary reader, however, insists on taking the subject of a tale very seriously, the artist takes his method of presentation more seriously still, and rightly so. For the art of 'Heart of Darkness' – as in every psychological masterpiece – lies in the relation of the things of the spirit to the things of the flesh, of the invisible life to the visible, of the sub-conscious life within us, our obscure motives and instincts, to our conscious actions, feelings and outlook. Just as landscape art implies the artist catching the exact relation of a tree to the earth from which it springs, and of the earth to the sky, so the art of 'Heart of Darkness' implies the catching of infinite shades of the white man's uneasy, disconcerted, and fantastic relations with the exploited barbarism of Africa; it implies the acutest analysis of the deterioration of the white man's *morale*, when he is let loose from European restraint, and planted down in the tropics as an 'emissary of light' (p. 28) armed to the teeth, to make trade profits out of the 'subject races'. The weirdness, the brilliance, the psychological truth of this masterly analysis of two Continents in conflict, of the abysmal gulf between the white man's system and the black man's comprehension of its results, is conveyed in a rapidly rushing narrative which calls for close attention on the reader's part. But the attention once surrendered, the pages of the narrative are as enthralling as the pages of Dost[o]evsky's *Crime and Punishment* (1866). The stillness of the sombre African forests, the glare of the sunshine, the feeling of dawn, of noon, of night on the tropical rivers, the isolation of the unnerved, degenerating whites staring all day and every day at the Heart of Darkness which is alike meaningless and threatening to their own creed and conceptions of life, the helpless bewilderment of the unhappy savages in the grasp of their flabby and rapacious conquerors – all this is a page torn from the life of the Dark Continent – a page which has been hitherto carefully blurred and kept away from European eyes. There is no 'intention' in the story; no *parti pris*, no prejudice one way or the other; it is simply a piece of art, fascinating and remorseless, and the artist is but intent on presenting his sensations in that sequence and arrangement whereby the meaning or the meaninglessness of the white man in uncivilized Africa can be felt in its really significant aspects.[8] □

Conrad himself was very pleased with Garnett's review, writing to him on 22 December 1902 to say that 'your brave attempt to grapple with the foggishness of H of D, to explain what I myself have tried to shape blindfold, as it were, has touched me profoundly. You are the Seer of the Figures in the Carpet'. Conrad may be alluding here, as the editors of Conrad's *Collected Letters* suggest, to Henry James's short story about the difficulties of critical interpretation, 'The Figure in the Carpet' (1896).[9] By the time Conrad wrote the letter, he had read other reviews and he mentioned to Garnett the difficulty he felt that reviewers had experienced in defining and evaluating 'Heart of Darkness': 'the H of D is this and that and the other thing – they aren't so positive because in this case they aren't intelligent enough to catch on to your indications'. He did, however, find the *Manchester Guardian* review of 10 December 1902 'fairly intelligent'.[10] This unsigned review sees both 'Heart of Darkness' and 'Youth' as having the 'quality', if not the 'scope and design', of Conrad's *Lord Jim* (1900), and applies Garnett's metaphor of the 'high-water mark' to both works (though in this case they both 'touch the high-water mark of English fiction' rather than being 'the high-water mark' of Conrad's talent). Both, however, offer 'an excitement' that is 'so prolonged' that it is bound to 'be something of a strain' and means that they will not be widely read. Here are its specific comments on 'Heart of Darkness':

■ 'Heart of Darkness' is, again [like 'Youth'], the adventure of youth, an adventure more significant than the mere knockabout of the world. It is youth in the toils, a struggle with phantoms worse than the elements, 'a weary pilgrimage amongst hints for nightmares' (p. 31), a destructive experience ... ...

It must not be supposed that Mr. Conrad makes attack upon colonization, expansion, even upon Imperialism. In no one is the essence of the adventurous spirit more instinctive. But cheap ideals, platitudes of civilization are shrivelled up in the heat of such experiences. The end of this story brings us back to the familiar, reassuring region of common emotions, to the grief and constancy of the woman who had loved Kurtz and idealizes his memory. It shows us how far we have travelled. [11] □

The anonymous *Times Literary Supplement* reviewer of 12 December 1902 also focuses on the final scene of 'Heart of Darkness', calling it 'crisp and brief enough for Flaubert', but judging that 'the effect – a woman's ecstatic belief in a villain's heroism – is reached by an indulgence in the picturesque horror of the villain, his work and his surroundings, which is pitiless in its insistence, and quite extravagant according to the canons of art'. The reviewer acknowledges, however, that 'the power, the success in conveying the impression vividly, without loss of energy is undoubted and is refreshing'.[12] The *Athenaeum*, in an unsigned review of 20 December 1902, judges 'Heart of Darkness' as 'the most important part' of the volume, 'a big and thoughtful conception'. The reviewer does not elaborate on this, however, 'deliberately abstain[ing]' from 'any attempt at analysis' that, in a limited space, 'would be a painful injustice where work of this character is concerned'. Like Edward Garnett, this reviewer stresses the need for the reader to pay Conrad the 'thoughtful attention' that he 'demands'.[13] 'Heart of Darkness' was rated less highly, however, by the poet John Masefield, who, like Conrad, had followed the sea, and whose first book of poems, *Salt-Water Ballads*, had, like the *Youth* volume, come out in 1902. In a review in *The Speaker* of 31 January 1903, Masefield calls each of the three stories in the volume 'a notable advance upon the technique and matter of his former work', but nonetheless finds 'a tendency towards the "precious"' in Conrad's prose, and a narrative that is 'most unconvincing', reminding one 'of a cobweb abounding in gold threads', giving 'a curious impression of remoteness and aloofness from its subject', and 'smell[ing] very palpably of the lamp', of conscious, laboured effort, with the result that it 'los[es] all spontaneity and becom[es] somewhat rhetorical'. Masefield judges 'Youth' the best of the three tales in the book, but finds that '[i]n 'Heart of Darkness' the author is too much cobweb, and fails, as we think, to create his central character'.[14]

A review from across the Atlantic, however, found 'Heart of Darkness' much less tenuous. The New York *Nation*, in an anonymous review attributed to Annie Logan,[15] called it 'a dreadful and fascinating tale, full as any of [Edgar Allan] Poe's of mystery and haunting terrors, yet with a substantial basis of reality that no man who had not lived as well as dreamed could conjure into existence'. The reviewer also found that the novel 'vibrate[d] with loathing of a land where primeval nature assumes the functions of a vengeful fate, and either kills invaders of her awful solitudes or reduces them to the condition of brutes'.[16] The sense of the power of the 'land' is echoed and reinforced in another American review, by Frederic Taber Cooper in the New York *Bookman* for November 1903. Cooper calls Conrad 'a writer second only to Rudyard Kipling in his sheer mastery of forceful English and virile audacity of style, second to none in unique, exotic flavour and oftentimes grotesque tragedy of his themes'. He also remarks on what he sees as a disproportionate relationship between Conrad's subjects and the space that he allows them, 'crumpling up a world-wide theme into the limits of a few pages, stretching out some transitory incident into the bulk of a portly volume'.[17] If, for Cooper, *The Nigger of the 'Narcissus'* (1897) is an example of the latter, 'Heart of Darkness' is an example of the former:

■ ... take *The Heart of Blackness* [*sic*], one of the shortest stories that Mr. Conrad has written, and at the same time containing the biggest, most suggestive of all his themes. It is nothing less than a presentment of the clashing of two continents, a symbolic picture of the inborn antagonism of two races, the white and the black. It pictures the subtle disintegration of the white man's moral stamina, under the stress of the darkness, the isolation, the promiscuity of the African jungle, the loss of dignity and courage and self-respect through daily contact with the native man and the native woman. The whole thing is a matter of a few score pages, and yet such is its strength, coupled with a certain indescribable trick of verbal foreshortening, that it gives an impression of measureless time and distance. We feel that we have spent years in his company, roaming through the murky atmosphere of physical and moral darkness – and still beyond stretch unexplored vistas, measureless, forbidding, unspeakable.[18] □

Cooper's substitution of 'blackness' for 'darkness' is a telling one, an index of his racist reading of the novel. Whereas *The Nation*'s use of the term 'invaders' implies that the whites might bear some responsibility for provoking the 'vengeful fate' that the 'land' visits upon them, Cooper's indictment does not concede that the whites might be at all culpable, and it extends to include not only the 'land' – what he calls 'the African jungle' – but also 'the native man and the native woman'. Cooper's response lends credence to Chinua Achebe's charge, over seventy years later, that 'Heart of Darkness' reinforces racist attitudes – a charge that will be considered in chapter three of this Guide (see pp. 71, 73–85).

Disturbing though Cooper's interpretation may be, however, his affirmation that 'Heart of Darkness' is a powerful, suggestive and compressed work that deals, in a short space, with large themes does anticipate the importance that the novel will come to assume in twentieth-century criticism. That sense of its importance is also evident, as has already been seen, in the reviews by Collins, Garnett and the *Athenaeum*. Indeed, it is possible to discern, in these first responses, a range of topics that future critics would develop. For example, while Clifford does not use the word 'psychological', his stress on Conrad's ability to show 'the "why of it"' – that is, of 'going Fantee', going native – links up with Garnett's emphasis on the novel's psychological penetration, as does Cooper's remark on 'the subtle disintegration of the white man's moral stamina'. Both Garnett and the *Athenaeum* stress the demands 'Heart of Darkness' makes on the reader's attention, and thus pose a kind of incitement and incentive to those who think of themselves as – to use Garnett's adjective – 'intelligent' readers, since they imply that an ability to appreciate the book is a measure of intelligence. Garnett's focus on the 'method of presentation', and Cooper's remark about 'a certain indescribable trick of verbal foreshortening', open up key aspects of the novel for further analysis. Clifford, by firmly identifying the setting of the story as the Congo, emphasises its link with contemporary events and controversies, even as he safely distances it from the British Empire. The 'loathing' of Africa that *The Nation* finds in 'Heart of Darkness', and Cooper's reading of the novel as 'a symbolic picture of the inborn antagonism of two races', highlight the relationship of Conrad's text to racist representations. Garnett's asser-tion that the story has no prejudice or *parti pris* and is 'simply a piece of art' anticipates the way in which an important strand of future criticism will play down the possible political dimensions of 'Heart of Darkness' and regard its supposed refusal to 'take sides' as one of the signs of its artistic quality. At the same time, that very assertion, and the *Manchester Guardian*'s claim that the novel does not attack colonisation, expansion and imperialism, sound like pre-emptive strikes, suggesting an awareness that the novel could be vulnerable to charges that it *is* prejudiced against, *is* mounting an assault on, colonisation, expansion and imperialism – that it is, in other words, political.

It would be some time, however, before critics would develop any of the issues raised in the early reviews of 'Heart of Darkness'. Conrad con-tinued to find intelligent admirers, and he achieved financial and popular success with *Chance* (1913) and *Victory* (1915); but his reputation declined after his death in 1924. One event occurred in 1925, however, that would later become significant: T. S. Eliot used a phrase from 'Heart of Darkness' – '"Mistah Kurtz – he dead"' (p.112) – as the epigraph to his poem 'The Hollow Men' (1925).[19] The impact of this juxtaposition would be delayed, since Eliot himself, then known only to a relative few as the notable, or notorious, author of 'The Waste Land' (1922), did not enjoy the acceptance that was later to come to him; but as his reputation as the major Modernist poet grew, 'Heart of Darkness' also seemed to gain extra signif-icance. Both Conrad and Eliot could be seen as writers who expressed, in complex and compact ways, the emptiness of modern man, and perhaps of all human life. In 1941, in an analysis that will be discussed later in this chapter, F. R. Leavis called 'Heart of Darkness' 'an appropriate source for the epigraph of "The Hollow Men"' (see p. 19);[20] in 1961, in an essay to be considered in the next chapter, Lionel Trilling remarked that 'Heart of Darkness' 'has been given a kind of canonical place in literature by Eliot's having it so clearly in mind when he wrote "The Waste Land" (1922) and his having taken from it the epigraph to "The Hollow Men"' (see pp. 41–42).[21]

But whatever the influence of Eliot's choice of epigraph on the repu-tation of 'Heart of Darkness', the general revival of Conrad's critical reputation in England began, according to J. H. Stape, with Edward Crankshaw's *Joseph Conrad: Some Aspects of the Art of the Novel* (1936; 2nd edn, 1976) and with M. C. Bradbrook's *Joseph Conrad: Poland's English Genius* (1941).[22] As Crankshaw recalls in his introduction to the second edition of his study, 'Conrad was unfashionable' when his book was first published; he was 'by no means firmly established among the unchal-lengeably great' and indeed 'was then seriously regarded by relatively few'.[23] Crankshaw's book makes only brief mentions of 'Heart of Darkness', however. On the other hand, M. C. Bradbrook's study, although short, singles out 'Heart of Darkness' as the 'masterpiece' of Conrad's early period.[24] Citing Conrad's own comment that the '"sombre theme . . . had to be given a sinister resonance"',[25] she finds that '[i]n this sinister resonance' 'Heart of Darkness' is 'supreme' and that the resonance 'is maintained almost wholly in terms of scene'.[26] Bradbrook contends:

■ The story carries this particular method of suggestion to its limits. It is most delicately counterpoised between what is seen and what is sensed or perceived, by means of similes which transform Conrad's powers of description into powers of analysis and creation. With no departure from the descriptive method, every incident yet deepens the force of the truth manifold and one which pervades the tale. There are contrasts and echoes: Marlow's aunt, for instance, in her illusion that he will be an apostle of progress in Darkest Africa provokes ironic reflections from her nephew on the feminine powers of self-deception, which would be wrong at the poignant interview with the fiancée of Kurtz, but which reverberate there with a 'sinister resonance'. Again the queer knitting women who inhabit the office in Belgium from which this chain of exploitation starts reoccur to Marlow at one of his worst moments as queer things to be at the other end of this affair (p. 105) – and they become shadowy Fates or at least *tricoteuses* in recollection [*tricoteuses* were the women who attended the meetings of the National Convention in the French Revolution and went on with their *tricotage* (knitting) while urging on the leaders to bloodshed]. The complexity is a living complexity; and Conrad's renunciation of the supernatural gives it all the close texture of actual life. There are no occult powers among the natives, Kurtz's adorers, who are just spied at their savage rites; in the day, they are pitiful creatures frightened off by the screech of the steamer's whistle. They are even more pitiful than the starved and dying negroes of the coast or the ship's crew who are paid with brass wire but given no food, so that when the steersman is killed Marlow has to throw him overboard at once before his carcase rouses the appetite of his fellows. Yet all these figures only deepen in garish splendour the death of Kurtz – the trappings of corruption.[27] □

Bradbrook's terms of approval accord with a set of ideas about the nature of artistic achievement in fiction that was becoming increasingly influential in the mid-twentieth century. These ideas included a preference for suggestive presentation – 'showing', or what Bradbrook calls 'description' – over 'telling', or explicit statement; an admiration for the novelist who could effect a kind of 'analysis' in this indirect way rather than through abstraction; a belief that all aspects of a fictional work should contribute to its overall unity; a concern for internal connections within a work – Bradbrook's 'contrasts and echoes' – that serve to deepen its unity and enrich its significance as one scene modulates or amplifies another; a complexity that is not mechanical but organic, or, as Bradbrook put it, 'living'; and a fidelity to 'the close texture of actual life'. In a brief compass, Bradbrook provides a basis for a rich critical agenda.

An even more potent basis was provided by F. R. Leavis's essay on Conrad, which first appeared in *Scrutiny* in the same year as Bradbrook's short book was published, and which was later given wider currency and greater authority by its incorporation into Leavis's *The Great Tradition* (1948). In *The Great Tradition*, Leavis included Conrad, along with Jane Austen, George Eliot and Henry James, in his highly selective 'great tradition' of English novelists, and this was a major reinforcement of Conrad's reputation; but while he claimed that 'Heart of Darkness' was, 'by common consent, one of Conrad's best things', he nonetheless judged it 'marred',[28] even if it did sometimes exemplify 'Conrad's art at its best'. Like M. C. Bradbrook, Leavis favoured indirect presentation in which authorial comment was implicit; but Leavis expresses this in his own distinctive vocabulary, with an acknowledged borrowing of T. S. Eliot's notion of the 'objective correlative', one of the most widely disseminated notions of mid-twentieth-century Anglo-American literary criticism. In an essay of 1919 on *Hamlet*, Eliot defined the 'objective correlative' as the 'only way of expressing emotion in the form of art'; such a correlative is 'a set of objects, a situation, a chain of events which shall be the form of [a] *particular* emotion'; when this set of objects, situation, or chain of events is presented to the audience, or the reader, they will produce a 'sensory experience' that will immediately evoke the relevant emotion.[29] Eliot's sets of objects, situations and chains of events become, in Leavis's idiom, 'the interaction of the particular incidents, actions, and perceptions that are evoked with such charged concreteness' and that 'carry specificities of emotion and suggestion'. It is when Conrad departs from particularity that the trouble arises. This is what Leavis says:

■ 'Heart of Darkness' is, by common consent, one of Conrad's best things – an appropriate source for the epigraph of 'The Hollow Men': '"Mistah Kurtz – he dead"' (p. 112) ... ... Borrowing a phrase from Mr. Eliot's critical writings, one might say that 'Heart of Darkness' achieves its overpowering evocation of atmosphere by means of 'objective correlatives'. The details and circumstances of the voyage to and up the Congo are present to us as if we were making the journey ourselves and (chosen for record as they are by a controlling imaginative purpose) they carry specificities of emotion and suggestion with them. There is the gunboat dropping shells into Africa ... ... There is the arrival at the Company's station ... ... There is the grove of death ... ...

By means of this art of vivid essential record, in terms of things seen and incidents experienced by a main agent in the narrative, and particular contacts and exchanges with other human agents, the overwhelming sinister and fantastic 'atmosphere' is engendered. Ordinary greed, stupidity, and moral squalor are made to look like behaviour in a lunatic asylum against the vast and oppressive mystery of the surroundings, rendered potently in terms of sensation. This means lunacy, [*sic.* Original *Scrutiny* version has 'This mean lunacy'] which we are made to feel as at the same time normal and insane, is brought out by contrast with the fantastically secure innocence of the young harlequin-costumed Russian ('"son of an arch-priest . . . Government of Tambov"' (p. 88)), the introduction to whom is by the way of that copy of Tower's (or Towson's) *Inquiry into some Points of Seamanship*, symbol of tradition, sanity, and the moral idea, found lying, an incongruous mystery, in the dark heart of Africa.

Of course . . . the author's comment cannot be said to be wholly implicit. Nevertheless, it is not separable from the thing rendered, but seems to emerge from the vibration of this as part of the tone. [Leavis's vocabulary here is close to that of Conrad's own 'Author's Note' to *Youth*, which Bradbrook quotes: '[t]hat sombre theme had to be given a sinister resonance, a tonality of its own, a continued vibration that, I hoped, would hang in the air and dwell on the ear after the last note had been struck'.[30]] At least, this is Conrad's art at its best. There are, however, places in 'Heart of Darkness' where we become aware of comment as an interposition, and worse, as an intrusion, at times an exasperating one. Hadn't he, we find ourselves asking, overworked 'inscrutable', 'inconceivable', 'unspeakable' and that kind of word already? – yet still they recur. Is anything added to the oppressive mysteriousness of the Congo by such sentences as:

> It was the stillness of an implacable force brooding over an inscrutable intention (p. 60) – ?

The same vocabulary, the same adjectival insistence upon inexpressible and incomprehensible mystery, is applied to the evocation of human profundities and spiritual horrors; to magnifying a thrilled sense of the unspeakable potentialities of the human soul. The actual effect is not to magnify but rather to muffle. The essential vibration emanates from the interaction of the particular incidents, actions, and perceptions that are evoked with such charged concreteness . . . . . . By such means . . . we are given a charged sense of the monstrous hothouse efflorescences fostered in Kurtz by solitude and the wilderness. It is a matter of such things as the heads on posts – a direct significant glimpse, the innocent Russian's explanations, the incidents of the progress up the river and the moral and physical incongruities registered; in short, of the charge generated in a variety of highly specific evocations. The stalking of the moribund Kurtz, a skeleton crawling through the long grass on all fours as he makes his bolt towards the fires and the tom-toms, is a triumphant climax in the suggestion of strange and horrible perversions. But Conrad isn't satisfied with these means; he feels that there is, or ought to be, some significance he has yet to bring out. So we have an adjectival and worse than supererogatory insistence on 'unspeakable rites' (p. 83), 'unspeakable secrets' (p. 101), 'monstrous passions' (p. 107), 'inconceivable mystery' (p. 108) and so on. If it were only, as it largely is in 'Heart of Darkness', a matter of an occasional phrase it would still be regrettable as tending to cheapen the tone. But the actual cheapening is little short of disastrous . . . . . .

. . . Actually, Conrad had no need to try and inject 'significance' into his narrative in this way. What he shows himself to have successfully and significantly seen is enough to make 'Heart of Darkness' a disturbing presentment of the kind he aimed at. By the attempt at injection he weakens, in his account of Kurtz's death, the effect of that culminating cry:

> He cried in a whisper at some image, at some vision, – he cried out twice, a cry that was no more than a breath –
> 'The horror! The horror!' (p. 112)

The '"horror"' there has very much less force than it might have had if Conrad had strained less.

This final account of Kurtz is associated with a sardonic tone, an insistent irony that leads us on to another bad patch, the closing interview in Brussels with Kurtz's 'Intended' . . . . . . It is not part of Conrad's irony that there should be anything ironical in this presentment of the woman. The irony lies in the association of her innocent nobility, her purity of idealizing faith, with the unspeakable corruption of Kurtz; and it is developed (if that is the word) with a thrilled insistence that recalls the melodramatic intensities of Edgar Allan Poe . . . . . . Conrad's 'inscrutable', it is clear, associates with Woman as it does with the wilderness, and the thrilling mystery of the Intended's innocence is of the same order as the thrilling mystery of Kurtz's corruption: the profundities are complementary. It would appear that the cosmopolitan Pole, student of the French masters, who became a British mastermariner, was in some respects a simple soul.[31] □

Leavis's judgement of 'Heart of Darkness' – especially his memorable and very Leavis-like phrase 'adjectival insistence' – became a key point of reference for later critics, whether in dissent or agreement; for example, it is cited, and interestingly challenged, by Albert J. Guerard in his 1958 study, which is discussed later in this Guide, and it is even deployed by Chinua Achebe, who summons Leavis as an unexpected ally in his assault upon the 'racism' of Conrad's novel (see p. 75). It is significant, however, that Leavis himself, like M. C. Bradbrook, never alludes to imperialism, in contrast to some of the first reviewers (see pp. 11, 12–13, 14). But if Leavis ignores the imperialist aspect, he does focus on another issue that will be taken up by future critics, not least feminist ones: the representation of the Intended. Leavis's suggestion of a link, for Conrad, between Woman, the wilderness and Kurtz's corruption is interesting, and could be open to interpretations other than the one that Leavis adopts, with his patronising reference to Conrad's simplicity of soul.

In 1950, a book called *Reading and Criticism* appeared, which devoted a whole chapter to an analysis of 'Heart of Darkness'. The book was by a Cambridge graduate and former Guards officer who was then an obscure adult education tutor in East Sussex, but who was to become famous later in the fifties as the author of *Culture and Society* (1958): Raymond Williams. The book appeared in a series called 'Man and Society' that was 'intended for use of students in adult classes, such as those promoted by the W. E. A. [Workers' Educational Association] and University Extra-Mural Departments, and by other readers requiring new introductory studies in the subjects covered'.[32] The purpose of Williams's book was, as he himself stated at the outset, 'to offer suggestions and material for the development of responsive and intelligent reading of literature'.[33] The terms 'responsive' and 'intelligent' echo Leavis, and Williams acknowledges his debt in his 'Preface' to a figure who, in Williams's words, 'has been largely responsible for the intelligent development of critical analysis as an educational discipline'.[34] Williams was one of those who, in the 1950s, carried an approach to literature strongly influenced by Leavis out of the universities and into other educational sites such as adult education classes and schools. But Williams also had his differences with Leavis, and it is notable that in his reading of 'Heart of Darkness', he contends that a phrase that might have been used to exemplify Leavis's charges of 'adjectival insistence' and empty abstraction – 'It [Kurtz's peroration] gave me the notion of an exotic immensity ruled by an august Benevolence' (p. 83) – is employed by Conrad ironically, to indicate the vacuity of Kurtz's peroration. Only in a footnote does Willliams concede that 'this specimen sentence of rhetoric . . . raises disturbing echoes from much of Conrad's work, including parts of "Heart of Darkness"'. Williams also agrees – though referring to it only in brackets – that the scene with the Intended is 'the least satisfactory part of the novel'. But otherwise his valuation of 'Heart of Darkness' is very positive; like Leavis he applauds the particularity of its writing and he strikes a further Leavisian note when he declares that '[t]he intention of "Heart of Darkness" is moral, in the sense that all great art proceeds from a moral centre'. Like M. C. Bradbrook, he commends the way in which the parts – which for him includes the scenes and the characters – contribute to a whole, 'the whole organization of words which is the work'. But Williams goes beyond both Bradbrook and Leavis in that he offers, within a relatively short chapter, a more refined analysis that makes a number of acute points worthy of further critical development: that Marlow's image of the meaning of a tale as a haze brought out by a glow is 'an implicit "preface" to the work', a kind of guide to how to read it that 'has a fine relevance to the method of Conrad's best work and to an important kind of prose fiction'; that the light/darkness opposition in the novel is 'conventional' but is given 'a precise and particular definition in the work as a whole' (notice once more the stress on particularity); that Marlow's picture of the decent young Roman forced to go to the remote colony of Britain is like the 'dumbshow' that used to precede some early Elizabethan plays, forecasting the main action; that Marlow is not Conrad (a distinction Leavis fails to make) but an interior narrator who is also the 'product' of the experience that he narrates; that the novel is not naturalistic; that the recurrent stress on 'dream' is significant; that the 'exploration to the heart of darkness has a clear spiritual reference' ('spiritual' is an adjective that would disappear from Williams's vocabulary later); and that 'Heart of Darkness' has elements of the old literary form of the 'Quest', though it would be wrong to describe the work in such terms. Here is Williams's analysis:

■ The central story of 'Heart of Darkness' is told aboard a cruising yawl near the mouth of the Thames. It begins and ends on this 'tranquil waterway leading to the uttermost ends of the earth' (p. 16), a waterway that in the last sentence of the work is conceived of as leading 'into the heart of an immense darkness' (p. 124). It is told by a 'seaman' (p. 18), Marlow, to four of his friends. We are quickly told something about Marlow which must also serve as an implicit 'preface' to the work. Certainly, it will tell us how to read the story ahead.

> The yarns of seamen have a direct simplicity, the whole meaning of which lies within the shell of a cracked nut. But Marlow was not typical (if his propensity to spin yarns be excepted), and to him the meaning of an episode was not inside like a kernel but outside, enveloping the tale which brought it out only as a glow brings out a haze, in the likeness of one of these misty halos that sometimes are made visible by the spectral illumination of moonshine. (p. 18)

The figure is perhaps difficult of initial apprehension, but when it is grasped it has a fine relevance to the method of Conrad's best work and to an important kind of prose fiction. The story is not an allegory, which must be 'opened up' for 'meaning'. The significance of a story like this is everywhere immanent [indwelling, inherent], and it is illuminated by a sharp realization of the *actual* story, which when it is 'heard, felt, seen' will carry its own significance [Williams alludes here to Conrad's statement in the 'Preface' to *The Nigger of the 'Narcissus'* (1897; first edition to include 'Preface', 1914): 'My task which I am trying to achieve is, by the power of the written word, to make you hear, to make you feel – it is, before all, to make you *see*'.[35] Williams cites (and slightly misquotes) the statement later in this extract (see p. 26 and p. 163, note 37).].

The initial emphasis, as the yawl waits for the turn of the tide, is on light. Attention is drawn to the lighthouse, to the lights springing up along the shore, to the glare of the great city behind:

> ... Lights of ships moved in the fairway – a great stir of lights going up and going down ...
> 'And this also,' said Marlow suddenly, 'has been one of the dark places of the earth.' (pp. 17, 18)

It is the first statement of an opposition with which throughout the work Conrad is concerned: the conventional opposition of light and darkness which will be given a precise and particular definition in the work as a whole: 'Light came out of this river ... [b]ut darkness was here yesterday'. Marlow imagines the Romans coming to the Thames when it was 'the very end of the world', and remarks of them: 'They were men enough to face the darkness' (p. 19). Why this insistence, which doubtless in this extraction appears almost crude, on certain keywords? Within the body of the work the objection of crudity disappears – the practical and the visual emphasis in Conrad's writing sees to that. But what is Conrad doing? It is clear that he is establishing a theme, an idea which is likely to be strange to readers who have been fed upon pronouncements by popular novelists that they 'never know the end of a novel when they begin it', but just 'create a character and follow where he leads'. The idea of a theme – not a 'subject' but a literary theme that exists in a certain arrangement of words – it is this that we must accept in this work of Conrad's. Having introduced the theme, he employs a method which reminds one of the dumbshow which used to precede certain early Elizabethan plays, giving a forecast of the action. Marlow pictures 'a decent young citizen in a toga' (p. 19) coming to the primitive Thames:

> Land in a swamp, march through the woods, and in some inland post feel the savagery, the utter savagery, had closed round him, – all that mysterious life of the wilderness that stirs in the forest, in the jungles, in the hearts of wild men. There's no initiation either into such mysteries. He has to live in the midst of the incomprehensible, which is also detestable. And it has a fascination, too, that goes to work upon him. The fascination of the abomination – you know. Imagine the growing regrets, the longing to escape, the powerless disgust, the surrender, the hate. (pp. 19–20)

The relevance of this to the fate of Kurtz will become evident. Marlow's narrative now increasingly occupies the work, and the reader might wonder why the interior narrative device is employed. For Conrad the device is not a mere convention. It is a method which allows comment yet retains impersonality. Marlow, for instance, is able to say:

> The conquest of the earth, which mostly means the taking it away from those who have a different complexion or slightly flatter noses than ourselves, is not a pretty thing when you look into it too much. What redeems it is the idea only. An idea at the back of it; not a sentimental pretence but an idea; and an unselfish belief in the idea – something you can set up, and bow down before, and offer a sacrifice to … (p. 20 [Conrad's ellipsis])

And this is not just an author putting his thumb into the scales [D. H. Lawrence's phrase, from 'Morality and the Novel'[36]], attempting didacticism. It is a dramatic device, as we shall see when we ponder the nature of this 'idea', relating it to the 'Idea' of Mr Kurtz, and the particular significance of 'bow down before and offer a sacrifice to', with its connotations of savagery. Marlow is not only a device for commentary. By being able to withdraw from him the author is given as it were an extra purchase on his material, a further refinement of viewpoint. Marlow now begins his story, and we see a further reason for the method. It was, Marlow says, this upriver journey, 'the farthest point of navigation and the culminating point of my experience. It seemed somehow to throw a kind of light …' (p. 21). One is reminded of this later, when Marlow breaks off his narrative to remark: '[o]f course in this you fellows see more than I could then. You see me, whom you know' (p. 50). Marlow is not only the narrator of his experience; he is also its *product*. Because he is an interior narrative character we are able to step back from him and survey him. It is this depth and variety of angle which makes Conrad's fiction *dramatic*, in the essential sense …

'It seemed … to throw a kind of light'. There is a journey, up a great river (the biographical reference will be obvious, but it is not relevant here). The area of this river has been to the boy Marlow 'a blank space of delightful mystery – a white patch' on a map (p. 22). Since then it had been charted, and undergone a 'fantastic invasion' (pp. 44, 58, 95); it 'had become a place of darkness' (p. 22). The easy association is with 'Darkest Africa', and the river is obviously the Congo. But the implications of the phrase 'Darkest Africa' are explicitly set aside. The area is not seen as one of savage darkness into which is brought light. On the contrary, in Marlow's words, it had 'become' a place of darkness. When Marlow receives his instructions at the headquarters of the great trading company, his 'excellent aunt' tells him that he is '[s]omething like an emissary of light, something like a lower sort of apostle' (p.28). But the '[o]ld knitter[s] of black wool' in the Company's Office guard the 'door of Darkness' (p.26) when they guard the door of the Company. Marlow does not bow down before this 'Idea' of light. At every point he treats it ironically, as when he talks of invading the homes of his friends on the yawl, 'just as though I had got a heavenly mission to civilize you' (p.21). Or again, when he talks of the disappearance of certain native hens: 'I should think the cause of progress got them' (p.24). In the ship approaching the first station he talks of this 'sordid farce' (p.30), 'the merry dance of death and trade' (p.31), and later, when he sees the 'Eldorado Exploring Expedition', he comments:

> [t]heir talk, however, was the talk of sordid buccaneers: it was reckless without hardihood, greedy without audacity, and cruel without courage; there was not an atom of foresight or of serious intention in the whole batch of them, and they did not seem aware these things are wanted for the work of the world. (pp.54–55)

But it is not a question of abstract denunciation . . . 'My task . . . is before all, to make you hear, to make you feel, to make you *see*'.[37] One sees the 'wanton smash-up' (p.34) of imported drainage pipes (and remembers '[w]hat saves us is efficiency' (p.20)), the absurd little warship '[i]n the empty immensity of earth, sky, and water . . . incomprehensible, firing into a continent. Pop . . . '(p.30) and the 'objectless blasting' at the quarry (p.33). One sees:

> . . . black shadows of disease and starvation, lying confusedly in the greenish gloom. Brought from all the recesses of the coast in all the legality of time contracts, lost in uncongenial surroundings, fed on unfamiliar food, they sickened, became inefficient, and were then allowed to crawl away and rest . . . glancing down, I saw a face near my hand. The black bones reclined at full length with one shoulder against the tree, and slowly the eyelids rose and the sunken eyes looked up at me, enormous and vacant, a kind of blind, white flicker in the depths of the orbs, which died out slowly . . . He had tied a bit of white worsted round his neck – Why? Where did he get it? Was it a badge – an ornament – a charm – a propitiatory act? Was there any idea at all connected with it? It looked startling round his black neck, this bit of white thread from beyond the seas. (p.35)

This is not only magnificently particular writing, but it is precisely set within the work as a whole. The 'bit of worsted' is at least one of the 'ideas you set up and bow down before and offer a sacrifice to' (p.20).

The word which begins to dominate the scene onshore is 'meaning-less', with its variants 'fantastic' and 'dreamlike'. To the chained negroes the law which has made them criminals is an 'insoluble mystery from over the sea'. And one remembers that there is 'no initiation . . . into such mysteries'; you have to be 'm[a]n enough to face the darkness' (p. 19). Like the 'legality of time contracts' applied to men who had 'no notion of time', it is the 'inapplicability' of everything about this 'fantastic invasion' which most appals. The perfect example is the first white man Marlow meets on this tropic shore:

> I saw a high starched collar, white cuffs, a light alpaca jacket, snowy trousers, a clear silk necktie, and varnished boots. No hat. Hair parted, brushed, oiled, under a green-lined parasol held in a big white hand. He was amazing, and had a penholder behind his ear . . . . . . he was devoted to his books, which were in apple-pie order . . . . . . Everything else in the station was in a muddle. (pp. 36, 37)

When an invalid agent is put to bed in his office, he remarks: '"The groans of this sick person . . . distract my attention. And without that it is extremely difficult to guard against clerical errors in this climate"' (p. 37). One notices about this scene, in spite of its extreme 'practicality', that there is no trace of 'naturalism', just as the narrative device of Marlow, who must speak some thirty-five thousand words without real pause, is not naturalistic. Instead of subservience to some (non-existent?) 'objective truth', Conrad selects and organizes, which amounts to the 'exaggeration and distortion' that is characteristic of the dramatic method.

The characters, also, are not isolated grotesques, or even 'real live persons', but rather the agents of communication of a particular and controlled experience, whose highest expression is the whole organization of words which is the work . . . . . .

And now we approach the fullest definition, which is Kurtz. Marlow says:

> He was just a word for me. I did not see the man in the name any more than you do. Do you see him? Do you see the story? Do you see anything? It seems to me I am trying to tell you a dream – making a vain attempt, because no relation of a dream can convey the dream-sensation, that commingling of absurdity, surprise, and bewilderment in a tremor of struggling revolt, that notion of being captured by the incredible which is of the very essence of dreams . . . . . . No, it is impossible . . . to convey the life-sensation of any given epoch of one's existence, – that which makes its truth, its meaning – its subtle and penetrating essence. (p. 50)

This recurrent emphasis of 'dream' is important. The approach to Kurtz, the movement into the heart of darkness which is the jungle, is perfectly realized in its own terms. But the significance of such a story is brought out by its very clarity. The exploration to the heart of darkness has a clear spiritual reference: '[w]e live, as we dream – alone' (p. 50). The discovery of what Kurtz represents has even something of the quality of that old literary-form, the Quest, although to describe the work as such would be misleading. Yet the reference is there: 'the approach to this Kurtz grubbing for ivory in the wretched bush was beset by as many dangers as though he had been an enchanted princess sleeping in a fabulous castle' (p. 72) ... ...

The humanity of the leaping negroes on the bank is

> truth stripped of its cloak of time. Let the fool gape and shudder – the man knows, and can look on without a wink. But he must at least be as much of a man as these on the shore. He must meet that truth with his own true stuff – with his own inborn strength . . . Principles won't do. Acquisitions, clothes, pretty rags – rags that would fly off at the first good shake. No; you want a deliberate belief. (p. 63)

The exploration is towards such a 'deliberate belief', towards such 'manhood' (which is a different concept from many ideas of masculinity as Conrad's concepts of light and darkness are different from accepted ideas of enlightenment) . . . And ahead is one who has made the exploration: Kurtz.

> The point was in his being a gifted creature, and that of all his gifts the one that stood out pre-eminently . . . was his ability to talk, his words – the gift of expression, the bewildering, the illuminating, the most exalted and the most contemptible, the pulsating stream of light, or the deceitful flow from the heart of an impenetrable darkness. (p. 79)

For 'light' and 'darkness' are closely related rather than opposed. The particular instance of their realization is Kurtz ... ... Kurtz was a gifted man. His voice! His pamphlet! 'The peroration was magnificent, though difficult to remember, you know. It gave me the notion of an exotic immensity ruled by an august Benevolence' (p. 83). [Williams's footnote at this point reads: 'It is necessary to comment, by way of limitation, that this specimen sentence of rhetoric, used here ironically, raises disturbing echoes from much of Conrad's work, including parts of "Heart of Darkness"'. This is Williams's only concession to Leavis's criticisms of the novel.] This was the 'light', but after the pieties, and forgotten by the writer, there came, 'like a flash of lightning', a scrawled note: "'Exterminate all the brutes!'". Certainly, Kurtz, '[w]hatever he was . . . was not common' (p. 84). He had made the exploration. But

> . . . there was something wanting in him . . . the wilderness had found him out early, and had taken on him a terrible vengeance for the fantastic invasion . . . it had whispered to him things about himself which he did not know, things of which he had no conception till he took counsel with this great solitude – and the whisper had proved irresistibly fascinating. It echoed loudly within him because he was hollow at the core . . . (p. 95)

Here one notices the retained verbal organization, running from the predominant strands: 'fantastic invasion . . . solitude . . . fascination'. The whole context of the moral definition with which the work is occupied is recreated at each point by this verbal organization.

Kurtz was a lie . . . Already, as will be announced in the unforgettable words of the negro servant, "'Mistah Kurtz – he dead'" (p. 112). What Kurtz did is defined, but at its practical level it does not greatly matter. The raids, the rites, the orgies, these are no more than tokens of 'the wilderness' (p. 106) which 'had beguiled his unlawful soul beyond the bounds of permitted aspirations'. 'He had kicked himself loose of the earth . . . he had kicked the very earth to pieces'. It is at once the local and the general dissolution of morality. That primitive journey, which it was necessary to undertake, that 'fantastic invasion' to the sound of 'words heard in dreams . . . phrases spoken in nightmares', had been too much for Kurtz. '[H]is soul . . . had gone mad', although 'his intelligence remained perfectly clear' (p. 107). He 'knew no restraint, no faith, and no fear' (p. 108).[38]

> One evening coming in with a candle I was startled to hear him say a little tremulously, 'I am lying here in the dark waiting for death.' The light was within a foot of his eyes . . . I . . . stood over him as if transfixed . . . . . . He cried in a whisper at some image, at some vision, – he cried out twice, a cry that was no more than a breath –
>   'The horror! The horror!'
>   . . . His was an impenetrable darkness. I looked at him as you peer down at a man who is lying at the bottom of a precipice where the sun never shines . . . . . . [He] was a remarkable man . . . Since I had peeped over the edge myself, I understand better the meaning of his stare, that could not see the flame of the candle, but was wide enough to embrace the whole universe, piercing enough to penetrate all the hearts that beat in the darkness . . . True, he had made that last stride, he had stepped over the edge, while I had been

permitted to draw back my hesitating foot. And perhaps in this is the whole difference; perhaps all the wisdom, and all truth, and all sincerity, are just compressed into that inappreciable moment of time in which we step over the threshold of the invisible (pp. 111, 112–13 [Williams has rearranged Conrad here: in 'Heart of Darkness', the passage which begins 'His was an impenetrable darkness . . .' and ends 'the sun never shines' comes before, not after, the passage that starts 'One evening coming in with a candle . . .']).

What comes into play then is 'your own inborn strength' (p. 63). 'There's no initiation . . . into such mysteries' (p. 20). Kurtz's essential moral failure, the lie at his heart, is not defined as the study of a person-ality. The intention of 'Heart of Darkness' is moral, in the sense that all great art proceeds from a moral centre. Kurtz 'open[ed] his mouth voraciously, as if to devour all the earth with all its mankind' (p. 117). His 'Intended' (a shadowy figure who occupies the least satisfactory part of the novel) is saved by her 'mature capacity for fidelity' (p. 119). But Kurtz's 'conquering' darkness (p. 117) leads out, 'to the uttermost ends of the earth', into the heart of an 'immense' darkness (p. 124).[39] □

Williams concludes by indicating that he feels his analysis is incomplete, and that he has not made explicit the evaluation that his analysis suggests – an evaluation that may be inferred to approach that of Leavis, but which would still perhaps be a more positive one, given that, as he says in his final paragraph, '"Heart of Darkness" is particularly close-knit, its moral statement controlled by a precise inter-relation of defined terms'.[40] He also says that lack of space prevents him from defining 'the extremely subtle identification of Marlow's destiny with Kurtz's'[41] – but clearly that is a hint for future critics to develop.

But for all the possibilities for further development that Williams's analysis offers, so also, today, can its exclusions be noted. Indeed, Williams himself provides an implicit key to those exclusions twenty years later, in his book *The English Novel from Dickens to Lawrence* (1970), where he observes that it is 'astonishing that a whole school of criticism has succeeded in emptying "Heart of Darkness" of its social and historical content, about which Conrad leaves us in no possible doubt'.[42] He omits to mention, however, that he was one of those critics responsible for such an 'emptying'. His analysis in *Reading and Criticism* is, to use his own term in that text, a very 'immanent' one, focusing only on what is supposedly inherent in the text and not moving beyond it to its contemporary histor-ical and ideological contexts – it is acknowledged that the river is 'obviously' the Congo, but then the matter is at once set aside. Whereas one of the early reviews of 'Heart of Darkness' felt it necessary, as was seen above (p. 14), to tell its readers that the novel was not a critique of imperialism, Williams does not seem to need to mention imperialism or colonialism at all. A possible critique is implied in his (questionable) remark that 'the area is not seen as one of savage darkness into which is brought light' but as having '*become* a place of darkness'; but he develops this point no further. It is significant that he cites the passage describing the French ship 'firing into a continent' on which, forty years later, Chinua Achebe would seize in his campaign against Conrad, pointing out that such an attack was not absurd at all, that it was one of the means by which imperial dominance was achieved and maintained. Achebe observes: 'By that crazy act of shelling the bush, France managed to acquire an empire in West and Equatorial Africa nine to ten times its own size'.[43] Williams, however, falls in with the mood of the passage and even reinforces it with his own remark about the 'absurd little warship'. Although Williams was politically committed to the left, he brings no political analysis to bear on Conrad's text, interpreting the story as one of 'essential moral failure' embodied in an individual, Kurtz, who is not located within specific colonialist and imperialist systems. In this silence about politics, he is very much a part of mainstream criticism of the 1950s. In terms of what later came to be called 'sexual politics', it is also notice-able that Williams seems to concur with Marlow's patronising remark about his 'excellent aunt' and that he dismisses the Intended in a much more summary way than Leavis, putting her in brackets, draining her of substance and relegating her to 'the least satisfactory part of the novel'. He makes the world of the novel into even more of a 'man's world' than Conrad does, even if he asserts that Conrad's notion of 'manhood' is dif-ferent from 'many ideas of masculinity'.

Williams's analysis had little direct influence, partly because he was still obscure at the time that it was published, and partly because it appeared as part of a textbook rather than as fully fledged criticism in its own right. But it remains a significant analysis, both for the elements of 'Heart of Darkness' that it acutely identifies and for its silences. In the 1950s and 60s, those elements were to be much more fully explored, and in the 1970s, 80s and 90s, those silences would start to be broken.

In his analysis, Williams alludes to the elements in 'Heart of Darkness' of 'that old literary-form, the Quest', although he contends that it would be misleading to describe the work in such terms. In 1955, however, Jerome Thale, in an essay first published in the *University of Toronto Quarterly*, affirmed that 'all the trappings of the conventional adventure tale' in 'Heart of Darkness' were only 'the vehicle of something more fun-damental', and that 'one way of getting at what they symbolize is to see the story as a grail quest'[44] – a quest that, however, is to be understood, for Thale, in humanist and existentialist rather than religious terms. The Grail that Marlow finds is not holy and offers no assurance of salvation. 'Kurtz is the grail at the end of Marlow's quest', and what Marlow discovers on his quest for that grail is 'the dreadful burden of human freedom'. Thus, Marlow's 'full illumination, his grail, is not transcendent being but the heart of man'.[45] In this kind of reading, 'the context of Africa' may be, as Thale asserts, 'important and necessary', but as a means for (white European male) self-discovery rather than in its own right: '[t]he journey to the heart of Africa is the journey into the depths of the self: Kurtz and Marlow travel into the heart of Africa and into the heart of man'.[46] Thale's approach was characteristic of a major strand of interpretation of 'Heart of Darkness': as Robert Burden points out, '[t]he Quest and the Journey of Discovery as mythic structures in ['Heart of Darkness'] are persistently discussed in Conrad criticism'.[47]

A different approach is taken by Thomas Moser in his study *Joseph Conrad: Achievement and Decline* (1957). Moser's overall thesis is that Conrad's writing is inferior in quality when he tries to write about love: '[t]he early Conrad's apprentice work and his failures strikingly resemble each other in subject matter and in symbolic imagery. Almost all deal in a major way with love'.[48] This approach leads Moser, in his account of 'Heart of Darkness', to focus on the novel's attitude to – or, more precisely, its exclusion of – women and sexuality. He sees 'Heart of Darkness' as the first work in which 'Conrad has been able to use material potentially related to sex in such a way as not to ruin his story and, in fact, in some respects to strengthen it'. The vegetation imagery, which Conrad, in his earlier work, has tended to associate with female menace, here takes on a wider range of meanings. Moser's interpretation remains interesting both in its own right and in relation to later feminist readings of 'Heart of Darkness'. This is his view of Conrad's novel:

■ [In 'Heart of Darkness', as] in 'Youth', all the principal characters are male. But Marlow, the narrator, makes some interesting comments on women; the last scene, between Marlow and Kurtz's Intended has considerable significance; and the jungle imagery raises some interesting problems. Marlow's most extended comment on women comes out apropos of his aunt's expostulations on the great missionary work of the Congo trading company. Marlow ventures to remind her that the company is run for profit, and then says in an aside to his male audience on board the yawl in the Thames estuary:

> It's queer how out of touch with truth women are. They live in a world of their own, and there had never been anything like it, and never can be. It is too beautiful altogether, and if they were to set it up it would go to pieces before the first sunset. Some confounded fact we men have been living contentedly with ever since the day of creation would start up and knock the whole thing over. (p. 28)

In the context of 'Heart of Darkness', with its theme of self-discovery, Marlow's assertion that women can take no part in the quest for truth is severe criticism indeed. Marlow says the same thing of Kurtz's Intended: 'Oh, she is out of it – completely. They – the women I mean – are out of it – they should be out of it. We must help them to stay in that beautiful world of their own' (p. 80).

Though 'Heart of Darkness' does not hint that Marlow has any sexual interest in the Intended, their scene together at the end certainly recalls in some respects scenes between the Herveys in 'The Return' (1898). For instance, though Marlow has been eager to meet her, he is filled with horror when he reaches her door. The fireplace in her drawing room has a 'cold and monumental whiteness' (p. 118). Marlow looks at the woman and wonders what he is doing there, 'with a sensation of panic in my heart as though I had blundered into a place of cruel and absurd mysteries not fit for a human being to behold' (p. 119). Their ensuing dialogue is halting and wooden, a 'bad patch' of prose as F. R. Leavis calls it [see p. 21 of this Guide]. Marlow has come there hoping to surrender to her the memory of Kurtz. She instead manoeuvres him into telling her a lie: that Kurtz's last words were, not '"The horror"' (p. 112), but her name: 'I heard a light sigh and then my heart stood still, stopped dead short by an exulting and terrible cry, by the cry of inconceivable triumph and of unspeakable pain' (p. 123). Marlow's lie certainly weakens the scene; he has made truth seem too important throughout the novel to persuade the reader now to accept falsehood as salvation.

The extended descriptions of the jungle remind us, not unnaturally, of the vegetation imagery of *Almayer's Folly* (1895) and *An Outcast of the Islands* (1896). Here, too, the 'vegetation rioted on the earth and the big trees were kings' (p. 59); the reader finds himself in a 'strange world of plants, and water, and silence' (p. 60). Yet 'Heart of Darkness' does not stress so heavily as the earlier works the strangling effects of tendrils and creepers. At one point, Marlow does mention the 'living trees, lashed together by the creepers' (p. 67), and at another he equates vegetation with woman just as he does not only in the Malay stories but also in *The Sisters* (1928 (unfinished)). The jungle woman is, of course, Kurtz's native mistress, 'savage and superb, wild-eyed and magnificent'. Marlow comments:

> And in the hush that had fallen suddenly upon the whole sorrowful land, the immense wilderness, the colossal body of the fecund and mysterious life seemed to look at her, pensive, as though it had been looking at the image of its own tenebrous and passionate soul. (p. 99)

Any reader of 'Heart of Darkness' must recognize that our analysis of it in terms of sexual love hardly scratches the surface. It means far more than this, and herein lies its significance. For the first time Conrad has been able to use material potentially related to sex in such a way as not to ruin his story and, in fact, in some respects to strengthen it. Our account of the imagery of the Congo jungle far from exhausts its meanings; rather, this imagery has the richness and tonality of the true symbol. The jungle stands for 'truth' (p.44), for an 'amazing reality' (p.48). Conrad equates it with the African natives who alone are full of vitality; the whites are but hollow men. Yet the jungle also means the 'lurking death', 'profound darkness' and 'evil' (p.58) which belong to the prehistoric life of man, our heritage. We cannot escape this heritage; going into the jungle seems to Marlow like travelling into one's own past, into the world of one's dreams, into the subconscious. Thus the vegetation imagery means much more than female menace; it means the truth, the darkness, the evil, the death which lie within us, which we must recognize in order to be truly alive. In the same way, while the scene between Marlow and Kurtz's Intended is imperfect, and while it does show the 'inconceivable triumph' (p.123) of woman over man, it has other, more important functions in the story. The scene can be read, for example, as an indictment of this woman, safe and ignorant in her complacent, Belgian bourgeois existence; she does not *deserve* to hear the truth. The scene can also be read as Marlow's reaffirmation of fellowship with Kurtz. To accept Kurtz's pronouncement, '"The horror"' (p.112), means accepting damnation; Marlow's sin, the lie, serves to confirm this.[49] □

Like Thale, then, Moser sees the novel as a kind of quest – 'a quest for truth' – even though he highlights, as Thale does not, the exclusion of women from that quest. Albert J. Guerard, in his very influential book *Conrad the Novelist* (1958), regards 'Heart of Darkness' not exactly as a quest, but certainly as a 'spiritual voyage of self-discovery' – more precisely, as Marlow's voyage of spiritual self-discovery; Guerard compares 'Heart of Darkness' to John Bunyan's novel *The Pilgrim's Progress* (Part 1: 1678; Part 2: 1684), calling it, in a famous formulation, 'a *Pilgrim's Progress* for our pessimistic and psychologizing age'.[50] Guerard acknowledges that 'Heart of Darkness' 'has its important public side, as an angry document on absurd and brutal exploitation'[51] and indeed makes a direct link with the politics of the 1950s: 'Conrad was reacting to the humanitarian pretences of some of the looters precisely as the novelist today reacts to the moralisms of cold-war propaganda. Then it was ivory that poured from the heart of darkness; now it is uranium'.[52] He also recognises the importance of Kurtz himself, and while he thinks that a 'little too much has been made . . . of the redemptive value' of Kurtz's '"The horror"' (p.112), he suggests that the 'redemptive view is Catholic' and contrasts Kurtz with a character from a mid-twentieth-century novel, Graham Greene's *The Power and the Glory* (1940): 'Kurtz can repent as the gunman of *The Power and the Glory* cannot'. Guerard affirms that, at a 'public and wholly conscious level', 'Heart of Darkness' 'combines a Victorian ethic and late Victorian fear of the white man's deterioration with a distinctly Catholic psychology'.[53] But for Guerard, 'the story is not primarily about Kurtz or about the brutality of Belgian officials but about Marlow its narrator'[54] – and, more specifically, about Marlow's 'night journey into the unconscious, and confrontation of an entity within the self'. It is a journey to be analysed as one might analyse 'the waking dream of a profoundly intuitive mind'. The extract below begins as Guerard develops his analysis of Marlow's inner voyage:

■ Substantially and in its central emphasis 'Heart of Darkness' concerns Marlow . . . and his journey towards and through certain facets or potentialities of self. F.R. Leavis seems to regard him as a narrator only, providing a 'specific and concretely realized point of view'.[55] But Marlow reiterates often enough that he is recounting a spiritual voyage of self-discovery. He remarks casually but crucially that he did not know himself before setting out, and that he likes work for the chance it provides to 'find yourself . . . what no other man can ever know' (p.52). The Inner Station 'was the farthest point of navigation and the culminating point of my experience' (p.21). At a material and rather superficial level, the journey is through the temptation of atavism [reversion to an earlier type]. It is a record of 'remote kinship' with the 'wild and passionate uproar', of a 'trace of a response' to it (p.63), of a final rejection of the 'fascination of the abomination' (p.20). And why should there not be the trace of a response? 'The mind of man is capable of anything – because everything is in it, all the past as well as all the future' (p.63). Marlow's temptation is made concrete through his exposure to Kurtz, a white man and sometime idealist who had fully responded to the wilderness: a potential and fallen self. 'I had turned to the wilderness really, not to Mr. Kurtz' (p.101). At the climax Marlow follows Kurtz ashore, confounds the beat of the drum with the beating of his heart, goes through the ordeal of looking into Kurtz's 'mad soul' (p.107 [the text actually reads: 'his soul was mad']) and brings him back to the ship. He returns to Europe a changed and more knowing man. Ordinary people are now 'intruders whose knowledge of life was to me an irritating pretence, because I felt so sure they could not possibly know the things I knew' (p.114).

On this literal plane, and when the events are so abstracted from the dream-sensation conveying them, it is hard to take Marlow's plight very seriously. Will he, the busy captain and moralizing narrator, also revert to savagery, go ashore for a howl and a dance, indulge unspeakable lusts? The late Victorian reader (and possibly Conrad himself) could take this more seriously than we; could literally believe not merely in a Kurtz's deterioration through months of solitude but also in the sudden reversions to the 'beasts' of naturalistic fiction. Insofar as Conrad does want us to take it seriously and literally, we must admit the nominal triumph of a currently accepted but false psychology over his own truer intuitions. But the triumph is only nominal. For the personal narrative is unmistakably authentic, which means that it explores something truer, more fundamental, and distinctly less material: the night journey into the unconscious, and confrontation of an entity within the self. 'I flung one shoe overboard, and became aware that that was exactly what I had been looking forward to – a talk with Kurtz' (p. 79). It little matters what, in terms of psychological symbolism, we call this double or say he represents: whether the Freudian id or the Jungian shadow or more vaguely the outlaw. And I am afraid it is impossible to say where Conrad's conscious understanding of his story began and ended. The important thing is that the introspective plunge and powerful dream seem true; and are therefore inevitably moving.

Certain circumstances of Marlow's voyage, looked at in these terms, take on a new importance. The true night journey can occur (except during analysis) only in sleep or in the waking dream of a profoundly intuitive mind. Marlow insists more than is necessary on the dreamlike quality of his narrative. 'It seems to me I am trying to tell you a dream – making a vain attempt, because no relation of a dream can convey the dream-sensation, that commingling of absurdity, surprise, and bewilderment in a tremor of struggling revolt . . . ' (p. 50). Even before leaving Brussels Marlow felt as though he 'were about to set off for the centre of the earth' (p. 29), not the centre of a continent.[56] The introspective voyager leaves his familiar rational world, is 'cut off from the comprehension' of his surroundings; his steamer toils 'along slowly on the edge of a black and incomprehensible frenzy' (p. 62). As the crisis approaches, the dreamer and his ship move through a silence that 'seemed unnatural, like a state of trance' (p. 67); then enter (a few miles below the Inner Station) a deep fog. 'The approach to this Kurtz grubbing for ivory in the wretched bush was beset by as many dangers as though he had been an enchanted princess sleeping in a fabulous castle' (p. 72).[57] Later, Marlow's task is to try to 'break the spell' (p. 106) of the wilderness that holds Kurtz entranced.

The approach to the unconscious and primitive may be aided by a savage or half-savage guide, and may require the token removal of civilized trappings or aids . . . In 'Heart of Darkness' the token 'relinquishment' and the death of the half-savage guide are connected.

The helmsman falling at Marlow's feet casts blood on his shoes, which he is 'morbidly anxious' to change (p. 78) and in fact throws overboard[58] . . . Here we have presumably entered an area of unconscious creation; the dream is true but the teller may have no idea why it is. So too, possibly, a psychic need as well as literary tact compelled Conrad to defer the meeting between Marlow and Kurtz for some three thousand words after announcing that it took place. We think we are about to meet Kurtz at last. But instead Marlow leaps ahead to his meeting with the 'Intended'; comments on Kurtz's megalomania and assumption of his place among the devils of the land; reports on the seventeen-page pamphlet; relates his meeting and conversation with Kurtz's harlequin disciple – and only then tells of seeing through his binoculars the heads on the stakes surrounding Kurtz's house. This is the 'evasive' Conrad in full play, deferring what we most want to know and see; perhaps compelled to defer climax in this way. The tactic is dramatically effective, though possibly carried to excess: we are told on the authority of completed knowledge certain things we would have found hard to believe had they been presented through a slow consecutive realistic discovery. But also it can be argued that it was psychologically impossible for Marlow to go at once to Kurtz's house with the others. The double must be brought on board the ship, and the first confrontation must occur there . . . The incorporation and alliance between the two becomes material, and the identification of 'selves'.

Hence the shock Marlow experiences when he discovers that Kurtz's cabin is empty and his secret sharer gone; a part of himself has vanished. 'What made this emotion so overpowering was – how shall I define it? – the moral shock I received, as if something altogether monstrous, intolerable to thought and odious to the soul, had been thrust upon me unexpectedly' (p. 104). And now he must risk the ultimate confrontation in a true solitude and must do so on shore. 'I was anxious to deal with this shadow by myself alone, – and to this day I don't know why I was so jealous of sharing with any one the peculiar blackness of that experience' (pp. 104–05). He follows the crawling Kurtz through the grass; comes upon him 'long, pale, indistinct, like a vapour exhaled by the earth'. ('I had cut him off cleverly . . .' (p. 105 [Guerard's ellipsis]).) We are told very little of what Kurtz said in the moments that follow; and little of his incoherent discourses after he is brought back to the ship. 'His was an impenetrable darkness. I looked at him as you peer down at a man who is lying at the bottom of a precipice where the sun never shines' (p. 111) – a comment less vague and rhetorical, in terms of psychic geography, than it may seem at a first reading. And then Kurtz is dead, taken off the ship, his body buried in a 'muddy hole' (p. 112). With the confrontation over, Marlow must still emerge from environing darkness, and does so through that other deep fog of sickness. The identification is not yet completely broken. 'And it is not my own extremity I remember best – a vision of greyness without form filled with physical pain, and a careless contempt for the evanescence of all things – even of this pain itself. No! It is his extremity that I seem to have lived through' (p. 113). Only in the atonement of his lie to Kurtz's 'Intended', back in the sepulchral city, does the experience come truly to an end. 'I laid the ghost of his gifts at last with a lie . . .' (p. 80).

Such seems to be the content of the dream. If my summary has even a partial validity it should explain and to an extent justify some of the 'adjectival and worse than supererogatory insistence' [see p. 21 of this Guide][59] to which F. R. Leavis (who sees only the travelogue and the portrait of Kurtz) objects. I am willing to grant that the unspeakable rites and unspeakable secrets become wearisome, but the fact – at once literary and psychological – is that they must remain *unspoken*. A confrontation with such a double and facet of the unconscious cannot be reported through realistic dialogue . . . when Marlow finds it hard to define the moral shock he received on seeing the empty cabin, or when he says he doesn't know why he was jealous of sharing his experience, I think we can take him literally . . . [Guerard's ellipsis] and in a sense even be thankful for his uncertainty. The greater tautness and economy of 'The Secret Sharer' (1910) comes from its larger consciousness of the psychological process it describes; from its more deliberate use of the double as symbol. And of the two stories I happen to prefer it. But it may be the groping, fumbling 'Heart of Darkness' takes us into a deeper region of the mind. If the story is not about this deeper region, and not about Marlow himself, its length is quite indefensible. But even if one were to allow that the final section is about Kurtz (which I think simply absurd), a vivid pictorial record of his unspeakable lusts and gratifications would surely have been ludicrous. I share Mr. Leavis's admiration for the heads on the stakes. But not even Kurtz could have supported many such particulars.[60] □

Guerard's account of 'Heart of Darkness' was not only a key interpretation in the Conrad criticism of the 1950s; it also anticipated a major cultural theme of the following decade. This was the theme of the 'inner voyage', the confrontation with the dark and split-off parts of the self, which found expression in books such as *The Divided Self* (1962) and *The Politics of Experience and The Bird of Paradise* (1968), by the existential psychiatrist R. D. Laing, and in novels like Doris Lessing's *The Golden Notebook* (1962) and *Briefing for a Descent into Hell* (1971). Improbable though it may seem, the work of the conservative Conrad could, through an interpretation such as Guerard's, strike chords with the 1960s counterculture – and this resonance was to produce perhaps its greatest result in Francis Ford Coppola's film *Apocalypse Now* (1979). In the 1960s, literary critics would often allude to Guerard's approach, enlarging on and dissenting from it; but they would also start to explore other aspects of 'Heart of Darkness' more deeply, such as its politics and its humour. The next chapter looks at these developments.

CHAPTER TWO

Metaphysics, Politics and a Hole in a Pail: 'Heart of Darkness' in the 1960s

BY 1960 CONRAD, and 'Heart of Darkness', were well-established as fitting subjects for literary study. 'Heart of Darkness' in particular provided a compact and manageable text that was rich in structural and stylistic complexity, in wide-ranging suggestiveness, and in allusions to other, more ancient canonical texts such as Bunyan's *The Pilgrim's Progress*, Dante's *Inferno*, the Holy Bible, and Virgil's *Aeneid*. It was ideal for seminar discussion in a way that longer novels, whether by Conrad or other writers, were not. Moreover, as was suggested at the end of the previous chapter, 'Heart of Darkness' could appeal to – perhaps even helped to contribute to – the ethos of the 1960s, especially when it was interpreted in terms like those of Guerard's, as an inner voyage of self-discovery.

The appearance right at the start of the decade of Jocelyn Baines's detailed, lucid and sensitive critical biography was a major boost to further Conrad studies. The 'critical' aspect of Baines's account of 'Heart of Darkness' is not particularly innovative, but it confirms and reinforces the novel's status. He contends that its 'power and fascination . . . rest upon the tale's moral elusiveness and ambiguity',[1] and it could be argued that its suitability as a teaching text also rests on those qualities. Baines is not uncritical; though his discussion of 'Heart of Darkness' does not cite Leavis explicitly, it echoes Leavis's objection to Conrad's 'adjectival insistence', finding that the 'epithets and phrases' such as 'inconceivable' and inscrutable' with which the novel's pages are 'spattered' are 'debased by their constant use'. He nonetheless sees 'Heart of Darkness' as 'one of the finest short stories that have been written',[2] though his definition of it as a 'short story' begs some questions. Kurtz's last words are interpreted as 'the crux of the story' in which, '[j]ust before he dies Kurtz is vindicated by a full emotional realization of his experience'. Marlow himself, and the whole story, are seen in Biblical terms: '[i]t is as if [Marlow] were re-enacting the legend of the Fall'.[3]

The high place 'Heart of Darkness' now enjoyed in the Anglo-American literary canon was confirmed by Lionel Trilling's discussion of it in 'On the Modern Element in Modern Literature', first published in *Partisan Review* in January–February 1961, and given wider circulation and authority by its appearance, under the title 'On the Teaching of Modern Literature', as the first essay in Trilling's *Beyond Culture: Essays on Literature and Learning* (1965). Trilling's earlier collection of essays, *The Liberal Imagination* (1950) had elevated him to 'pundit status' among the Anglo-American intelligentsia, and his pronouncements, particularly when they came out in book form, were likely to be listened to. 'On the Teaching of Modern Literature' has two concerns. One is the response of students to modern literature; the other is the definition of modern literature itself. With regard to student response, Trilling worries that his students, about whom he writes in a rather patronising way, seem not to be 'taken aback' by their study of modern literature, that they appear all too ready 'to engage in the process that we might call the socialization of the anti-social, or the acculturation of the anti-cultural, or the legitimization of the subversive'[4] – although he acknowledges that he 'must think it possible that in ways and to a degree which they keep secret they have responded directly and personally to what they have read'.[5] The question of the definition of modern literature itself involves Trilling in a number of broad generalisations: that 'the characteristic element of modern literature, or at least of the most highly developed modern literature, is the bitter line of hostility to civilization which runs through it';[6] that 'the chief intention of all modern literature' is 'to free [it]self from the middle class'; and that 'the means of freedom which in effect all of modern literature prescribes' is that of 'losing oneself up to the point of self-destruction, of surrendering oneself to experience without regard to self-interest or conventional morality, of escaping wholly from the societal bonds'.[7] In his quest for definition, Trilling twice uses the 'nothing is more characteristic than' formula, seeming to offer, in fairly quick succession, two somewhat different candidates for one vacancy – that of the most definitive characteristic of modern literature. He first contends that '[n]othing is more characteristic of modern literature than its discovery and canonization of the primal, non-ethical energies'[8] and later that '[n]othing is more characteristic of the literature of our time than the replacement of the hero by what has come to be called the anti-hero'.[9] It may be that 'modern literature' is not quite identical with 'the literature of our time', but Trilling does not make the distinction explicit. In the light of such definitions, however, questionable though they may be, 'Heart of Darkness' shines forth as a model of a modern literary text. Trilling sums up the novel in this way:

■ This very great work has never lacked for the admiration it deserves, and it has been given a kind of canonical place in the legend of modern literature by Eliot's having it so clearly in mind when he wrote 'The Waste Land' and his having taken from it the epigraph to 'The Hollow Men'. But no one, to my knowledge, has ever confronted in an explicit way its strange and terrible message of ambivalence towards the life of civilization. Consider that its protagonist, Kurtz, is a progressive and a liberal and that he is the highly respected representative of a society which would have us believe it is benign, although in fact it is vicious. Consider too that he is a practitioner of several arts, a painter, a writer, a musician, and into the bargain a political orator. He is at once the most idealistic and the most practically successful of all the agents of the Belgian exploitation of the Congo. Everybody knows the truth about him which Marlow discovers – that Kurtz's success is a result of a terrible ascendancy he has gained over the natives of his distant station, an ascendancy which is derived from his presumed magical or divine powers, that he has exercised his rule with an extreme of cruelty, that he has given himself to unnameable acts of lust. This is the world of the darker pages of [J. G.] Frazer's *The Golden Bough* (1890; 1900; 1911–15). It is one of the great points of Conrad's story that Marlow speaks of the primitive life of the jungle not as being noble or charming or even free but as being base and sordid – and for *that* reason compelling: he himself feels quite overtly its dreadful attraction. It is to this devilish baseness that Kurtz has yielded himself, and yet Marlow, although he does indeed treat him with hostile irony, does not find it possible to suppose that Kurtz is anything but a hero of the spirit. For me it is still ambiguous whether Kurtz's famous deathbed cry, '"The horror! The horror!"' (p. 112) refers to the approach of death or to his experience of savage life. Whichever it is, to Marlow the fact that Kurtz could utter this cry at the point of death, while Marlow himself, when death threatens him, can know it only as a weary greyness, marks the difference between the ordinary man and a hero of the spirit. Is this not the essence of the modern belief about the nature of the artist, the man who goes down into that hell which is the historical beginning of the human soul, a beginning not outgrown but established in humanity as we know it now, preferring the reality of this hell to the bland lies of the civilization that has overlaid it?[10] □

It can be seen that, for Trilling, 'Heart of Darkness' is, unequivocally, a 'very great work'. Like Leavis, Trilling alludes to its association with T. S. Eliot, but he expresses none of Leavis's reservations about Conrad's 'adjectival insistence'. Indeed, that insistence seems to produce the required response in Trilling, with his assumption that 'the primitive life of the jungle' is 'base', 'sordid' and 'devilish'. Although Trilling asserts that Kurtz's society is 'vicious', there is little of Raymond Williams's sense that Africa has *become* a place of darkness, that if it is base, sordid, and devilish, this is, partly at least, because of the white man's intervention. Trilling posits a binary opposition between civilisation and primitivism, without any apparent awareness that 'the primitive life of the jungle' could have its own kind of indigenous culture and civilisation. He mentions 'exploitation', but he does not use the word 'imperialism', although this absence is also evident, as has been seen, in both Williams (in 1950) and Leavis. Trilling reduces the possible interpretations of Kurtz's last words to two options, whereas there are other possibilities – for example, Kurtz could be uttering a judgement on his own actions, and thus reaffirming 'the life of civilization'. Altogether, Trilling offers one interesting but limited and selective reading of 'Heart of Darkness' that is very much in line with the kind of interpretation of the novel that was becoming dominant in the later 1950s and early 1960s, despite his implicit claim that he is doing something new because no one, prior to himself, had ever explicitly confronted the novel's 'strange and terrible message of ambivalence towards the life of civilization'.

A different, more worldly and historical approach is taken by Eloise Knapp Hay in a long chapter on 'Heart of Darkness' in her critical study *The Political Novels of Joseph Conrad* (1963). Here Trilling's ahistorical antinomies of 'civilization' and 'the primitive' are relocated in an imperialist context. Conrad, Hay contends, was a didactic, political writer who produced, in 'Heart of Darkness', 'a vehement denunciation of imperialism and racialism' that nonetheless did not damn 'all men who through the accident of their birth in England were committed to these public policies'. This, of course, is a rather different judgement from the one that Chinua Achebe would later express (see pp. 71, 73–84). Hay inverts the subordination of the political to the mythological practised by critics such as Feder, Thale and Guerard; in her perspective, it is the pressure of Conrad's political concern that produces the mythological references:

■ To a man for whom 'race' meant 'nation' more than 'pigmentation', and for whom 'nation' was a sacred image, the nineteenth-century cultivation of racialism as a means of commercial profit through tyranny was history's most agonizing chapter. In conveying the effect upon his mind, he could only imagine the worst torments of hell, invoke Virgil and Dante who had seen hell as if with their own eyes (knowing it as a place where evil is not justified by the morality of the moment), and add to their testimony what he had seen with *his* eyes in the Congo.[11] □

Hay sets out the contemporary historical context of 'Heart of Darkness', pointing to the 'crisis in South Africa which, from the point of view of the public at large, was at once the most dramatic trial of British imperial claims and the clearest test of the very idea of imperialism', and suggesting that Cecil Rhodes, in 'his combination of titanic idealism with daemonic egotism . . . appears the prototype of a Conrad character', particularly perhaps of Kurtz.[12] Homing in on 'Heart of Darkness' itself, Hay argues that Marlow should be seen as an impercipient narrator, rather than as a figure whose experiences in the Congo have matured him; she suggests that a fundamental challenge to imperialism emerges from the discrepancy between what Marlow says and what Conrad presents. Whereas Raymond Williams saw Marlow's attitude to the 'idea' of Western civilisation bringing 'light' as one of constant irony (p. 26), Hay sees Marlow – though not Conrad – as partly complicit with it. She takes issue directly with the view that, as she puts it, 'the jungle and all it signifies for Conrad in "Heart of Darkness" is evil in the sense of intrinsically alien to man's social instincts' – a view that is, she suggests, implied by two critics discussed in the previous chapter – Moser and Guerard – and which, as was seen earlier in this chapter, is shared by Lionel Trilling. The following extract shows how Hay develops her case; it begins by stressing that there is another narrator in the story besides Marlow, the first narrator who opens and closes the novel and creates the 'frame' for Marlow's tale:

■ As the novel begins, both the first narrator and Marlow give voice to the same thoughts with subtle differences. 'And this also . . . has been one of the dark places of the earth' (p. 18), says Marlow, implying that this England, this London, are no longer dark, though the first narrator has just noted that they are quite hidden beneath the gloom. Then, looking at the Thames, Marlow puts in his own words what the other [the first narrator] has just said about the 'great knights-errant' of Elizabethan exploration, the '[h]unters for gold or pursuers of fame . . . bearing the sword, and often the torch . . . bearers of a spark from the sacred fire' (p. 17). Answering, Marlow says:

> Light came out of this river since – you say Knights? Yes; but it is like a running blaze on a plain, like a flash of lightning in the clouds. We live in the flicker – may it last as long as the old earth keeps rolling! But darkness was here yesterday. (p. 19)

Both voices give us the curious picture of torch-carriers issuing out of darkness. To the first voice it is 'a spark from the sacred fire', which like the gloom this voice described over London will have a later resonance, for 'sacred' in this story is a highly fraught word. Marlow, the English seaman, is modestly aware that the light of England's achievements and civilization was struck by men long dead, that he and his contemporaries bask in the reflection of their glory, but his unwary optimism proposes an absurdity: that the light shed by a grass fire or a flash of lightning might last to the end of time! Marlow seems little affected at this point by the experience he is about to recount.

Reading this story repeatedly, as we must for anything like its full effect, we know that the dark English coast before him recalls for Marlow the darkness of modern Africa, which is the natural darkness of the jungle but more than that the darkness of moral vacancy, leading to the atrocities he has beheld in Africa. In a second reading we may wonder even this early whether the moral darkness Marlow saw in Africa is, as he implies, the same as the precivilized darkness of England, or if Marlow's insight is incomplete. For the moral darkness of Africa, we learn later, is not the simple darkness of native 'ignorance', but of white men who have blinded themselves and corrupted the natives by their claim to be light-bearers. If I am not mistaken, the reader must very early begin to question Marlow's ultimate 'discovery', for we are from the start treated to several questionable examples of his wisdom, this Marlow who has been matured, supposedly, by his Congo experience . . . . . .

Although Marlow admits that English conquest, like all others, 'means the taking [of the earth] away from those who have a different complexion or slightly flatter noses than ourselves', he claims that the English form is redeemed by an idea: '[a]n idea at the back of it; not a sentimental pretence but an idea; and an unselfish belief in the idea – something you can set up, and bow down before, and offer a sacrifice to' (p. 20).

All critics have read this astonishing passage as a straightforward, unambiguous apology for British imperialism, spoken from Conrad's heart through Marlow's mouth. No one seems to hear the reverberations of Marlow's bitter emphasis later on figures of religious devotion, especially the worship of ideas. [It was not, in fact, the case that 'all critics', at the time at which Hay was writing, had interpreted the passage in the way that Hay suggests – as was seen in the previous chapter, Raymond Williams, in 1950, recognised the link between Marlow's apology for British imperialism and the reverberations of Marlow's later 'bitter emphasis' on the worship of ideas (see p. 25). But there is no sign that Hay had read Williams's book.] He will himself finally say that he had to lay the ghost of Kurtz's 'gifts' with a lie, but it is left to the reader to perceive that Marlow must kill off a part of his own self-knowledge with lies in order to save the 'beautiful world' (p. 80) of British civilization along with the beautiful world of Kurtz's Intended.

Before his last insight the cadaverous Kurtz will speak of right motives and redeeming ideas, too: '"[o]f course you must take care of the motives – right motives – always"' (p. 110). Marlow then wonders if Kurtz is preparing phrases for some newspaper as he speaks, even while dying, of '"the furthering of my ideas. It's a duty"' (p. 111). At the beginning of the tale, Marlow's words about redeeming ideas must have a jarring effect if we follow his curious notion that the British 'idea' has to become a sort of idol, reducing the minds that hold it to the posture of worshippers. The mind that masters the idea is to become its slave? Why this association of ideas and idols? ... ...

At the first company station, Marlow is shown a picture painted by the remarkable Mr. Kurtz, 'representing a woman, draped and blind-folded, carrying a lighted torch. The background was sombre – almost black. The movement of the woman was stately, and the effect of the torchlight on the face was sinister' (pp. 46–47). Stately *and* sinister, in Marlow's descriptive, unanalytical words – not stately *but* sinister. Only much later in the story will the reader learn that Kurtz saw his mission in Africa as that of torchbearer for white civilization ...

Marlow never interprets the allegory of the painting or asks why the face appears sinister. He does not connect the light of the torch-bearers that came out of England with the light on the lady's face. We remember, of course, that it was the first narrator who compared England's light to the brand of a torchcarrier. The reader may suspect that darkness – the black of the natives as well as of 'ignorance' in uncivilized portions of the earth – is innocent; and hence the corollary holds, that light may have an evil influence.

We have, then, even in the first pages of the novel, repeated rever-sals or inversions of normal patterns of imagery, warning us to perceive that what appears to be bright and white may turn out to be dark or black in many different senses [this echoes Raymond Williams's point – see pp. 24, 25–26, 28–29]; that what seems holy and sacred may prove to be idolatrous and even diabolical; that what is clothed may be stripped. The reversal works both for the European whites and the African blacks. For Marlow will establish in his more lucid moments (and we must admit he has many) that what is black in Africa is what has a right to be there. If whiteness finally emerges as moral vacuity, blackness finally appears as reality, humanity, and truth ... ...

It is typical of Marlow's dilemma that while he claims to be con-cerned above all with self-knowledge and truth, he progresses towards deception and denial; while disdainful of the staves which all the European civilizers carry in the Congo, he obsessively frets that they and he himself lack anything to support them; and while priding him-self on the power of his English belief in an idea, he can find no 'real' idea in his head to support him when he needs it.

Marlow cannot interpret clearly the question of what supports a man, though he can sense the different aspects of social life that should put something solid 'behind' a man. The European parasites in Africa are hollow, we are made to believe, because they have no personal moral vision of their inhumanity and folly, but they are also collapsible because they have nothing 'behind them' – in their society's institu-tions – to hold them up.[13] Marlow shares the onus, and he is conscious of doing so. For his own reasons, he becomes a pretender like the others. He lets the brickmaker think he is an important emissary of the company, higher in status than the brickmaker, closer to Kurtz. 'I became in an instant as much of a pretence as the rest of the bewitched pilgrims. This simply because I had a notion it somehow would be of help to that Kurtz whom at the time I did not see – you understand' (p. 50). Instead of stopping the foolish 'papier-mâché Mephistopheles' (p. 48), Marlow says, 'I let him run on . . . and think what he pleased about the powers that were behind me. I did! And there was nothing behind me' (pp. 50–51).

Just when men have most need of the institutions their civilization boasts of – particularly in 'backward' lands – they find nothing available. The corner policeman and the reassuring pressures of public opinion are not only too far away, but their strength has been built on men's ability to forget the very things they would have to know in order truly to conquer a wilderness. Like one hydrogen-filled balloon tied to another, when Kurtz's diabolism is revealed to him, Marlow says Kurtz 'had kicked himself loose of the earth . . . and I before him did not know whether I stood on the ground or floated in the air' (p. 107).

Marlow's sharpening awareness of 'reality' suffers a bifurcation early in the story. On one side is his consciousness of what is real for the Africans, which turns out to be their natural lives and surroundings in Africa. What is real for the Westerners reduces itself quickly to their reasons for being there. 'The word "ivory" rang in the air, was whispered, was sighed. You would think they were praying to it' (p. 44). But the ivory, which is white like the men, is the mean side of another aim that is at once more exalted and more pernicious. As ivory has become the idol of the foolish run of European pilgrims, the ideal of racial whiteness and all it supposedly stands for has become the idol of 'superior' white men like Kurtz. Marlow was prepared to find Kurtz a man for whom the ivory was only the outward sign of an inward grace. The allegoric picture and the reports of Kurtz's artistic, intellectual, and persuasive powers whetted his appeal for the Marlow who described himself as a man that would offer sacrifices to an idea, as a man who imagined his best weapon against the jungle was his 'voice', his power of speech – 'for good or evil mine is the speech that cannot be silenced' (p. 63).

Progressively Conrad tangles the Marlow who will surrender to Kurtz in his own yarn. The irony is Conrad's, not Marlow's, when Marlow reveals that Kurtz had 'appropriately' been entrusted with the job of giving guidance to the International Society for the Suppression of Savage Customs. ('All Europe contributed to the making of Kurtz', and likewise the society for suppressing the natives is 'International'.)

Marlow's comment on the report is characteristically confusing: 'eloquent . . . but too high-strung, I think'. While he spins the yarn, the thought seems to occur to him that there was something a bit 'ominous' in Kurtz's paragraph asserting that the white men must necessarily appear to the savages as '"supernatural beings"', who by the '"simple exercise of our will"' can exert practically unbounded power '"for good"'. This same report, he says, made him 'tingle with enthusiasm' (p.83). And when he finally does express irony, he rises to it considerably later than the quick reader gives him credit for. It is only when he ironically calls the report's 'valuable' postscript ('"Exterminate all the brutes!"' (p.84)) 'the exposition of a method' (p.83) that we know Marlow has at last reached Conrad's level of irony. Even now, however, Marlow (aboard the *Nellie*, supposing himself freed of Kurtz's influence and 'gifts') has missed an important aspect of the story he is telling. His perception that Kurtz in his madness was driven to an ultimate insight which was, in the report, the 'exposition of a method' does not suggest to Marlow, even while he comments wryly on it, that all talk of method – efficiency – is in itself despicable in a report that from beginning to end is vicious by its premises that all savage customs should be suppressed and that there is something almost supernatural about white men . . . . . .

At the moment of greatest crisis, when Marlow is faced with 'a choice of nightmares' (p.101) and will side with the diabolical Kurtz against the flabbier devils of the European trading company, we may too quickly assume that there is some radical difference between the two nightmares. Reading more cautiously, we discover that Kurtz's characteristics can be found in diluted solution in all the other Europeans, and Marlow himself, in his own way, betrays his kinship. What Marlow with incomplete irony calls the accountant's 'achievements of character' (p.36) are revealed by the meticulously white linen he wears. Marlow, as marveler, registers but never questions or later recalls that when he asked the clerk 'how he managed to sport such linen', the clerk answered with 'just the faintest blush' (p.36), that he had '"been teaching one of the native women about the station. It was difficult. She had a distaste for the work"'. Kurtz, too, had influence with a native woman. Hearing the clerk's explanation, Marlow – the moralist who sanctifies Britain's efficient imperialism – comments, 'Thus this man had verily accomplished something' (p.37).

Clearly the accountant's devotion to his job is successful only because he can obliterate from his mind all conflicting intrusions from the African wilderness. When he tells Marlow about Kurtz, more efficient than all other agents in sending out ivory, a dying European who has just come out of Kurtz's territory is lying within earshot. His groaning distracts the accountant, but the sick man is too ill to offer any correcting information on the subject of Kurtz. The enchanted silence protecting Kurtz from the inquiries of his fellow workers is thus protected by the celebrated job sense of the efficient clerk, compartmentalizing himself against all disruptive knowledge.

This scene prepares us for the superbly dramatic last pages of the story when Marlow, too, will close off a sentimental lady – and not only a lady but himself and all Europe – against the disruptive truth of Kurtz's experience.

'Everything else in the station', of course, 'was in a muddle, – heads, things, buildings' (p. 37), except only this miracle of neatness, who significantly is the first to mention the name of Kurtz. He is in fact a clue to Kurtz, who is also a creature standing in the forefront of his kind, distinguished by special 'virtues'. Marlow insists that these superior individuals, to whom will be added the Russian 'harlequin' (p. 87), in some way relieve the stupidity of the farce. Finally, taken together, they merely define the only alternative choice to the nightmare of delusion in which the manager of the company is the main figure.

In the design of the novel there are, thus, the extremes represented on one hand as efficiency and intellectual superiority, signalled by the accountant and the 'harlequin' respectively, pointing to Kurtz as head, and on the other extremes of inefficiency and inanity, represented by the anonymous officials of the company, by the 'brickmaker' (pp. 47, 101) and the manager. When Marlow chooses the nightmare dominated by Kurtz in preference to the nightmare of the inferior traders, he gravitates to the pole of his own values, without fully exploring his kinship with Kurtz.

A further exposé of Marlow's devotion to efficiency is built up around the handbook of seamanship which Marlow discovers in an abandoned hut, in front of which hung a 'flag of some sort' and a 'neatly stacked wood-pile' (p. 64) – the one a symbol of yet another nation planting its claim in Africa, the other a fine exemplum of good method. The manual, '"An Inquiry into some Points of Seamanship," by a man Tower, Towson – some such name',[14] inspires Marlow with its 'singleness of intention, an honest concern with the right way of going to work'. And he experiences another of his moments of relief, the 'delicious sensation of having come upon something unmistakably real' (p. 65). In the margins, however, are unreadable notes, which he learns only later are not ciphers but notations in Russian. It turns out that the owner of the book, like the accountant 'wonderfully neat' (p. 87), is the son of an archpriest, who has run away to sea and then to Africa in search of experience and ideas . . . like Marlow, this young man is capable of marvelling without discernment and is a worshipper at the shrine of efficiency and ideas, which is the altar over which Kurtz, the most 'successful' of all the ivory hunters, is God.

As the 'hairdresser's dummy' accountant (p. 36) had some of the virtues that hallow Kurtz, so too this Russian 'harlequin' – another figure from make-believe worlds, with whom belongs also the 'papier-mâché Mephistopheles' (p. 48). The marvellously mended suit of the Russian might remind us of the patchwork talents of Kurtz, the 'universal genius', whom Marlow thinks of as 'draped nobly in the folds of a gorgeous eloquence' (p. 117), the Kurtz who is also the patchwork of all Europe. [In a 1966 essay, Mario D'Avanzo points out the resemblance between the harlequin's patches and the map with the European colour codes Marlow sees in Brussels (p. 25). Perry Meisel (1978),[15] see p. 90, and Hampson (1995), p. 137, note 102, also draw attention to this similarity.] And the glamorous young Russian is indeed a thing of patches – a snatch of several different explorers (Mungo Park, as Conrad describes the fair youth in 'Geography and Some Explorers',[16] the quixotic Roger Casement, and Conrad himself) all possessed by the 'absolutely pure, uncalculating, unpractical spirit of adventure' (p. 90). Is he not, too, a remnant of earlier history and the earlier part of Marlow's tale, of those 'knights-errant of the sea' who bearing 'a spark from the sacred fire' (p. 17), had first opened the dark places of the earth? In him we see man's continuing expansive energy, gullibly innocent of its association with all the despotisms intruding on the integrity of Africa.[17]

When Conrad saw what the young Russian saw in Africa, it changed his life. ('Before the Congo I was just a mere animal'.[18]) But in 'Heart of Darkness' not one of these intruders is changed into a moral being by what he sees. Or rather, only Kurtz – ultimately, when it's too late – becomes a moral agent. Marlow then sides with him in his 'victory' (p. 114) but only imperfectly: 'I was within a hair's-breadth of the last opportunity for pronouncement, and I found with humiliation that probably I would have nothing to say . . . He had summed up – he had judged . . . After all, this was the expression of some sort of belief' (p. 113).

If taken as evidence of Marlow's moral enlightenment after meeting Kurtz, this is most unsatisfactory. Much earlier Marlow was convinced that Kurtz 'had come out equipped with moral ideas of some sort' (p. 55). Now Marlow has only been reassured, after frightful disillusionment, that indeed Kurtz achieved 'some sort of belief'.

Kurtz may in the end see himself even as he is seen. But Marlow? We watch him cling to Kurtz as a fugitive clings to a foothold above an abyss. Having clutched at one inadequate support after another among the hopeful symbols of his culture in Africa: the efficient accountant, the work he himself has been trained for, the manual of seamanship – all comforts having to do with good method – at perhaps the most critical moment in the story, when the general manager uses just this standard for judging Kurtz, Marlow is revolted.

In answer to the manager's remark that '"Mr. Kurtz's methods had ruined the district"' (for trading purposes), Marlow confusedly mumbles

'"No method at all"' (p. 101 [the remark Hay attributes to the manager is in fact Hay's condensed paraphrase of what he is represented as saying]), meaning what it is hard to guess, unless that at this point he refuses to think at all of Kurtz's methods in collecting ivory, this spokesman for British efficiency. Of course, it is because the manager cannot see that there is more than a question of method in Kurtz's madness that Marlow feels he has 'never breathed an atmosphere so vile' and turns 'mentally to Kurtz for relief' (p. 101). Kurtz has discovered (in himself) evil unsimulated, though until his very last words he goes on posing as a standard-bearer of European superiority in matters of efficiency and ideas . . . . . .

Identifying Marlow closely with Conrad, Guerard suggests that the novel expresses a deferred collision between 'the adventurous Conrad and Conrad the moralist'.[19] But surely *that* collision is conveyed better in Marlow's meeting with the Russian than in his meeting with Kurtz. Face to face with Kurtz, Marlow experiences a more serious collision, between Conrad the British subject and Conrad the moralist. The question left hanging is whether good work any more than evil work justifies the empire-builder in Africa.

In the iconography of the novel, Marlow's talk of 'devotion to efficiency' has a religious overtone no less menacing than his reference to an 'unselfish belief in the idea – something you can set up, and bow down before, and offer a sacrifice to' (p. 20). We cannot separate these images altogether from the 'pilgrims', the ivory ('[y]ou would think they were praying to it' (p. 44)), the young Russian's worship of Kurtz's ideas, and Kurtz himself, self-apotheosized, 'insatiable of splendid appearances, of frightful realities' (p. 117).

Of course I am speaking of the public or political logic of Marlow's narrative. As Moser and Guerard have shown, the same material lends itself to psychological analysis on a more private level. But whether or not the latter is 'deeper' as far as the significance of the novel is concerned, it is unlikely that the tale's psychological content can contradict what Guerard calls the 'more superficial' meanings of the story.[20] It is important to decide, most crucially, whether 'the jungle' and all it signifies for Conrad in 'Heart of Darkness' is evil in the sense of intrinsically alien to man's social instincts, as both Guerard and Moser imply, or whether primitive life represents the 'existential' truth of human relationships which has had to be suppressed by racialist 'civilizers'.

Moser writes that 'going into the jungle seems to Marlow like travelling into one's own past, into the world of one's dreams, into the subconscious'. Finding the jungle described in the story as 'lurking death', 'profound darkness', and 'evil' (p. 58) (all these separate from their contexts), he concludes that 'the vegetation imagery means much more than female menace; it means the truth, the darkness, the evil, the death which lie within us, which we must recognize in order to be truly alive'[21] [see p. 34 of this Guide]. The implication is that in siding with Kurtz, Marlow is in some Freudian or Nietzchean way attracted into a revolt against the cage that society has made for him. But he makes plain that the savages in their jungle are as 'virtuous' and humane in their society as he is in his own. His revolt is only against the false-hoods that are ruining his society. If he finally suppresses the truth he has seen, it is not because it is evil but because he is by nature conserv-ative in the political sense and suppresses it for the good of white society, as [Joseph] Chamberlain suppressed the truth about Rhodes.[22]

Cannibalism and sexual perversion exist in the jungle, as in differ-ent forms they exist in cities. But one must read something foreign into Conrad's text . . . if one is to conclude that familiarity with the 'dark' races breeds contempt for one's 'better' in the sense of 'more social' instincts. Marlow puts it clearly, that 'the wilderness' had found Kurtz out early, 'had taken on him a terrible vengeance', had 'echoed loudly within him *because he was hollow at the core*' (p. 95 [Hay's italics]). There is a condition. Freud, denying the possibility of moral hollowness, would say that primitive nature is 'morally' dangerous to all men living in more advanced societies. In his tentative way, Marlow sees that it is dangerous only to the man who is not 'at least . . . as much of a man as these on the shore' (p. 63).

Time is treacherous. This is part of the truth that Marlow says is 'hidden – luckily, luckily' (p. 60). The river that carried Marlow in time 'to the earliest beginnings of the world' (p. 59) also carried him forward to civilization's superman, Kurtz. And this conquering genius, by the might of his Nietzchean will, had not conquered but surrendered to the savage customs he most hated. The implication is that he and the people that contributed to his making will disappear into the reality of Africa as torchlight disappears in sunlight.

Marlow, who will not allow that Kurtz's experience in the Congo is vitally relevant to Europe's future action, is yet aware that its 'shadow' can follow him home. Into the lady's house with him goes the sound of savage drums, like the heartbeats 'of a conquering darkness' (p. 117). In spite of the darkness, the wilderness is vibrantly alive and throbbing, while in her 'radiance', the lady inhabits a 'sarcophagus' (p. 118 [in Conrad's text, the word 'radiance' does not appear, and it is the grand piano, rather than the Intended's house itself, which is compared to a sarcophagus]). She is a 'familiar Shade' (p. 122), recalling Dido in Virgil's underworld [in *The Aeneid*, Book 6]. And it is her Europe that is the underworld. Marlow's interview with Kurtz's Intended, like everything else in the story, approaches allegory in its suggestiveness without departing from the concrete experience a man like Marlow would have registered in such a situation.

Marlow has made too much of lying all through the story to con- vince us at the end that he lies only to save the woman . . . The story, for all its length, is bound from start to finish by the repetitions in Marlow's random observations which Marlow is not himself able to correlate. In his half-awareness, at the beginning of the tale, Marlow informed his listeners that there was an aunt – the lady who pulled strings to secure his Congo job with the 'Continental concern' (p. 22) – who lived in a make-believe world, 'too beautiful altogether', that 'would go to pieces before the first sunset' (p. 28) if it were to be set up. Yet we learn, too, that the aunt is merely expressing illusions held by most people in the city like a whited sepulchre, particularly the people in the trading house where Marlow is hired, a house as still as the 'city of the dead' (p. 26). Then in the moment before Marlow's meeting with Kurtz, we are reminded again that there is a world, a woman's world, that must be kept inviolate 'lest ours gets worse' (p. 80); that the knowledge of Kurtz we are about to gain is going to have to be killed with a lie so that the woman's world, now the world of the Intended, will remain intact.[23]

Shortly after Kurtz's death – far enough from this disclosure for Marlow's oversight not to seem absurd – we learn that Marlow feels compelled to lie about Kurtz not to a woman, to save a woman's world, but to men, representatives of commerce and finance who have a right to know about Kurtz but could not possibly, Marlow thinks, be allowed to know. He assures one of them that 'Mr. Kurtz's knowledge, however extensive, did not bear upon the problems of commerce or administration' (p. 115).[24] Not a direct lie, perhaps, but certainly an effort to keep them in a beautiful world which is not a real world.

It should be clear when Marlow's lies for Kurtz are considered together – and they are given us in good order for a proper perspective on the final scene with the Intended – that the male world of civilized Europe no less than the woman's world is entirely 'out of it' (p. 80). The house of the Intended in the final scene (as the sun sets on it) is a good image for the 'house' of all Europe. Morton Dauwen Zabel keenly observes that the Intended is merely 'the vestal of the ideal to which [Kurtz's] genius has been dedicated'.[25] As the allegorical female torch-carrier embodies more meaning than the painter [Kurtz] intended, so his Intended is more than the representative of the woman's world that Marlow takes her for.

Thus critics conclude too hastily that she is only one more example of Conrad's ineptitude in treating the subject of romantic love; they do not trust Conrad to have seen the effect his words create . . . .

Although Marlow is conscious that 'sunlight can be made to lie' (p. 116), he is never able to see that darkness, too, may be deceptive, and that what is dark may not be kept so. He thinks it is only his own

memory of Kurtz's '"horror"' (p.112) that accompanies him like a living shadow into the European scene of death, as still as 'a well-kept
alley in a cemetery' (p.117). No wonder he has to kill this ghost with
the lie which he said before, when lying for Kurtz to a man, has always
for him 'a taint of death, a flavour of mortality' (p.49). Anything so
much alive as the dead Kurtz (and, we may add, as the 'half-shaped
resolve' (p.99) beginning to mobilize in Africa) seems a threat to the
'whiteness' of the lady's house, the 'cold and monumental whiteness'
(p.118). Conrad plays intricately with his design. Against her white
background, the lady is in black mourning, and the daylight begins to
recede. Metaphysical darkness fades into the ordinary; metaphorical
light into what can be precisely seen. The blonde and sentimental lady
exerts her depressing radiance over the closing story. Almost aware of
his impotence before this encroaching 'radiance', this inversion of real
light and darkness, 'with a dull anger stirring' in him, as if repeating
his spontaneous gesture when he blew out the candle on Kurtz's dying
words, Marlow blows out the candle of truth in a final pretence of saving the lady from what 'would have been too dark . . . altogether'
(p.123). But he and his fellow Englishmen sit looking at the Thames,
which ominously is a 'tranquil waterway leading . . . into the heart of
an immense darkness' (p.124) . . . . . . [They seem] to see its course run
back into the Congo, which Marlow compared to 'an immense snake
uncoiled' (p.22). The snake is motionless, perhaps, but venomous,
ready to recoil in the heart of that immense darkness. Marlow continues
to sit like a meditating Buddha, but we are left to meditate on what he
has failed to see: that England's efficiency and ideas will not save her
from the half-shaped resolve in Africa which will hardly distinguish
one white man from another when Africa's moment comes. All Europe
contributed to the making of Kurtz, Marlow said (p.83). It seems the
major burden of the story to reveal what Marlow has failed to see – that
England is in no way exempt.[26] □

Hay's account of 'Heart of Darkness' is important and interesting in a
range of ways: it offers a powerfully argued alternative to the mythical
and psychological interpretations that dominated in the 1950s and 1960s;
it alerts the critic to any over-easy identification of Marlow with Conrad;
it draws attention to Marlow's possible unreliability as a narrator; it questions the validity of some of the values, such as efficiency, that Marlow
upholds; it challenges the extent to which the novel exempts Britain from
colonialist and imperialist guilt; and it suggests that it is the English and
European men, no less than the women, who are excluded from contact
with reality – an argument that it is interesting to consider in relation to
later feminist critiques of the novel, such as that of Nina Pelikan Straus,
which is considered in chapter four of this Guide (see pp.134–39). But it is

also possible to see that Hay's determination to read 'Heart of Darkness' as a consciously anti-imperialist work involves making a rigid distinction between Marlow and Conrad and mounting a strong indictment against Marlow himself. Undoubtedly this provides a useful corrective to approaches that more or less identify Marlow with Conrad and which assume that Marlow's account is to be trusted; but it is questionable whether the presentation of Marlow in 'Heart of Darkness' has quite the degree of critical detachment that Hay's reading suggests.

Like Hay, J. Hillis Miller, in *Poets of Reality: Six Twentieth-Century Writers* (1965), locates Conrad in an imperialist context. Indeed, he asserts that in 'Conrad's fiction the focus of the novel turns outward from its concentration on relations between man and man within civilized society to a concern for the world-wide expansion of Western man's will to power. Conrad is the novelist not of the city but of imperialism'.[27] But for Miller, as the phrase 'will to power' suggests, imperialism is less a product of politics than of psychology and metaphysics. Ultimately, imperialism is to be understood not in economic or political terms, but as the expression of the will to power that emerges untrammelled once belief in God has gone. What Miller calls the 'special place of Joseph Conrad in English literature' lies primarily, not in the fact that he is the novelist of imperialism, but in the fact that 'in him the nihilism covertly dominant in modern culture is brought to the surface and shown for what it is'.[28] In doing this, Conrad 'point[s] the way towards the transcendence of nihilism by the poets of the twentieth century', especially those whom Miller considers in the rest of his book – Yeats, Eliot, Dylan Thomas, Wallace Stevens and William Carlos Williams. Coming at the end of 'a native tradition' of the English novel in which, from 'Dickens and George Eliot through Trollope, Meredith, and Hardy the negative implications of subjectivism become more and more apparent', Conrad is also 'part of European literature and takes his place with Dostoevsky, Mann, Gide, Proust, and Camus as an explorer of modern perspectivism and nihilism'.[29] Miller thus elevates Conrad to a position of supreme importance, a writer who bridges the gaps between the nineteenth and the twentieth centuries, between English, European and Russian fiction, between poetry and prose, and between nihilism and new affirmation. And in this process, 'Heart of Darkness' is a crucial text, as Miller says in the first chapter of his book:

■ In 'Heart of Darkness' Conrad shows how imperialism becomes the expansion of the will towards unlimited dominion over existence. What begins as greed, the desire for ivory, and as altruism, the desire to carry the torch of civilization to the jungle, becomes the longing to '"wring the heart"' of the wilderness (p. 111) and '"[e]xterminate all the brutes"' (p. 84). The benign project of civilizing the dark places of the world becomes the conscious desire to annihilate everything which opposes man's absolute will. Kurtz's megalomania finally becomes limitless. There is 'nothing either above or below him'. He has 'kicked himself loose of the earth', and in doing so has 'kicked the very earth to pieces' (p. 107).

It is just here, in the moment of its triumph, that nihilism reverses itself . . . Conrad's work does not yet turn the malign into the benign, but it leads to a reversal which prepares for the daylight of later literature. When Kurtz's will has expanded to boundless dimensions, it reveals itself to be what it has secretly been all along: nothing. Kurtz is 'hollow at the core'. Into his emptiness comes the darkness. The darkness is in the heart of each man, but it is in the heart of nature too, and transcends both man and nature as their hidden substance and foundation . . . . . . When the wilderness finds Kurtz out and takes 'a terrible vengeance for the fantastic invasion' (p. 95), then the dawn of an escape from nihilism appears, an escape through the darkness. By following the path of nihilism to the end, man confronts once again a spiritual power external to himself. Though this power appears as an inexpressibly threatening horror, still it is something beyond the self. It offers the possibility of an escape from subjectivism.[30] □

In his second chapter, Miller focuses his general discussion of Conrad around 'Heart of Darkness' and *The Secret Agent* (1907), and key extracts from his discussion of 'Heart of Darkness' are given below. It is interesting to note that Miller, in contrast to Hay, assumes that there is no distinction between Conrad and Marlow in their admiration for work, efficiency and 'the idea', and that Conrad unequivocally endorses Marlow's values in these areas:

■ Conrad respected those who could keep up appearances in a wilderness. He admired people who could keep their heads clear in any circumstances and remain single-mindedly faithful to a job to be done. The elegantly dressed accountant at a trading station halfway to the heart of darkness is a symbol of this equilibrium in the midst of demoralization. His artificiality of dress and manner is the exact correlative of the artificiality of his accounts. The precision and enumeration of the latter stand against the blur of the surrounding jungle as light stands against darkness in the dominant symbolism of the novel. The accountant represents the triumph of an unceasing act of will, a will to keep the darkness out and to keep what is within the charmed circle of civilization clear, distinct, and inventoried.

The starched and scented accountant is not only an example of one kind of human life. He represents the human enterprise generally as it appeared to Conrad at a certain stage of history. That stage was not the mid-nineteenth century, the time of the triumph, in the Western world, of the middle class, industrialism, and the scientific interpretation of nature. Nor was it our darker time when these forces have reached out to dominate the world, and seem about to reverse themselves and destroy their makers. It was the time of imperialism, when the middle class and the commercial spirit, having conquered the countries of their birth, were spreading outward to conquer the world . . . There were still blank places on the map, *terrae incognitae* [unknown or unexplored regions] offering themselves to man's greed for power and knowledge, as the white patch of the Congo fascinated Conrad's Marlow. In the imperialist epoch European countries were still aware of the existence of areas which had not yet submitted to their ideals. Primitive places and primitive peoples still existed . . . . . .

In Conrad's view civilization is the metamorphosis of darkness into light. It is a process of transforming everything unknown, irrational, or indistinct into clear forms, named and ordered, given a meaning and use by man. Civilization has two sides, curiously in contradiction. To be safe, civilized man must have a blind devotion to immediate practical tasks, a devotion which recalls the Victorian cult of work. For Conrad as for [Thomas] Carlyle work is protection against unwhole-some doubt or neurotic paralysis of will . . . So Marlow in 'Heart of Darkness' is protected from the wilderness by the hard work necessary to keep his river steamer going: 'I had to watch the steering, and circumvent those snags, and get the tin-pot along by hook or by crook. There was surface-truth enough in these things to save a wiser man' (p. 63). When Marlow finds in a jungle hut a battered copy of 'An Inquiry into some Points of Seamanship', the book seems to him an expression of man's power to keep possession of himself through concentrated attention on practical problems: 'The simple old sailor, with his talk of chains and purchases, made me forget the jungle and the pilgrims in a delicious sensation of having come upon something unmistakably real' (p. 65).

Devotion to work is real, with a specifically human reality and sanity, but there is more to the humanizing of the world than 'devotion to efficiency' (p. 20). Behind the efficiency and directing it must be 'the idea'. Sometimes this idea is the simple one of obedience and fidelity . . . Sometimes Conrad means by the idea the grandiose goal of bringing light and civilization to the unillumined peoples of the earth. The idea is civilized man's protection against the anarchic power of atavistic ways of life. It is the guide of devoted work, directing that work as it transforms the world to man's measure. The idea gives meaning to what is wrested from the wilderness, and it builds a barrier making the circle of civilization secure, as . . . Kurtz is an 'emissary of light' (p. 28) imposing his 'ideas' (pp. 96, 100, 110, 111), his 'plans' (100, 106, 117, 121) on the jungle, or as Marlow's voice, 'the speech that cannot be silenced' protects him against the 'fiendish row' of the savages (p. 63). The idea is man's armour against the darkness, and it is the source of the form and the meaning he gives the world.

Civilization is at once a social ideal and an ideal of personal life ... As a personal ideal, submission to civilization may mean being one of the stolid, unimaginative people, like Captain MacWhirr in *Typhoon* (1903). It may also mean setting up for oneself an ideal of glory, the winning of power and fame for the accomplishment of some difficult project. A man who does this accepts as the meaning of his life the value he has in the eyes of other people ...

To live in this way means substituting some goal in the future for gratification in the present. A man who makes glory his aim makes of the present a means to an end, and lives always beyond himself. So ... Kurtz's goal is the power he will win in Europe for the successful con- quering of the jungle. He wants 'to have kings meet him at railway-stations on his return from some ghastly Nowhere, where he intend[s] to accomplish great things' (p. 110). There is more than a nominal form of speech in the way Kurtz refers to his fiancée as his 'Intended' (pp. 81, 115, 117). That lady, with her 'pure brow' (p. 119), 'smooth and white ... illumined by the unextinguishable light of belief and love' (p. 120), and her 'soul as translucently pure as a cliff of crystal' (p. 114), is a symbol of the orientation of Kurtz's life. He faces towards an ideal intention which depends on the faith and respect of other people. He lives in terms of an expectation.

Perhaps the intention can never be fulfilled. Perhaps a society based on progress can never reach the far-off divine event when all the darkness will be turned to light. Nevertheless, the project of humaniz- ing the world has in some places been successful, and to dwell in such a place means, as Marlow says, living 'with solid pavement under your feet, surrounded by kind neighbours ready to cheer you or to fall on you, stepping delicately between the butcher and the policeman, in the holy terror of scandal and gallows and lunatic asylums' (pp. 81–82). All the strangeness and danger has been removed or covered up. Everything has been labelled, transformed into a utensil or a signifi- cance. The lower regions of human consciousness have been forgotten or buried deep out of sight ... Civilization is the triumph of the human, of the all too human ... ... [But] [t]he human world is a lie. All human ideals, even the ideal of fidelity, are lies. They are lies in the sense that they are human fabrications. They derive from man himself and are supported by nothing outside him. There is a gap between man and the world, and what remains isolated within the human realm is illusory and insubstantial ... Kurtz is not really devoted to a worthy ideal. He is 'avid of lying fame, of sham distinction, of all the appearances of success and power' (p. 110).

Collective social ideas are no less unreal . . . . . . If civilization and each man in it move farther from reality the more completely the humanizing of the world succeeds, is there any chance to escape from the falsity of the human? How can man be liberated from his dream? The aim of all Conrad's fiction is to destroy in the reader his bondage to illusion, and to give him a glimpse of the truth, however dark and disquieting that truth may be. His work might be called an effort of demystification . . . . . . The first step in his method of demystification consists, strangely enough, in accentuating the lucidity of vision typical of civilized man. The characteristic stance of Conrad's narrators is one of cold, clearheaded, ironic objectivity . . . His habit of multiplying narrators and points of view, so that sometimes an event is told filtered through several consciousnesses, his reconstruction of the chronological sequence to make a pattern of progressive revelation, his use of a framing story – all these techniques increase the distance between the reader and the events as they were lived by the characters.

The avowed purpose of this detachment is to permit a clarity of vision which will reach the truth of things, but detachment has, in Conrad's most striking and characteristic passages, another surprising effect. It leads the reader to experience the story with a dreamlike and hallucinatory intensity, to see things as irreducibly strange, separated from their usual meaning. Conrad, more than any other English novelist, is a master of this way of showing things, and the narrators of all his novels could say what Marlow says in 'Heart of Darkness': 'It seems to me I am trying to tell you a dream – making a vain attempt, because no relation of a dream can convey the dream-sensation, that commingling of absurdity, surprise, and bewilderment in a tremor of struggling revolt, that notion of being captured by the incredible which is of the very essence of dreams' (p. 50) . . . . . .

Though all men live in a dream, many people are lucky enough to go on with their illusions untouched, in the serene and peaceful state of being deceived. 'Of course', says Marlow, 'a fool, what with sheer fright and fine sentiments, is always safe' (p. 63). Some men, like Conrad himself and like most of his heroes, are not so lucky. An experience of solitude, of failure, of adventure, of intense emotion, or simply of unfortunate perspicuity breaks the illusion, and leads such people to see that the dream is a dream . . . . . .

In all his novels Conrad makes images of things and people which cause them to appear mysterious, but perhaps no novel makes a more strategic use of this technique than 'Heart of Darkness'. That novel is structured as a passing of portals, a travelling through states which leads the reader ever deeper into the darkness. The method of this presentation is to put in question whatever Marlow reaches, to show it as a misleading illusion, something which must be rejected for the sake of

the truth behind it. Conrad succeeds in this way in showing civilization as a 'fantastic invasion' (p.44) directed by a 'flabby devil' (p.40),
as a 'sordid farce acted in front of a sinister backcloth' (p.30). The two
silent women knitting in the office of the company in Belgium, 'introducing, introducing continuously to the unknown' (p.26 [in fact, it is
only one of the women who is described as doing this – the other is
described as 'scrutinizing the cheery and foolish faces with unconcerned
old eyes']); the French ship firing shells one after another into the
immensity of Africa; the disorder of the first station Marlow reaches,
with its dying natives, its aimless dynamiting, its machinery lying
broken and useless in ditches [in fact, it is the drainage-pipes, rather
than the machinery, which are lying broken and useless in 'a very narrow
ravine' (p.34), which could be called a ditch; the machinery, however, is
on the surface – 'a boiler wallowing in the grass', and 'an undersized
railway-truck' with one wheel missing and 'a stack of rusty rails' on the
hillside (p.32)]; the perfectly dressed accountant keeping up appearances in the jungle; the stout man with moustaches trying to put out a
blazing warehouse fire with water carried in a tin pail with a hole in it;
the Eldorado expedition with its 'absurd air of disorderly flight with
the loot of innumerable outfit shops and provision stores' (p.54) – each
of these is another example of the absurdity of the imperialist invasion.

The first stage in the reader's liberation from his customary dream is
a way of presenting human activities and intentions which holds them
at arm's length and shows each one as 'a mournful and senseless delusion' (p.30). What is uncovered when the veil of forms is lifted? ... ...

To see the world without interpretations is to see it reduced to pure
quality ... ... Conrad habitually calls attention to the conflict between
the qualitative aspect of things and the interpretation of what is seen
into recognizable objects. The world is often perceived simultaneously
as colours or incomprehensible sounds and as things which can be
identified ... ... One aim of ['Heart of Darkness'] is to make it possible
for the reader to see the wilderness outside the frail fences guarding
the outposts of imperialism, the 'silent wilderness surrounding this
cleared speck on the earth ... something great and invincible, like evil
or truth, waiting patiently for the passing away of this fantastic
invasion' (p.44).

The culmination of the vision of the world as pure quality is the
recognition that behind 'the overwhelming realities of this strange
world of plants, and water, and silence' (pp.59–60) is something else,
something more than human and more than natural, an 'implacable
force brooding over an inscrutable intention' (p.60). This is the darkness. The impressions things make on the senses are no more ultimate
reality than their interpretation into meanings and objects. Qualities
are a thin layer of scintillating light spread over the formless stuff of

things, like the moonlight's silvery glitter on the jungle river or on the primeval mud. The famous sentence in the 'Preface' to *The Nigger of the 'Narcissus'* about making the reader see is followed by another text not so often quoted: 'If I succeed, you shall find there according to your deserts: encouragement, consolation, fear, charm – all you demand – and, perhaps, also, that glimpse of truth for which you have forgotten to ask'.[31] The attempt to render the exact appearances of things is not an end in itself. Its aim is to make the truth of life, something different from any impression or quality, momentarily visible. Not colours or light, but the darkness behind them, is the true reality . . . . . .

The crucial experience for Conrad's characters is the moment when they escape from their enclosures in the sane bounds of everyday life and encounter the heart of darkness which beats at the centre of the earth and in the breast of every human being on earth. The darkness is everywhere, like Kurtz's last words, which Marlow hears whispered in the air even when he is back in Europe and safe in a city: 'The dusk was repeating them in a persistent whisper all around us, in a whisper that seemed to swell menacingly like the first whisper of a rising wind. "The horror! the horror!"' (p. 123). The experience of knowing the darkness takes many forms in Conrad's work, but the darkness remains the same in all manifestations, as a point reached by diverse radii remains the same centre. In any of its forms the darkness causes the collapse of daylight intentions and ideals, the rational forms by which civilized man lives.

The darkness is present in the sheer materiality of things, in the primeval mud of the jungle, but also in the 'asphalt and bricks . . . blind houses and unfeeling stones' of the city.[32] It is the wild animal clamour of the wilderness or of savagery, which modern man has gone beyond to become civilized. In one way the scrawled note ('"Exterminate all the brutes!"' (p. 84)) at the bottom of Kurtz's pamphlet on 'The Suppression of Savage Customs' does not reverse his former eloquence but only states it in another way. The civilizing of the world is the transformation of brute men into restrained human beings. Primitive man and civilized man are related to one another . . . The human world is made by the extermination of its source, the substitution of Marlow's clarity for the irrational emotion of the native life he sees on the shore.

The darkness is the present nature of man, too, for no man has out-grown his beginning. The heart of darkness exists beneath Apollonian clarity, ready to burst out and change the most civilized man into a savage, as, at the deepest point of his penetration of the darkness, Marlow 'confound[s] the beat of the drum with the beating of [his] heart' (p. 105). The shock to Marlow of his sight of the dancing, howling natives is 'the thought of your remote kinship with this wild and passionate uproar', 'just the faintest trace of a response to the terrible frankness of that noise, a dim suspicion of there being a meaning in it which you – you so remote from the night of first ages – could comprehend'. At this moment Marlow must recognize that '[t]he mind of man is capable of anything – because everything is in it, all the past as well as all the future' (p. 63).

Kurtz's return to savagery is striking proof of this terrible law of Conrad's universe. With his plans, his genius, his eloquence, his ideals, he is an example of civilized man at his highest point of development. In spite of this he is swallowed up by the jungle. The fantastic invader is himself invaded and destroyed by the wilderness.

This invasion takes a number of forms, forms which reveal Conrad's sense of what the darkness means as a possible condition of even the most civilized man. Kurtz is driven to substitute the immediate moment of self-forgetful gratification for the satisfaction he has sought in dreams of fame and power. The native woman, apparently Kurtz's mistress, who stands on the shore with her arms upraised, 'like the wilderness itself, with an air of brooding over an inscrutable purpose' (p. 99), is a symbol of the present as Kurtz's Intended with her crystalline brow is a symbol of the future. Sexual abandon, as opposed to spiritualized love, belongs to the darkness. Conrad's misogyny, present in his work from *An Outcast of the Islands* and *Almayer's Folly* onward, derives from his identification of sexual experience with the loss of mental clearness and self-possession. Sex is descent into the darkness of irrational emotion, the blurring of consciousness or its extinction. It is not surprising to find that Conrad identifies sex with the jungle.[33] Both mean the same thing to him: the destruction of lucid consciousness. Kurtz's return to the jungle is 'the awakening of forgotten and brutal instincts' (p. 107). He becomes a god in the wilderness, and is worshipped by his native followers. This means putting absolute sovereignty in place of submission to any law or authority. Religious experience, like sex, is for Conrad a loss of rationality. Kurtz's willingness to think of himself as a god is a special form of that perversion. He replaces reasonable dreams of political or commercial power with a desire for the omnipotence of a god. The riotous dances and unspeakable rites offered to him are forms of the Dionysiac abandon to which he has succumbed.

Kurtz has even unleashed the power of death. Marlow's first understanding of Kurtz's condition comes through his view of the shrunken heads on poles around Kurtz's hut, each 'smiling continuously at some endless and jocose dream of that eternal slumber' (p. 94). If the mind of man is capable of anything this is because it contains all the future as well as the past. The future is death, the return of all created things to the night from which they have sprung. To say that the darkness is the end of all things is to identify the darkness with death, and to realize that the truth of the universe can only be recognized by those who have entered the realm of death . . . In 'Heart of Darkness' . . . death is another form of the darkness. Kurtz's victory comes at the moment of his death and depends on his proximity to death. So Marlow compares his own inconclusive '[wrestle] with death' (p.113) to Kurtz's: 'True, he had made that last stride, he had stepped over the edge, while I had been permitted to draw back my hesitating foot. And perhaps in this is the whole difference; perhaps all the wisdom, and all truth, and all sincerity, are just compressed into that inappreciable moment of time in which we step over the threshold of the invisible' (pp.113–14) . . . . . .

Is there no way to remain in touch with the darkness without being engulfed by it, no way to be actively engaged in life without becoming part of an empty masquerade? . . . . . . Apparently there is no way. Even those who are not destroyed by their recognition of the darkness seem to have no satisfactory course open to them. Marlow comes back from the darkness. Now he can look down on the citizens of the sepulchral city because, as he says, 'I felt so sure they could not possibly know the things I knew' (p.114). What good does his wisdom do him? He knows that the lie is a lie, and confirms his allegiance to civilization by the lie he tells Kurtz's Intended. Action which is taken with awareness that the lie is a lie is the only action which is not a mournful and sombre delusion, but this authenticity is based on a contradiction. Action is authentic only insofar as it is recognized that no action is authentic. True action must be based on that which denies it. Its hope is its despair, its meaning its meaninglessness, its reality its proximity to the uninterrupted night, the horror. It is a mistake to define Conrad's solution to the ethical problem by the phrase the 'true lie'.[34] There is nothing true about any action or judgement except their relation to the darkness, and the darkness makes any positive action impossible. Marlow, in a moment of insight, recognizes the pointlessness of life: 'it occurred to me that my speech or my silence, indeed any action of mine, would be a mere futility. What did it matter what any one knew or ignored? What did it matter who was manager? One gets sometimes such a flash of insight. The essentials of this affair lay deep under the surface, beyond my reach, and beyond my power of meddling' (pp.66–67) . . .

Nevertheless, there is someone else present in 'Heart of Darkness', someone besides Kurtz, even someone besides Marlow who has come back from the darkness to sit like a dreaming Buddha, contemplating his empty truth and preaching it. There is the narrator, one of those on board the *Nellie*, a passive listener whose understanding of the world, it may be, is radically transformed by the story he hears.[35] And there is Conrad himself, the author of the book, the man who after years of active life at sea settled down to decades of solitude, covering thousands upon thousands of blank sheets of paper with words . . . . . . To devote oneself to writing, however, is to engage in the most unreal action of all . . . . . . Words, the medium of fiction, are a fabrication of man's intellect. They are part of the human lie. One way to define the darkness is to say that it is incompatible with language. As Marlow gets closer to the heart of darkness he also gets further from it, for he more and more recognizes the gap between words and the darkness they can never express. The expression of Kurtz's genius is his eloquence: 'Kurtz discoursed. A voice! a voice! It rang deep to the very last. It survived his strength to hide in the magnificent folds of eloquence the barren darkness of his heart' (p. 110). The hollowness of Kurtz's eloquence exposes the incompatibility between language and truth, and shows that of all the superficial films putting a glittering surface between man and the darkness, language is the most ephemeral. So Conrad is tormented not only by the unreality of words, but also by a sense of guilt for the mendacity of language . . .

In spite of this, the separation from the daylight world involved in the act of writing, its forgetting of life in order to penetrate into a realm which does not exist, is the only safe means of reaching truth. Language faces two ways. Words are a sign of man's imprisonment within illusions, but the language of fiction is the substance of a story which has no existence outside words. This detachment of words from their utilitarian function as signs puts language in touch with the unworded darkness. It brings to light the fact that words have always been detached from the everyday world. Language is that which is most intimate to man and therefore flows from the profound dark rather than from the daylight of rationality. The 'gift of expression' is double. It is 'the bewildering, the illuminating, the most exalted and the most contemptible, the pulsating stream of light, or the deceitful flow from the heart of an impenetrable darkness' (p. 79).

How, in a novel, can words flow from the darkness and name the nameless? The form of Conrad's fiction gives the answer. Words can name the darkness by describing a double motion of descent into the darkness and return from it. To descend directly into the dark is to be destroyed. The writer must structure the experience of some surrogate in such a way as to reveal its truth. This truth will either destroy that other self, as Kurtz or Decoud [in *Nostromo* (1904)] are destroyed, or will be hidden from them, as it is hidden from Lord Jim or from Flora de Barral in *Chance*. Conrad's novels are an elaborate manipulation of data in order to make the truth behind the facts appear, and the relation of Marlow to Kurtz may be seen as a dramatization of the writer's relation to his subject. Marlow's real experience, he says, is not his own but Kurtz's: '[i]t is his extremity I seem to have lived through' (p. 113). Each writer must bring the truth back from the darkness, as Marlow carries

CRIT GDE HEART DARK SPLIT

POSIO (COD) #7

I began to feel slightly uneasy. You know I am not used to such ceremonies, and there was something ominous in the atmosphere. It was just as though I had been let into some conspiracy – I don't know – something not quite right; and I was glad to get out. In the outer room the two women knitted black wool feverishly. People were arriving, and the younger one was walking back and forth introducing them. The old one sat on her chair. Her flat cloth slippers were propped up on a foot-warmer, and a cat reposed on her lap. She wore a starched white affair on her head, had a wart on one cheek, and silver-rimmed spectacles hung on the tip of her nose. She glanced at me above the glasses. The swift and indifferent placidity of that look troubled me. Two youths with foolish and cheery countenances were being piloted over, and she threw at them the same quick glance of unconcerned wisdom. She seemed to know all about them and about me too. An eerie feeling came over me. She seemed uncanny and fateful. Often far away there I thought of these two, guarding the door of Darkness, knitting black wool as for a warm pall, one introducing, introducing continuously to the unknown, the other scrutinizing the cheery and foolish faces with unconcerned old eyes. *Ave!* Old knitter of black wool. *Morituri te salutant* ['Hail! . . . Those who are about to die salute you' – the Roman gladiator's salute to the Emperor on entering the arena before combat (Hampson (1995), p. 131, note 39)]. Not many of those she looked at ever saw her again – not half, by a long way (pp. 25–26).

Several critics have made the two knitters a primary basis for a large-scale symbolic interpretation of 'Heart of Darkness' in which Marlow's whole journey becomes a version of the traditional descent into hell, such as that in the sixth book of Virgil's *Aeneid* [see Feder (1955)], and in Dante's *Inferno* [see Evans (1956)]. This kind of critical interpretation assumes that the symbolic reference of the verbal sign must be closed rather than open, and that it arises, not from the natural and inherent associations of the object, but from a preestablished body of ideas, stories, or myths. The present passage certainly makes symbolic reference to associations of this kind; Marlow presents his own experience in the general perspective of the pagan and Christian traditions of a journey to the underworld: this is made sufficiently explicit when he talks of the knitters 'guarding the door of Darkness', and of the two youths 'being piloted over'. But this is not the only symbolic reference of the passage, nor the most important; and there is no reason to assume that the movement from the literal to the symbolic must be centripetal [moving or tending to move towards a centre]. Only some such assumption could have impelled one critic to assert that there is a 'close structural parallel between "Heart of Darkness" and the *Inferno*', and proceed to equate the company station with Limbo and the central station with the abode of the fraudulent, while making Kurtz both a 'traitor to kindred' and a Lucifer.[47]

One obvious practical objection to this kind of symbolic interpretation is that it alerts our attention too exclusively to a few aspects of the narrative – to those which seem to provide clues that fit the assumed unitary and quasi-allegorical frame of symbolic reference. This leads us to interrogate the text only in those terms, and to ask such questions as: Why does Conrad give us only two fates? Which one is Clotho the spinner? and which Lachesis the weaver? Did the Greeks know about knitting anyway? Where are the shears? [In Greek and Roman mythology, there are three Parcae, or Fates, originally represented as three old women spinning: Clotho, Lachesis and Atropos. Later poets varied their activities; for example, according to Lemprière's *Classical Dictionary* (3rd edn, 1984), p. 445, and contrary to Watt, Clotho is the weaver and Lachesis the spinner: Clotho presides over the moment in which we are born and holds in her hand a distaff (a cleft stick holding wool or flax wound for spinning by hand), while Lachesis spins out all the events and actions of our life; Atropos, the third Fate, cuts the thread of life with a pair of shears.] What symbolic meaning can there be in the fact that the thin one lets people *in* to the room and then *out* again – a birth and death ritual, perhaps? Lost in such unfruitful preoccupations, our imaginations will hardly be able to respond to the many other symbolic clues in the passage, or even to the many other meanings in those details which have secured our attention.

In fact a multiplicity of historical and literary associations pervades the scene in the anteroom; and this multiplicity surely combines to place the two knitters in a much more universal perspective. There is, most obviously, the heartless unconcern manifested throughout the ages by the spectators at a variety of ordeals that are dangerous or fatal to the protagonists. This unconcern is what the fates have in common with the two other main historical parallels evoked in the passage – the French *tricoteuses* callously knitting at the guillotine, and the Roman crowds to whom the gladiators address their scornful farewell in Marlow's rather pretentious interjection: '*Ave*! Old knitter of black wool. *Morituri te salutant*' (p. 26).

Within the context of 'Heart of Darkness' as a whole the function of these three examples of symbolic reference is local and circumscribed; like Marlow's earlier historical allusions to Drake and Franklin (p. 17 [In fact, the first narrator, not Marlow, makes these allusions]) they are dropped as soon as made; they are not intended to link up with other allusions into a single cryptographic system which gives the main symbolic meaning of the work as a whole. One reason for this is surely that any continuing symbolic parallel would undermine the literal interest and significance of the narrative at every compositional level, from the essential conflict of the plot, to the details of its narrative presentation.

The present passage, then, gives clear evidence of how Conrad aimed at a continuous immediacy of detail which had symbolic reference that was primarily of a natural, open, and multivocal kind. Marlow presents a highly selective but vivid series of details; they are for the most part given as raw and unexplained observations, and the autonomy and isolation of each particular image seems to impel the reader to larger surmise. There is, for instance, the approach of the thin knitter who 'got up and walked straight at me – still knitting with downcast eyes – and only just as I began to think of getting out of her way, as you would for a somnambulist, stood still, and looked up. Her dress was as plain as an umbrella-cover' (pp. 24–25).

If we submit ourselves to the evocative particularity of these intensely visualized details, their symbolic connotations take us far beyond our primary sense of the fateful, uncanny, and impassive atmosphere of the scene; we are driven to a larger awareness of a rigid, mechanical, blind, and automatized world. If we attempt to explain the sources of this awareness we can point to the way that the thin knitter does not speak to Marlow, nor even, apparently, see him; her movements are unrelated to other human beings. The knitter's appearance increases this sense of the nonhuman; her shape recalls an umbrella and its tight black cover; there has been no effort to soften the functional contours of its hard and narrow ugliness with rhythmic movements, rounded forms, or pleasing colours. It is not that the knitter reminds us of the classical Fates which really matters, but that she is herself a fate – a dehumanized death in life to herself and to others, and thus a prefiguring symbol of what the trading company does to its creatures.

Some of the images in the passage are representative in a limited and mainly pictorial way; the older knitter, for example, with her wart and her flat cloth slippers, becomes a stark visual image of physical and spiritual deformity combined with imperturbable self-complacence. But there is another, larger, and to some extent contrary, tendency, where the extreme selectivity of Marlow's memory draws our attention to his state of mind at the time. For instance, when Marlow comments about the tycoon: '[h]e shook hands, I fancy' (p. 25), his uncertainty suggests that his consciousness was occupied with other matters. Marlow omits much that would certainly be mentioned in an autobiography, or a naturalist novel; we are not, for instance, given the details of Marlow's contract, or the name of the people. This omission of proper names is a particularly typical symbolist procedure – in Maeterlinck, for instance, or in Kafka. The general reason for the strategy is clear: most of the details about the narrative object are omitted, so that what details remain, liberated from the bonds and irrelevancies of the purely circumstantial and contingent, can be recognized as representatives of larger ideas and attitudes.

Marlow despecifies the tycoon to reveal his essence; he calls him merely a 'pale plumpness' (p. 25) because big bureaucrats typically eat too much, don't exercise outdoors, are featureless and somewhat abstract. But there is another essence involved in the situation; if Marlow so often despecifies the external and the factual aspects of the scene, it is because his own hierarchy of attention at the time was primarily internal and moral; what Marlow was actually registering with benumbed incredulity was his spiritual reaction to being initiated into the most universal and fateful of modern society's rites of passage – the process whereby the individual confronts a vast bureaucracy to get a job from it.

Marlow begins his rite of passage with a representative ecological sequence: approach through unfamiliar streets and arid staircases; passive marshalling from waiting room to grand managerial sanctum; and, forty-five seconds later, a more rapid return thence through the same stages, with a delayed and demoralizing detour for medical examination. The sequence of routinized human contacts is equally typical: the impassive receptionists; the expert compassion of the confidential secretary; the hollow benevolence of the plump tycoon; the shifty joviality of the clerk; and the hypocritical pretences of the medical examiner.

Marlow registers but rarely comments; and we are thus left free to draw our deductions about the symbolic meanings of the passage. They are multiple, and they are not expounded but suggested; consequently our interpretative priorities will depend on our literary imagination as readers, and on our own way of conceiving reality.

One possible direction of larger symbolic reference concerns the implicit view of civilization suggested in the passage. Some of the details of the scene suggest the way Marx saw one result of modern capitalism as the turning of people into mere objects in a system of economic relations; human beings become things and so their personal relationships take on a 'spectral objectivity'.[48] This interpretation is also consistent with Max Weber's related view that modern bureaucratic administration brings with it 'the dominance of a spirit of formalistic impersonality'.[49] Since both these interpretations find some support in the literal meanings of the passage, as well as in other parts of 'Heart of Darkness', they can reasonably be regarded as tributes to Conrad's power not only to penetrate the essential moral meaning of the institutions of the modern world, but to communicate that meaning symbolically.

The passage also implies a good deal about the unspoken subjective meaning of the ordeal for Marlow. When the scene ends we can look back and see that Marlow is left with a sense of a doubly fraudulent initiation: the company has not told him what he wants to know; but since Marlow has been unable to formulate the causes of his moral discomfort, much less ask any authentic question or voice any protest, his own tranced submission has been a betrayal of himself. These implications prefigure what we are to see as one of the larger and more abstract themes of the story – the lack of any genuinely reciprocal dialogue; even Marlow cannot or does not speak out. In this passage, for instance, Marlow's most extended dialogue at the company's offices is with the doctor. In part it merely typifies this particular aspect of bureaucratic initiation: the formulaic insult ('"Ever any madness in your family?"'); the posture of disinterested devotion to scientific knowledge (measuring Marlow's cranium); and the pretendedly benevolent but actually both impractical and deeply disquieting counsel ('"Avoid irritation more than exposure to the sun"' (p.27)). Such details might be said to operate partly in a centripetal way, since they point to specific later issues in the narrative – to Kurtz's skull and those on his fenceposts, and to the physical and mental collapse of Kurtz and Marlow at the end; but the details also have larger and more expansive centrifugal overtones [centrifugal, the opposite of 'centripetal' (see p.97), means 'moving or tending to move away from a centre']. The horrors of the modern secular hell are not merely the affronting mumbo-jumbo of the medical priesthood; Marlow has illumined the haze which hangs like a pall over the society of which the doctor, the clerk, the knitters and the pale plumpness are the symbolic representatives; and we are led outwards to discern the ramifying absences of human communion.

We are left with an overpowering sense of Marlow's fateful induction into the vast overarching network of the silent lies of civilization. No one will explain them – not the servants of the company certainly, if only because the jobs of the personnel depend on their discretion; the great corporate enterprise has no voice, yet Marlow cannot help attributing moral meanings and intentions to all the tangible manifestations of the power which controls his life.

The absence of shared understanding exists at an even higher level of abstraction. Marlow hardly knows the meaning of what is happening to him; there is no Virgil in sight, much less a Beatrice; and no one even seems aware that the problem exists. Later the narrative reveals that this gap extends throughout Marlow's world; we go from the silent, lethal madness of the trading company to that of the civilization for which it stands; Marlow is confronting a general intellectual and moral impasse whose narrative climax is enacted when he is forced to lie to the Intended; and this gap, in turn, can be seen in a wider historical and philosophical perspective as a reflection of the same breakdown of the shared categories of understanding and judgement, as had originally imposed on Conrad and many of his contemporaries the indirect, subjective, and guarded strategies that characterized the expressive modes of Symbolism.

One could argue that the distinctive aim, not only of Conrad but of much modern literature, is not so much 'to make us see' [Conrad's stated aim in the 'Preface' to *The Nigger of the 'Narcissus'*[50]], but, somewhat more explicitly, 'to make us see what we see'; and this would ultimately involve a view of narrative in which every detail is inherently symbolic. The reader and the critic of such literature, therefore, must assume that since each individual text generates its own symbolic meaning, only a primary commitment to the literal imagination will enable him to see the larger implications of all the particularities which confront him. Thus in the present scene the knitters suggest many ideas which are essentially generalized forms of the literal or inherent qualities which Marlow has recorded; and each of these symbolic meanings can in turn be extended in a centrifugal way to a larger understanding of the world Conrad presents. The opposite kind of critical reading starts from an esoteric interpretation of particular objects – the knitters are 'really' the fates – and combines them into a centripetal and crypto-graphic interpretation which is based, as in allegory, on a single and defined system of beliefs, and is largely independent of the literal meanings of the details presented and of their narrative context. But the primary narrator's image has warned us against proceeding as though there is a single edible kernel of truth hidden below the surface; and it is surely curious, even saddening, to reflect that, out of the dozen or more studies of the scene with the knitters, none has interpreted it as part of a larger symbolic vision of the great corporation and its civilization.[51] □

It is possible to see in these extracts how Watt moves between a close focus on specific passages and a broader discussion of technique, theme, symbolism and critical approach. Old-fashioned though he may be in some ways, his readiness to discuss his own critical approach makes him a very modern critic, in that he does not assume that the grounds and methods of his critical practice can be taken for granted, but tries to explain and justify them; he offers not only interpretations of 'Heart of Darkness', but also accounts of the means by which he arrived at those interpretations – and thus, of course, exposes both the interpretations themselves, and the interpretative means, to challenge. Moreover, Watt's attempt to restrict interpretation by an appeal to the 'literal meaning' is in tension with other emphases in his account that find echoes in decon-struction and post-structuralism: his challenge to 'centripetal' symbolic interpretation could be linked to the idea of 'decentring' developed by Perry Meisel; his objection to the limitations of the attempt to apply a 'unitary' frame of reference might be related to the deconstructionist and post-structuralist view that a text has no unitary meaning (not even, or especially not, a 'literal' one); his stress on 'a multiplicity of historical and literary associations' has similarities to the post-structuralist notion of intertextuality, of the way in which any text takes its place within, and alludes and refers to, a multiplicity of other texts; and his notion of 'open' and 'multivocal' symbolic reference could be associated with the idea of the 'heteroglossic', many-voiced text derived from the Russian critic Mikhail Bakhtin. But while it is important to note the ways in which Watt's approach might be linked with the kinds of critical practices that were to become widespread in the 1980s and 1990s, it is no less important to note the ways in which it is distinct from, and opposed to, those practices, the ways in which it presents an anticipatory challenge to them.

Watt and Achebe, in their very different fashions, shook up the Conrad consensus in the 1970s, fragmenting and extending it, posing new and challenging questions; and Perry Meisel's analysis both offered an interpretation of great interest in its own right and gave a hint of what was to come in the next decade, as deconstruction and post-structuralism transformed the whole landscape of literary studies in the UK and the USA. In relation to 'Heart of Darkness', one other event of the 1970s should be highlighted, which took place outside the usual province of literary criticism at that time: the appearance in 1979 of Francis Ford Coppola's film *Apocalypse Now*. This loose adaptation of Conrad's story to the Vietnam War was, in its way, as provocative as Achebe's lecture, and produced much the same range of responses, from 'How dare you!' to a sense of truly seeing a familiar text for the first time. Since 1979, with the opening of literature courses to alternative texts and media, and the expansion of film studies and cultural studies, *Apocalypse Now* has increasingly been discussed alongside 'Heart of Darkness': by the 1990s, comparisons of novel and film have become, like responses to Achebe, an established sub-genre of 'Heart of Darkness' criticism (see Bibliography). But in 1979, that development lay in the future.

It was not all that lay in the future. As the 1980s approached, it still seemed, in literary criticism, that the centre would hold; but Achebe's cultural bomb, Meisel's covert deconstructive sabotage, and even Watt's last stand on the quicksand of literal meaning, were, in their different ways, signs of the times. Things were starting to fall apart; and, in the next decade, rough critical beasts would emerge – and, not surprisingly, some of them would seize on 'Heart of Darkness'. The results shall be seen in the next chapter.

CHAPTER FOUR

New Maps of Hell: Rereading 'Heart of Darkness' in the 1980s

NEW AND powerful readings of 'Heart of Darkness' emerged in the 1980s. If Conrad's novel had looked like a text well suited to the symbolic, mythological, psychological, political and metaphysical approaches of the 1950s and 1960s, it had never quite been contained by them, and it seemed to gain a new lease of life in the heady climate of the 'critical decade' that saw a revolution in literary studies in the UK and USA.[1] Indeed, in this decade, activity around 'Heart of Darkness' seemed to grow more intense, as if a text born in the era of high imperialism could speak with increased urgency to a world undergoing globalisation and witnessing the collapse of a great communist empire. It was no longer a secure classic; Achebe's cultural bomb had blown Conrad from his pedestal, and more bombs were soon to be lobbed by feminist critics. But this only made 'Heart of Darkness' more exciting. Critics no longer had to bow down before an idol and perform predictable rites; interpreting 'Heart of Darkness' became more like a dangerous journey up a strange river with hidden currents, keeping the eyes strained for snags and closed in at moments by fog, under attack from the banks and trying to control the inept squirtings of panicking Conradophile pilgrims.[2]

One of the first important interpretations of the decade appeared in 1983, in Benita Parry's *Conrad and Imperialism: Ideological Boundaries and Visionary Frontiers*. Parry was alert to the ideological and political implications of 'Heart of Darkness', and to its complexity and contradictoriness as a fictional text that is 'a militant denunciation and a reluctant affirmation of imperialist civilization' that both 'exposes and colludes in imperialism's manifestations'. Thus the first part of her discussion explores the complex ways in which the conventional notions of light and dark are subverted but finally confirmed in the novel. This links up with her view of Marlow as a sceptic who implicitly calls into question his own affirmation of the redemptive idea of imperialism and observes actualities with graphic precision, but who is also a fantasist possessed by a lurid imperialist mythology; while Kurtz as colonialist and racialist disappears into Kurtz the 'repentant iconoclast' who finally acknowledges his sin against European civilisation. The extract begins as Parry develops her analysis of the way in which, in Conrad's tale, fantasy absorbs history:

■ It is . . . Marlow's own narration that negates his thesis on the redemptive dimensions to imperialism. His confusions about the substance of his narration, his misrecognitions, the discrepancies between what he shows and what he sees, his positing of certainties which prove to be dubious, these are the fiction's means of exhibiting that his endeavour to devise an ethical basis for imperialism is destined to fail. With the advent of Kurtz, another narrative mode supervenes, submerging the existing discourse in material that originates a new legend for colonial mythology. Since the intercession of ironic disproof is here suspended, the problem for the reader becomes one of distinguishing between what is spontaneously revealed and the formal constructions brought to the evidence by Marlow's interpretative commentary and, in the absence of a countermanding viewpoint, implicitly endorsed by the fiction. From the information imparted by Marlow, Kurtz emerges as exorbitant and grotesque because of the excesses rather than the essence of his conduct, a figure existing at the far end of the colonial continuum, the bizarre features of which are noted by Marlow in language that is precise and severe, registering his astonishment and outrage while remaining coherent. He recalls watching a French man-of-war in 'the empty immensity of earth, sky, and water . . . firing into a continent' (p. 30), looking on the 'wanton smash-up' (p. 34) caused by the Company's exploitation of physical and human resources, seeing an emaciated, diseased and starving chain-gang 'in all the attitudes of pain, abandonment, and despair' (p. 35), and meeting agents lacking in principle, imagination and intelligence who boasted that '"[a]nything – anything can be done in this country"' (p. 57). A passage abundantly signposted with absurdities and atrocities leads to Kurtz, the Company's most successful agent and one reputed to have gone out to Africa with moral ideas of some sort. It is with misgivings that the sceptical Marlow reads the Report commissioned from Kurtz by the International Society for the Suppression of Savage Customs, unwillingly electrified by its magniloquence and chilled by its final call to a holocaust: 'at the end of that moving appeal to every altruistic sentiment it blazed at you, luminous and terrifying, like a flash of lightning in a serene sky: "Exterminate all the brutes!"' (pp. 83–84). On meeting Kurtz, Marlow confronts a man impersonating imperialism's will to expand its domain over the earth and all its creatures, a spectacle for which his previous sights of a ravenous colonialism had prepared him: 'You should have heard him say, "My ivory." . . . "My Intended, my ivory, my station, my river, my – " everything belonged to him' (p.81); even his cannibalistic mien speaks of that insatiable appetite for conquest elevated to a principle by imperialism: 'I saw him open his mouth wide – it gave him a weirdly voracious aspect, as though he had wanted to swallow all the air, all the earth, all the men before him' (p.97).[3]

All this is before Marlow and is the 'objective' substance of his graphically told story, but what he *sees*, and this remains uncontroverted by the text, belongs not to history but to fantasy, to the sensational world of promiscuity, idolatry, satanic rites and human sacrifices unveiled in nineteenth-century travellers' tales as the essence of an Africa without law or social restraint, a representation that was embroidered into colonial romances and charted by an ethnography still innocent of a discipline's necessary rules of evidence.[4] It is this mythological cosmos, an invention essential to imperialism's rationale, which fascinates Marlow and as the lurid images from colonialism's gallery take possession of his vision these, in the absence of a dissenting discourse, come to occupy the fiction's space. With this, there is a displacement of the perspective on Kurtz as a Prospero figure [Prospero, political exile and magician, is the protagonist of Shakespeare's play *The Tempest* (1611)] who had fled the society of his peers to enter a universe where the thunder and lightning of his technological magic had made him appear a god to the lakeside tribe of the wilderness; and the symbiotic relationship between Kurtz and his acolytes, which from Marlow's account had appeared as an extreme form of that sadomasochistic political nexus celebrated in colonial legend as a natural bond between a master-race and peoples born to servitude, is relegated to the margins of a vista now wholly filled by enactments of rituals that are native to Africa and violations of Western taboos.[5]

What appals the much-travelled and worldly Marlow, who shows himself to be a convinced cultural-relativist since he is untroubled by 'uncomplicated savagery' (p.95), able to accept cannibals as men one could work with, and not deeply disturbed at identifying the round knobs on the posts surrounding Kurtz's house as shrunken heads, is rumour of the rites initiated by Kurtz in his own honour. It is the atavistic regression of a cultivated European which alone elicits 'moral shock' in Marlow, 'as if something altogether monstrous, intolerable to thought and odious to the soul, had been thrust upon me unexpectedly' (p.104). As Marlow struggles to explain Kurtz's defection from civilization, so does his already opaque portrayal become hidden by a jungle of tropes [that is, figures of speech, such as personification, in which something which is not a person is given human attributes – for example, 'the wilderness had patted him on the head'; or simile, in which one thing is explicitly compared to another using the words 'like' or 'as' – for instance, 'it [Kurtz's head] was like a ball']:

> The wilderness had patted him on the head, and, behold, it was like a ball – an ivory ball; it had caressed him, and – lo! – he had withered; it had taken him, loved him, embraced him, got into his veins, consumed his flesh, and sealed his soul to its own by the inconceivable ceremonies of some devilish initiation (p. 81) . . . I think it had whispered to him things about himself which he did not know, things of which he had no conception till he took counsel with this great solitude – and the whisper had proved irresistibly fascinating (p. 95) . . . I tried to break the spell – the heavy, mute spell of the wilderness – that seemed to draw him to its pitiless breast by the awakening of forgotten and brutal instincts, by the memory of gratified and monstrous passions. (pp. 106–07)

Discernible through the thicket of the prose is the wilderness as a metonym for dangerous appetites curbed by civilization [a 'metonym' is a word used in a 'metonymy', a figure of speech, or trope, in which the name of an attribute or adjunct of a thing is used to refer to that thing itself, for instance, crown for king, Downing Street for the British Government, or, as here, the wilderness for 'dangerous passions'] . . . Kurtz's liberation from repression, his 'forgetting himself' amongst the peoples of the tribe is seen as a capitulation to an enslavement in which he hates the life and is unable to get away. With this composite representation, Marlow's academic tolerance of savagery is overwhelmed by articulations of a visceral revulsion towards the other that obliterate the fiction's existing definitions of that historical condition in which Kurtz's pursuit of profit and power had been nurtured and the specific circumstances where the 'bounds of permitted aspirations' (p. 107) had appeared illimitable. Thus what finally commands attention is not the consummate exploiter poisoned by a diet too lavish and too rich, but the daemonic hero who had embraced outlawed experiences and who, because of gratifying illegitimate desires, was privileged to confirm the value of what he had profaned: 'Better his cry . . . It was an affirmation, a moral victory paid for by innumerable defeats, by abominable terrors, by abominable satisfactions. But it was a victory!' (p. 114).[6] The call to genocide uttered by the megalomaniac extremist who 'could get himself to believe anything' (p. 116), the rhetoric of the self-infatuated colonialist who having witnessed and committed atrocities had gone on to extol these as festivals of racial power, is finally drowned by the last whisper of the repentant iconoclast attaining heroic stature by acknowledging his sin in desecrating the commandments of his civilization . . . . . .

Marlow's mythopoeic [myth-constructing] narration of a journey in time to specified places in Africa's interior follows a route that had already been taken by the western mind through the alien world Europe set out to conquer, and if it arrives at the same destination, it selects other landmarks for scrutiny and locates the roots of western shock and antipathy in new areas. The fiction's inclusive view is derived from spanning both Marlow's conscious apprehensions and the information he unconsciously mediates; and it is by inventing meanings for Africa that he exhibits the geography and boundaries of the imperialist imagination, while also illuminating the dislocating effects of a foreign mode on a mind formed by the western experience and devoted to its forms.[7] His voyage along a formless, featureless coast, 'as if still in the making' (p. 29), past rapids whose rushing noise sounds 'as though the tearing pace of the launched earth had suddenly become audible' (p. 34), and into the virgin forest where the vegetation seems 'like a rioting invasion of soundless life . . . ready to topple over the creek, to sweep every little man of us out of his little existence' (p. 54), maps a mythic return of modern civilization to an imagined primal condition and images a dream of the conscious mind regressing to its archaic ground: 'Going up that river was like travelling back to the earliest beginnings of the world (p. 59) . . .We were cut off from the comprehension of our surroundings . . . We could not understand, because we were too far and could not remember, because we were travelling in the night of first ages, of those ages that are gone, leaving hardly a sign – and no memories' (p. 62).

From being a blank place on a map once seen by Marlow when a boy dreaming of the adventures to come, Africa is experienced by the man who is now a servant of colonialism, as an alien cosmos whose every aspect violates his concepts of intelligibility and congruity. Its vacant landscape, without form or feature, is deaf, mute and petrified. 'An empty stream, a great silence, an impenetrable forest (p. 59) . . . It was not sleep – it seemed unnatural, like a state of trance. Not the faintest sound of any kind could be heard' (p. 67). In this proliferation of negatives, Marlow communicates a recoil from what he intuitively senses to be an immanent quietism annulling the rational orderings and moral discriminations imposed by western thought, and repudiating that affirmative activism to which as a sailor he is heir and which he considers the essential human attribute and appropriate field of endeavour:

> We penetrated deeper and deeper into the heart of darkness . . . We were wanderers on a prehistoric earth, on an earth that wore the aspect of an unknown planet. We could have fancied ourselves the first of men taking possession of an accursed inheritance, to be sub-dued at the cost of profound anguish and excessive toil . . . . . . The

earth seemed unearthly. We are accustomed to look upon the shackled form of a conquered monster, but there – there you could look at a thing monstrous and free. (p. 62)

For Marlow Africa is the negation of his own humanly-dominated and dynamic social order, a domain where archaic energies are rampant and nature's exercise of an autonomous will is unlimited. However, competing with this perception which sets nature against culture as adversaries, is Marlow's insight that what is 'true' and 'real' is the human presence as modifier and modified within the material world, a relationship exhibited by Africans paddling a boat in the surf and violated by the careless greed of victors who savage what they have appropriated. In Kurtz, a man driven by a hunger to engorge the universe, the fiction displays the conqueror who despoils the planet he craves to possess, points to his fate as victim of its 'terrible vengeance for the fantastic invasion' (p.95), and with this delivers a judgement on imperialism's awesome triumphalism:

> . . . I had to deal with a being to whom I could not appeal in the name of anything high or low. I had, even like the niggers, to invoke him – himself – his own exalted and incredible degradation. There was nothing either above or below him, and I knew it. He had kicked himself loose of the earth . . . he had kicked the very earth to pieces. (p. 107)

Because the fiction does not dramatize a political struggle between colonizer and colonized – indeed the human material for such a treatment is absent as the blacks are not functional protagonists but figures in a landscape who do not constitute a human presence – the confrontation between Europe and Africa is realized wholly as the conflict between two polarized and incompatible epistemologies, an encounter which displays the insufficiencies of positivism without endorsing metaphysics as an alternative. The one disposition, articulated in ways austere and ornamental by the primary narrators, Marlow and Kurtz, represents the philosophy underpinning the project of an expansionist Europe mobilized to conquer and remake the earth;[8] the other, silently manifest in Africa's primordial wilderness, intimates the existence of transcendental knowledge. For Marlow the voyage through this other universe exposes the poverty of his own outlook, and the man who is at home in the turbulence of the temporal world, who abhors unreconstructed nature, is without a religious sensibility and finds poetry in proficiency, is led to make a distinction between the surface truths and accurate likenesses accessible to empirical observation, which he contrasts favourably with senseless delusion, splendid appearances and unreal pretence, and the 'hidden truths' [this is not a direct quotation; the closest the text comes to this phrase is 'the truth is hidden' (p. 60)] and 'overwhelming realities' (pp. 59–60) which can only be approached asymptotically and experientially [an 'asymptote' is a line that continually approaches a given curve but does not meet it at a finite distance]. [Marlow's] journey comes to mimic an epistemological passage taking him from faith in 'the unmistakably real' (p. 65), the 'redeeming . . . straightforward facts of life' [This last quotation conflates terms from two different parts of the text: 'redeeming facts of life', p.43; 'straightforward facts', p. 30], the world of rivets and steamboats, mechanics and explicit navigational manuals where chronology and duration prevail and work dignifies existence, to intimations of other meanings manifest in a landscape he can only perceive metaphorically. The silent wilderness strikes him 'as something great and invincible, like evil or truth' (p. 44); 'the silence of the land went home to one's very heart, – its mystery, its greatness, the amazing reality of its concealed life' (p. 48); the woods seem to have an 'air of hidden knowledge' (p. 93) and in the stillness of the jungle Marlow senses 'an implacable force brooding over an inscrutable intention' (p. 60).

The ornate and obscurantist language both intimates and conceals Marlow's intuition that there may be non-phenomenal 'realities' and alternative ways of perceiving 'truth', since this apprehension must contend with his commitment to pragmatism as necessary to efficiency: 'When you have to attend . . . to the mere incidents of the surface, the reality – the reality, I tell you – fades. The inner truth is hidden – luckily, luckily' (p. 60). On the threshold of new ways of seeing, Marlow draws back from the dangers of too much reality to the boundaries of that restricted consciousness he had ventured to criticize. In turning away from the amorphous and indefinable absolutes perceived as indwelling in Africa, Marlow repudiates the wilderness to whose being he had responded with awe and humility, disparaging it as the habitation of those malignant energies his civilization had defused: 'never, never before, did this land, this river, this jungle, the very arch of this blazing sky, appear to me so hopeless and so dark, so impenetrable to human thought, so pitiless to human weakness' (p. 91). His recoil from its 'tenebrous and passionate soul' (p. 99), 'the lurking death . . . the hidden evil . . . the profound darkness of its heart' (p. 58), 'the unseen presence of victorious corruption, the darkness of an impenetrable night' (p. 101), coalesces with the revulsion he feels for its indigenous peoples whose very presence in that desolation had amazed him. Together, the effluences from the spirit of the place and the sights of the human inhabitants giving corporeal form to that essence provide Marlow with an explanation of Kurtz's fall, an interpretation in which the fiction, for want of a dissenting viewpoint, concurs. Having crossed to the frontiers of the imperialist imagination and looked back on its narrow territory, Marlow retreats to its heartland taking the text with him and, in the range of his repugnance and opprobrium, initiating a new chapter in colonialist mythology.

For what the fiction validates is Marlow's conviction that the choice before a stranger exposed to an alien world lies between a rigorous adherence to ethnic identity, which carries the freight of remaining ignorant of the foreign,[9] or embracing the unknown and compromising racial integrity. His way, a posture that was traditionally enjoined by British imperialism on its servants, is opposed to Kurtz's dangerous intimacy with the other. However, both Kurtz and Marlow look upon blacks as another genus, the one psychotically hating those to whom he is tied by an illegitimate bond, the other reluctantly recognizing a remote and distant kinship with people he sees ambivalently to be 'not inhuman' (p. 62) and whom he perceives either as noble savages aloof from the degradations of modern civilization – the statuesque chain-gang walking slow and erect, the superb bearing of the barbarous woman, the profound, lustrous and enquiring look of the dying helms-man – or as a subspecies that has failed to realize its human potential.[10] If Marlow does formally acknowledge the unity of humankind and declares the human mind to be the repository of 'all the past as well as all the future' (p. 63), he also distances himself from the blacks, seeing their faces as grotesque masks, judging their souls to be rudimentary and their minds as belonging to the beginnings of time, and hearing their speech as a black and incomprehensible frenzy. It is finally by denying them the faculty of 'human' speech (p. 108) that Marlow de-lineates his cognition of the real and unbridgeable gulf, since apart from the laconic but eloquent announcement of Kurtz's death made by a servant in broken English, and the cannibal headman's curt request that hostile tribesmen be given to the crew for food, the blacks coming within his vista express themselves either in the 'violent babble of uncouth sounds' (p. 38) or through mime. [Compare Achebe, p. 78.] It is language that draws Marlow towards Kurtz because he can speak English and it is Kurtz's voice that entices him into his orbit; on the other hand, it is his response to the 'terrible frankness' of the Africans' 'wild and passionate uproar' that for Marlow confirms verbal utter-ances as the primary form of consciousness and one in which the blacks do not partake: 'An appeal to me in this fiendish row – is there? Very well; I hear; I admit, but I have a voice too, and for good or evil mine is the speech that cannot be silenced' (p. 63). This intrusion of testament into Marlow's narrative registers a powerful affirmation of faith in reason over instinct and passion, which in the context is a declaration of allegiance to Europe and an assertion of its stature.[11] That is why Marlow, who had accepted the cannibal helmsman as a partner and acknowledged the 'claims of distant kinship' in his dying look, can sacrifice this obligation to the greater loyalty owing a man who has disobeyed every tenet of his creed but to whom he is bound through the umbilical cord of culture, and in this he demonstrates an act of solidarity with a world whose values he suspects and whose practices he disavows . . . . . .

The scornful voices in 'Heart of Darkness' castigating the 'dead cats of civilization' and the 'dust-bin[s] of progress' (p.84) echo the fears expressed by Conrad's contemporaries, optimistic socialists and authoritarian pessimists alike, that the West was embarking on a course that would lead to its own destruction. In the fiction's universe, Europe does not manifest itself as the vital force of progress proposed by imperialist propaganda, but as the parent of degenerate progeny, of sordid ambitions pursued by corrupt human agents. Yet, having detached readers from spontaneous trust in imperialism's rationale, the fiction introduces themes valorizing [fixing or raising the value of] the doctrine of cultural allegiance as a moral imperative which is independent of the community's collective moral conduct. It is to this end that the adumbrations of racist views, the denigration of a foreign structure of experience and the commendation of submission to civilization's discontents are directed, strategies that clear the way for sanctioning Marlow's lie in defence of Europe. Since the historical and mythopoeic modes intersect and diverge, the fiction can register ethical stances as disconnected from social circumstances, so that Marlow's negotiation of his dilemma is not acknowledged as constituting a political choice. Attention is instead focused on Marlow as the dissident hero who stands by the dying renegade and solaces his spellbound betrothed, and the principled traitor whose honourable behaviour entails a violation of his own creed. On every score but one, Marlow can be seen to be placed in situations where his austere standards are compromised and his beliefs sacrificed; to the code of gallantry alone does he remain defiantly faithful and the recipients of his chivalry are the contrary and complementary incarnations of a Europe formally committed to humanism and humanitarianism while negating these in the pursuit of imperialist ambitions.

That Marlow admits to an inconsequential lie and makes this the occasion for a peroration on the malignancy of falsehood, while failing to recognize the import of the real lie when he protects Kurtz's reputation in Europe with evasions and by deliberate deception abets the exalted fantasies of the Intended, is the fiction's means of showing up Marlow's capacity for self-delusion and the strength of a commitment to Europeanism which blinds him to the act as one that is a betrayal of his principles. If Kurtz, musician and poet, orator and artist, writer and colonial agent, to whose making '[a]ll Europe contributed' (p.83), is the embodiment of the West's secular culture and the incarnation of its expansionist impulse, then the Intended with her fair hair, pale visage and pure brow, her mature capacity for fidelity, belief and suffering, is the emblem of Europe's religious traditions and the symbol of an imperialism saved by visionary desires. Of his faithfulness to Kurtz, Marlow speaks as if this had been predestined, 'it was ordered I should never betray him – it was written I should be loyal to the nightmare of my choice' (p. 104), and he does not apply to himself the stern judgement he had made on the intrepid Russian sailor's dangerous and fatalistically accepted devotion to Kurtz. Marlow, however, had resisted the seduction of Kurtz's magnetic presence and offered his support to one who despite transgressions was a sentient product of the western world. Drawn to the Intended by 'an impulse of unconscious loyalty' (p. 117), Marlow defers to this figure of a virtuous Europe in full knowledge that the object of his homage is a fantasy representation of a real social order. In delivering to her the lie about her beloved and colonialism's civilizing mission, carried out as she believes by great and good men of generous minds and noble hearts, Marlow is fulfilling a romantic obligation to protect bourgeois ladies like the Intended and his aunt, who also confidently mouths imperialist cant, within 'that beautiful world of their own, lest ours gets worse' (p. 80), a world which if set up 'would go to pieces before the first sunset' (p. 28).

While this suggests the gallant defence of idealism against pragmatism, Marlow's motivation, like the notion of chivalry itself, is tainted with suspect attitudes since he evokes two contrasting but related images of women to serve respectively as figures of Europe's casuistry and its delusions. Just as Kurtz's sketch of a blindfolded woman carrying a lighted torch which has a sinister effect on her face represents an unseeing Europe confidently holding a beacon on to it knows not what in Africa, so does the Intended, whose features bear the delicate shade of truthfulness, and who demands confirmation of her mistaken beliefs, stand as the false prophetess of imperialism's utopian impulse. All the same it is 'before the faith that was in her, before that great and saving illusion that shone with an unearthly glow in the darkness' (p. 121), that Marlow bows his head, a reverent gesture evoking his earlier exhortation of fealty [fidelity, allegiance] to an unselfish belief in an idea, 'something you can set up, and bow down before, and offer a sacrifice to . . .' (p. 20). But now[,] because the eulogies to blind devotion are not undercut by the ironies attaching to its enactment by the vile agents worshipping ivory or the adorers crawling before Kurtz, the fiction invites a positive response to Marlow's action which its cumulative discussion has countermanded.

Marlow assents to the fantasies of an ignorant woman, but confesses to his knowing companions, men themselves connected with colonial ventures and therefore fellow-conspirators whose absolution from the lie he seeks and whose complicity in the lie he solicits and will receive, since on that silence about imperialism's practice depends the utterance of its high-minded and mendacious justifications. The address of the primary narrator to a contemporary British audience began with the appearance of flattering their self-esteem as a nation of intrepid and virtuous empire-builders, and ended by disturbing their conscience and undermining their confidence. Marlow on the other hand makes known at the outset his contempt for imperialism's sententious verbiage, and although his narration abundantly validates his view of colonialism as robbery with violence, his story concludes with an affirmation of loyalty to Europe's illusory pure form. Since Marlow is an unreliable witness and his tale the unburdening of a nonconformist moralist who has by his own standards compromised his individual integrity in the name of a higher corporate obligation, neither his admonition nor his approbation carry the seal of textual approval, and the contradictions in his stance are made transparent through the ironic juxtapositions of the 'facts' he is narrating and his own interpretation of these situations. That Marlow the adherent of an austere code of serious service and Kurtz the flamboyant practitioner of the triumphalist aspiration are products of the same social order and servants of the same official social ends, is an unacceptable reality that Marlow is unable to assimilate and that the text itself intimates but does not confront. The fact of the book's existence does give credence to the argument that 'Heart of Darkness' is ultimately a public disavowal of imperialism's authorized lies. But although the central dialogue is conducted by Marlow's two voices speaking in counterpoint, one the sardonic and angry dissident denouncing imperialism's means and goals as symptoms of the West's moral decline, the other the devoted member of this world striving to recover a utopian dimension to its apocalyptic ambitions, the fiction's relationship to its principal intelligence is equivocal, giving and withholding authority to his testimony, exposing and occluding his inconsistencies. The joining of disparities in unorthodox and unexpected conjunctions is a deliberate and ostentatious feature of the novel's discourse, and the phrases 'abominable satisfactions' (p. 114), 'exalted . . . degradation' (p. 107) and 'diabolic love' (p. 110) are overt signs of its heterogeneous and incompatible meanings. These discontinuities have evoked conflicting readings and to proffer an interpretation of 'Heart of Darkness' as a militant denunciation and a reluctant affirmation of imperialist civilization, as a fiction that exposes and colludes in imperialism's mystifications, is to recognize its immanent contradictions.[12] □

Clearly, Parry agrees, to some extent, with Chinua Achebe. She does not denounce Conrad as a racist, but she does contend that 'Heart of Darkness' contains, among other things, 'adumbrations' – representations in outline, faint indications, or typifications – of 'racist views'; and, like Achebe, she sees the text as denying human speech to the African natives. In a note to the first chapter of her book, she affirms, in fact, that Achebe's 'protest at Conrad's insulting representations of Africa should be listened to by critics for the "truth" this registers' but calls his 'attack' a 'blunt' one that 'dispenses with the recognized language of critical discourse'.[13] Despite the use of the adjective 'bloody', however, and a certain polemical intemperance, it is not altogether true that Achebe dispenses with such language – his positive invocation of F. R. Leavis is a sign of that (see p. 75); but it is the case, as was indicated in the previous chapter of this Guide (pp. 85–86), and as indeed the invocation of Leavis further signifies, that Achebe's critical assumptions were, in 1975, starting to become old-fashioned, and they had become more so by the 1980s.

A key difference between the assumptions that underlie Achebe's attack and those that underlie Parry's analysis is that Parry, in contrast to Achebe, does not assume that a literary text has a single, unitary message; she is thus able to suggest contradictions in Conrad's text that challenge its racist and imperialist aspects, although, in her view, they do not finally overthrow them. Parry's sense of textual contradiction has some affinities with the post-structuralist and deconstructionist approaches to literary interpretation that were becoming more widespread in the UK and USA in the 1980s; in her interpretation of 'Heart of Darkness', however, she does not appear to share the post-structuralist and deconstructionist view that all texts are, necessarily and inherently, contradictory. It is, rather, specific contradictions produced in the context of imperialism with which she is concerned. Parry, like Achebe, thinks that 'Heart of Darkness' exemplifies a much more widespread Western image, or what she sees as a mythology, of Africa, but she also regards Conrad's text, not merely as repeating that image or mythology with particular vividness, but also as revising it, even if finally reconfirming it – 'select[ing] other landmarks for scrutiny and locat[ing] the roots of western shock and antipathy in new areas', as she puts it in the extract that has just been quoted. Parry's interpretation is important both in its own right and in the way in which it exemplifies a new kind of approach to the interpretation of 'Heart of Darkness'; an approach that is able to acknowledge both the pro- and anti-racist and imperialist aspects in Conrad's text, to see ways in which that text rewrites, and does not merely inertly reproduce, those aspects; to grasp the contradictions between them; to locate those contradictions historically, and to place them in the context of a wider image or mythology of Africa – or what was starting to be called, as a result of the growing influence of Edward W. Said's path-breaking book *Orientalism*

(1978), a 'discourse' that constructed an image or mythology of Africa. Christopher L. Miller's study of 'Heart of Darkness' in relation to Africanist discourse will be considered later in this chapter (pp. 127–34).

But it was certainly not the case that innovative interpretation of 'Heart of Darkness' in the 1980s was wholly dominated by considerations of imperialism, colonialism, racism, or the discursive construction of Africa. Another original approach to 'Heart of Darkness', which mentions the imperialist aspect but does not make it central, first appeared in English[14] in 1984 in Peter Brooks's seminal book *Reading for the Plot*. Brooks's study produced powerful new readings of a range of canonical novels, including one that is the subject of another Icon Critical Guide, Dickens's *Great Expectations*.[15] In his concern with plot, Brooks brings together psychoanalysis and narratology – the study of the way stories are told – to try 'to talk of the dynamics of temporality and reading, of the motor forces that drive the text forward, of the desires that connect narrative ends and beginnings, and make of the textual middle a highly charged field of force'.[16] One key feature of 'Heart of Darkness', sometimes forgotten in critical discussion, is that it is a compelling story – a feature that may be crucial to its continuing popularity among critics and students, but which perhaps makes it more dangerous for those, like Achebe, who see its message as a dehumanising one. 'Heart of Darkness' is both an adventure story, and, as Brooks points out, a detective story, with mysteries, clues and a quest for a solution – but it is a detective story rewritten in the terms of an emerging modernism, a detective story in which crime, suspect and solution remain unresolved. Marlow and his listeners on the Thames would not dispel the gathering darkness at the end of his narrative by making their way to 221B Baker Street to seek the help of Sherlock Holmes in finding out the truth about Kurtz or Africa. It is 'Heart of Darkness' as a modernist detective story that Brooks explores in an account hardly less compelling than the narrative that is his subject.

A number of the terms that Brooks uses should be defined at the outset. The terms *fabula* and *sjužet* were employed by the Russian Formalist critics who were active in the early twentieth century – not long after 'Heart of Darkness' was first published – but whose work did not enter significantly into European critical discourse until the 1960s and 1970s. The *fabula* is the events of a story as they would proceed if told in straightforward chronological order; the *sjužet* is the order in which the events of a story are actually told, which may, and usually does, depart to a greater or lesser extent from straightforward chronological order. The *sjužet* of the classic detective novel, for example, departs from its *fabula* because it does not tell us who committed the murder at the time at which the murder occurs; the identity of the murderer is not revealed until the end of the novel, and it is only when the identity is known that it is possible for the reader to reconstitute the *fabula*, to tell the events in the order in which they would have occurred in actual life. In English, *fabula* is often translated as 'story' and *sjužet* as 'plot', a translation Brook partly accepts and employs, but with an added dimension: for Brooks, 'plot' is, in a sense, the interpretative activity that is prompted by the distinction between *fabula* and *sjužet*: it is an aspect of the *sjužet* in that it is the 'active shaping force' of the *sjužet*,[17] but as it shapes the *sjužet*, compelling a particular arrangement of events, it also makes us try to grasp and understand the *fabula*, to rearrange the events in a straightforward chronological order. In reading a detective story, for instance, the plot both contributes to the *sjužet*, by prompting an ordering of events that partly conceals the *fabula*, but also drives us towards the *fabula* as that which we eventually want to discover.

In French narratology, the *fabula* may be referred to as the *histoire* (story), and the *sjužet* as the *récit* (account), or sometimes, the *discours* (discourse).[18] As Brooks points out, the French narratologist Gérard Genette adds to the *histoire/récit* or *fabula/sjužet* distinction a third category, which he calls *narration* – 'narrating': this means, in Brooks's paraphrase, 'the level at which narratives sometimes dramatize the means and agency (real or fictive) of their telling'.[19] This third category is relevant for 'Heart of Darkness' because of the way in which, at various points, the narrative draws attention to the kind of story Marlow is telling: there is, for example, the famous description by the first narrator of Marlow's story as a 'glow' that brings out a 'haze' (p. 18), or Marlow's own remark that '[i]t seems to me I am trying to tell you a dream' (p. 50).

Bearing these terms and definitions in mind, the extract below is from one of the stories about stories that make up Brooks's book – his fruitfully tangled tale of the narrative complexities and inconclusive ending of 'Heart of Darkness':

■ Joseph Conrad's 'Heart of Darkness' – published in the last year of the nineteenth century – poses in an exemplary way central questions about the shape and epistemology of narrative. It displays an acute self-consciousness about the organizing features of traditional narrative, working with them still, but suspiciously, with constant reference to the inadequacy of the inherited orders of meaning. It suggests affinities to that preeminently nineteenth-century genre, the detective story, but a detective story gone modernist: a tale of inconclusive solutions to crimes of problematic status. In its representation of an effort to reach endings that would retrospectively illuminate beginnings and middles, it pursues a reflection on the formal limits of narrative, but within a frame of discourse that appears to subvert finalities of form. Most of all, it engages the very motive of narrative in its tale of a complexly motivated attempt to recover the story of another within one's own, and to retell both in a context that further complicates relations of actors, tellers, and

117

listeners. Ultimately, all these questions, and everything one says about the tale, must be reconceived within the context of Marlow's act of narration aboard the *Nellie* at the moment of the turning of the tide on the Thames, in the relation of this narrator to his narratees and the relation of the narrative situation to the stories enacted within it.

'Heart of Darkness' is . . . a framed tale, in which a first narrator introduces Marlow and has the last word after Marlow has fallen silent; and embedded within Marlow's tale is apparently another, Kurtz's, which never quite gets told – as perhaps Marlow's does not quite either, for the frame structure here is characterized by notable uncertainties. Referring . . . to Gérard Genette's tripartite distinction of narrative levels, it is evident that in 'Heart of Darkness' everything must eventually be recovered on the plane of narrating, in the act of telling which itself attempts to recover the problematic relations of Marlow's narrative plot to his story, and of his plot and story to Kurtz's story, which in turn entertains doubtful relations with Kurtz's narrative plot and its narrating. Marlow's narrative plot will more and more as it proceeds take as its story what Marlow understands to be Kurtz's story. Yet Kurtz's story has other plots, ways in which he would like to have it told: for instance, in his [Report to the International Society for the Suppression of Savage Customs] (a plot subverted by the scribbled and forgotten footnote '"Exterminate all the brutes!"' (p.84)); or else the manner in which posthumously he commands Marlow's 'loyalty' (pp.112, 117) in retelling it – as lie – to his Intended. Ultimately, we must ask what motivates Marlow's retellings – of his own and Kurtz's mortal adventures – in the gathering dusk on the Thames estuary.[20]

One way to begin to unpack the dense narrative layerings of 'Heart of Darkness' may be through the various orders of signification and belief – ready-made life plots – that the text casts up along the way: orders that marshal reality and might explain it if only one could believe them, if only there did not always seem to be something subverting them. One such order, for instance, is the Company, its door flanked by the two knitters of black wool, one of whom – or is it by now a third, to complete the suggestion of the Parcae [the Greek Fates – see p.98]? – obtrudes herself upon Marlow's memory at the moment of maximum blackness 'as a most improper person to be sitting at the other end of such an affair' (p.105).[21] In the knitted web – shroud, pall, or is it rather Ariadne's thread into a dark labyrinth? – the Company's design reaches to the depths of the dark continent. [In Greek mythology, Ariadne followed Theseus into the labyrinth of the Minotaur trailing a thread behind her which she and Theseus later used to find their way out.] The Company as [a form of] ordering is related to the 'idea':[22] 'The conquest of the earth . . . is not a pretty thing when you look into it too much. What redeems it is the idea only' (p.20). The 'idea' is the fiction of the mission, which upon inspection is seen to cover up the most rapacious and vicious of imperialisms. Here surely is one relation of order as ready-made plot to story in 'Heart of Darkness': a relation of cover-up, concealment, lie. Yet one should note a certain admiration in Marlow for the idea in itself: a recognition of the necessity for plot, for signifying system, even in the absence of its correspondence to reality (which may, for instance, suggest a reason for his effacing Kurtz's scribbled footnote before passing on the [Report to the International Society for the Suppression of Savage Customs] to the press). The juxta-position of ready-made order to reality, and Marlow's capacity to see both the admirable and the absurd in such attempted applications of order, is well suggested by the Company's chief accountant in the lower station, in high starched collar and cuffs, 'bent over his books . . . making correct entries of perfectly correct transactions; and fifty feet below the doorstep I could see the still tree-tops of the grove of death' (p. 38). The building of the railroad, with its objectless blasting of a path to nowhere, would be another example; even more com-pelling is perhaps the picture of the French warship shelling an incomprehensible coast:

> Once, I remember, we came upon a man-of-war anchored off the coast. There wasn't even a shed there, and she was shelling the bush. It appears the French had one of their wars going on there-abouts. Her ensign dropped limp like a rag; the muzzles of the long eight-inch guns stuck out all over the low hull; the greasy, slimy swell swung her up lazily and let her down, swaying her thin masts. In the empty immensity of earth, sky, and water, there she was, incomprehensible, firing into a continent. Pop, would go one of the eight-inch guns; a small flame would dart and vanish, a little white smoke would disappear, a tiny projectile would give a feeble screech – and nothing happened. Nothing could happen. There was a touch of insanity in the proceeding, a sense of lugubrious drollery in the sight; and it was not dissipated by somebody on board assur-ing me earnestly there was a camp of natives – he called them enemies! – hidden out of sight somewhere. (pp. 30–31)

The traditional ordering systems – war, camp, enemies – lead to the logical consequences – men-of-war, cannonades – which are wholly incongruous to the situation requiring mastery. There is an absurd disproportion between the ordering systems deployed and the trivial-ity of their effect, as if someone had designed a machine to produce work far smaller than the energy put into it. And there are many other examples that conform to such laws of incongruous effect.

The question of orderings comes to be articulated within the very heart of darkness in an exchange between Marlow and the manager on the question of Kurtz's 'method' in the acquisition of ivory, which, we have already learned from the Russian – Kurtz's admirer, and the chief teller of his tale – Kurtz mainly obtained by raiding the country. The manager's rhetoric is punctuated by Marlow's dissents:

> '. . . I don't deny there is a remarkable quantity of ivory – mostly fossil. We must save it, at all events – but look how precarious the position is – and why? Because the method is unsound.' 'Do you,' said I, looking at the shore, 'call it "unsound method"?' 'Without doubt,' he exclaimed, hotly. 'Don't you?' . . . [Conrad's ellipsis] 'No method at all,' I murmured after a while. 'Exactly,' he exulted. 'I anticipated this. Shows a complete want of judgement. It is my duty to point it out in the proper quarter.' 'Oh,' said I, 'that fellow – what's his name? – the brickmaker, will make a readable report for you.' He appeared confounded for a moment. It seemed to me I had never breathed an atmosphere so vile, and I turned mentally to Kurtz for relief – positively for relief. (p. 101)

The result of this exchange is that Marlow finds himself classified with those of '"unsound method"', which, of course, is a way of moralizing as lapse from order any recognition of the absence of order, using the concept of disorder to conceal the radical condition of orderlessness. The manager's language – '"unsound method"', '"want of judgement"', '"duty to point it out in the proper quarter"' – refers to ordering systems and in so doing finds a way to mask perception of what Kurtz's experience really signifies. The '"readable report"', which Marlow notes to be the usual order for dealing with such deviations as Kurtz's, would represent the ultimate system of false ordering, ready-made discourse. What we really need, Marlow seems to suggest, is an *unreadable* report – something like Kurtz's [Report], perhaps, with its utterly contradictory messages, or perhaps Marlow's eventual retelling of the whole affair.

The text, then, appears to speak of a repeated 'trying out' of orders, all of which distort what they claim to organize, all of which may indeed cover up a very lack of possibility of order. This may suggest one relationship between story and narrative plot in the text: a relationship of disquieting uncertainty, where story never appears to be quite matched to the narrative plot that is responsible for it. Yet the orders tried out in 'Heart of Darkness' may in their very tenuousness be necessary to the process of striving towards meaning: as if to say that the plotting of stories remains necessary even where we have ceased to believe in the plots we use. Certain minimum canons of readability remain necessary if we are to be able to discern the locus of the necessarily unreadable.

Marlow's own initial relationship to the matter of orderings is curious, and recognized by himself as such. Marlow is eminently the man of work, proud of his seamanship, concerned with what he calls the 'surface-truth' (p. 63) of steering, mechanics, repairs, devoted to the values of the master mariner codified in Towson's (or Towser's) 'An Inquiry into some Points of Seamanship': 'Not a very enthralling book; but at the first glance you could see there a singleness of intention, an honest concern for the right way of going to work, which made these humble pages . . . luminous with another than a professional light' (p. 65). Yet as he presents his decision to undertake his African journey, it appears capricious, irrational, unmotivated. The decision reaches back to his boyhood passion for maps – which are another external ordering of reality – yet particularly his attraction to the unmapped within them, to their blank spaces. The space to which he will journey in the story recounted in 'Heart of Darkness' – for convenience, we may call it the Congo, though it is never so named, never named at all, in the text – appeared 'the biggest, the most blank, so to speak' (p. 22). By the time of his journey, the blank has been filled in, 'with rivers and lakes and names'; indeed, possibly it has been filled overfull with 'ideas', for '[i]t had become a place of blackness' [sic – Hampson's text has '[i]t had become a place of darkness', echoing Conrad's title, not 'blackness' (p. 22)[23]]. But blackness appears to motivate as strongly as blankness. Marlow in fact appears to recognize that his explanation lacks coherence, when he goes on to describe the 'mighty big river . . . resembling an immense snake uncoiled', and himself as the 'silly little bird' that is 'fascinated' by the snake (p. 22) – so fascinated that he began to have recourse, as he never had before, to women relatives on the Continent, in order to have a captaincy in the Company trading on the river. The desire for the journey is childish, absolute, persistent through contradictions; the journey itself appears compulsive, gratuitous, unmotivated. In the manner of Marlow himself, the reader must, in the absence of clear purpose or goal to the journey, be content with a general 'fascination'. The point bears some insistence, for Marlow's description of his trip up the river will in fact be also a description of how the journey came to be motivated: of the precipitation of a motivating plot within the originally unmotivated journey, and narrative.

'Going up that river was like travelling back to the earliest beginnings of the world . . .' (p. 59). The way up is the way back: Marlow's individual journey repeats, ontogenetically [in terms of individual development], a kind of reverse phylogeny [evolution of the human race], an unravelling of the threads of civilization. His quest, we might say, is also an inquest, an investigation leading towards beginnings and origins; and the traditional story line of the journey comes to be doubled by the more specifically goal-oriented plot line of the inquest.

What makes it so is his discovery that he has been preceded in his journey by the 'remarkable' (pp. 37, 101, 112, 113, 120) Mr. Kurtz, who becomes the object of inquest, providing a motive for the previously gratuitous voyage. Kurtz in fact provides a magnetizing goal of quest and inquest since he not only has led the way up the river, he has also returned upriver instead of coming back to the central station as he was supposed to do: Marlow indeed is able to 'see Kurtz for the first time', in his imagination, in this return upriver, 'setting his face towards the depths of the wilderness' (p. 57). It can in fact be pieced together from various remarks of the Company officials that the very reason for Marlow's being sent on his journey upriver is to detect the meaning and the consequences of Kurtz's return upriver – a presiding intention to his voyage of which Marlow becomes aware only in its midst, at the central station. It is thus gradually impressed upon Marlow, and the reader, that Marlow is in a state of belatedness or secondariness in relation to the forerunner; his journey is a repetition, which gains its meaning from its attachment to the prior journey. Marlow's plot (*sjužet*) repeats Kurtz's story (*fabula*), takes this as its motivating force – and then will seek also to know and to incorporate Kurtz's own plot for his story.

So it is that Marlow's inquest, in the manner of the detective's, becomes the retracing of the track of a precursor . . . No more than the detective's, Marlow's narrative is not primary: it attaches itself to another's story, seeking there its authority; it retraces another's path, repeats a journey already undertaken.

In Marlow's narrative, then, we witness the formation of motivation in the middle of the journey, though in his act of narration this motivation may stand at its very inception, as part of the very motive of telling, since his own story has become narratable only in relation to Kurtz's. In a phrase that marks his first explicit recognition of a goal to his journey, and hence of a plot to his story, Marlow states: 'Where the pilgrims imagined it [the steamboat] crawled to I don't know. To some place where they expected to get something, I bet! For me it crawled towards Kurtz – exclusively' (p. 61). The reason for Marlow's choice of this 'exclusive' and seemingly arbitrary motivation is made more specific following the attack on the steamboat, in a manner that helps us to understand the uses of plot. Thinking that the attack may betoken the death of Kurtz (later we learn that Kurtz himself ordered the attack), Marlow feels an 'extreme disappointment', as if 'I had travelled all this way for the sole purpose of talking with Mr Kurtz. Talking with. . . .' (p. 79 [Conrad's ellipsis]). His choice of terms to image his anticipated meeting with Kurtz now leads him to recognition that it was indeed Kurtz as talker that he sought . . . . The definition of Kurtz through his 'gift of expression' (p. 79) and as a 'voice' (pp. 79, 80, 98. 110, 112), and Marlow's postulation of this definition of Kurtz as the motivating goal of his own journey, serve to conceptualize the narrative end as expression, voice, articulation, or what Walter Benjamin [in his essay 'The Storyteller' (1936)] termed simply 'wisdom':[24] the goal of all story-telling which, with the decline of traditional oral transmission, has in the 'privatized' genre of the novel come to be defined exclusively as the meaning of an individual life. And . . . in Benjamin's argument, the meaning of a life cannot be known until the moment of death: it is at death that a life first assumes transmissible form – becomes a completed and significant statement – so that it is death that provides the authority or 'sanction' of narrative. The deathbed scene of the nineteenth-century novel eminently represents the moment of summing-up of a life's meaning and a transmission of accumulated wisdom to succeeding generations. Paternal figures within novels write their own obituaries, transmitting to the younger protagonists something of the authority necessary to view the meaning of their own lives retrospectively, in terms of the significance that will be brought by the as yet unwritten end.

To Marlow, Kurtz is doubly such a deathbed figure and writer of obituary. In the first place, he has reached his journey's end, he is lodged in the heart of darkness and it is from that 'farthest point of navigation' (p. 21) that he offers his discourse, that 'pulsating stream of light' or 'deceitful flow' (p. 79). Kurtz has reached further, deeper than anyone else, and his gift for expression means that he should be able to give articulate shape to his terminus. 'Kurtz discoursed. A voice! a voice!' (p. 110) Marlow will later report. But by that point Kurtz's report on the meaning of his navigation into the heart of the jungle will be compounded with his journey to his life's end, and his terminal report on his inner descent into darkness. So that Kurtz's discourse stands to make sense of Marlow's voyage and his life, his journey and his inquest: to offer that final articulation that will give a meaning to journey and experience here at what Marlow has doubly identified as 'the farthest point of navigation and the culminating point of my experience' (p. 21). Kurtz is he who has already turned experience into Benjamin's 'wisdom', turned story into well-formed narrative plot, matter into pure voice, and who stands ready to narrate life's story in significant form. Marlow's own narrative can make sense only when his inquest has reached a 'solution' that is not a simple detection but the finding of a message written at and by the death of another. The meaning of his narrative plot has indeed come to depend on Kurtz's articulation of the meaning of *his* plot: Marlow's structuring of his own *fabula* as *sjužet* has attached itself to Kurtz's *fabula*, and can find its significant outcome only in finding Kurtz's *sjužet*.

For Kurtz, in the heart of darkness and at life's end, has 'stepped over the edge' and has 'summed up'. Since it is a 'summing up' that Marlow has discovered to be what most he has been seeking – that summary illumination that retrospectively makes sense of all that has gone before – his insistence that Kurtz has summed up is vitally important. At the end of the journey lies, not ivory, gold, or a fountain of youth, but the capacity to turn experience into language: a voice. But here we are forced to give closer scrutiny to Marlow's affirmations and their curious self-cancellations. Noting that after Kurtz's death he almost died himself, Marlow continues in reflection on ultimate articulations:

> I was within a hair's-breadth of the last opportunity for pronounce-ment, and I found with humiliation that probably I would have nothing to say. This is the reason why I affirm that Kurtz was a remarkable man. He had something to say. He said it. Since I had peeped over the edge myself, I understand better the meaning of his stare, that could not see the flame of the candle, but was wide enough to embrace the whole universe, piercing enough to pene-trate all the hearts that beat in the darkness. He had summed up – he had judged. "The horror!" He was a remarkable man. After all, this was the expression of some sort of belief; it had candour, it had con-viction, it had a vibrating note of revolt in its whisper, it had the appalling face of a glimpsed truth – the strange commingling of desire and hate. And it is not my own extremity I remember best – a vision of greyness without form filled with physical pain, and a careless contempt for the evanescence of all things – even of this pain itself. No! It is his extremity that I seem to have lived through. True, he had made that last stride, he had stepped over the edge, while I had been permitted to draw back my hesitating foot. And perhaps in this is the whole difference; perhaps all the wisdom, and all truth, and all sincerity, are just compressed into that in-appreciable moment of time in which we step over the threshold of the invisible. Perhaps! I like to think my summing-up would not have been a word of careless contempt. Better his cry – much better. It was an affirmation, a moral victory paid for innumerable defeats, by abominable terrors, by abominable satisfactions. But it was a victory! That is why I have remained loyal to Kurtz to the last, and even beyond, when a long time after I heard once more, not his own voice, but the echo of his magnificent eloquence thrown to me from a soul as translucently pure as a cliff of crystal (pp. 113–14).

The passage is one that epitomizes all our difficulties with Marlow as narrator, for the resonance of its ethical pronouncements seems some-how to get in the way of the designation of a starker and possibly contradictory truth: the moral rhetoric appears in some measure a cover-up. Marlow explicitly confirms Benjamin's argument concerning storytelling and wisdom, and confirms his need for Kurtz as the paternal figure whose final articulation transmits wisdom. Kurtz 'had summed up'. And this summary articulation, which concerns not only Kurtz's individual experience but also penetrates 'all the hearts that beat in the darkness', comes from 'over the edge', on the other side, beyond life, or more accurately, on the threshold of the beyond, with one foot on either side; whereas Marlow has only 'peeped' over the edge. In his hypothesis that 'all the wisdom, and all truth' are compressed into this moment of termination and threshold, Marlow evokes the tradition of the 'panoramic vision of the dying': as he says just before the passage I quoted at length, 'Did he [Kurtz] live his life again in every detail of desire, temptation, and surrender during that supreme moment of complete knowledge?' (p. 112). The supremacy of the moment should inform Kurtz's *ultima verba* [last words], his summing-up: in his discourse is wrought his 'victory'.

And yet, when after considering that 'all the wisdom, and all truth' may lie compacted in that last moment, that 'last opportunity for pronouncement', Marlow states: 'I like to think my summing-up would not have been a word of careless contempt', he may subvert the rhetorical system of the passage quoted by inculcating a major doubt concerning the proper characterization of Kurtz's 'word'. The uncertainties of Marlow's argument here are suggested by other curiosities of diction and rhetoric. 'Better his cry' is a curious comparative to use in regard to a word that Marlow claims was *not* spoken (the word of careless contempt). 'But it was a victory' appears somewhat strange in that one doesn't ordinarily introduce a clause by a concessive when the previous clause is ostensibly making the same affirmation. Marlow's discourse seems to shape itself in opposition to the anticipated objections of an imagined interlocutor. By protesting too much, he builds those putative objections dialogically into his own discourse, making it (in Mikhail Bakhtin's terms) 'double voiced'.[25] Double voicing indeed is suggested by the evocation of the 'echo' of Kurtz's voice. This 'echo of his magnificent eloquence' becomes the most highly problematic element of the passage when, later, we understand that the 'soul as translucently pure as a cliff of crystal' is Kurtz's Intended, and that the 'echo' which she hears is a pure fiction in blatant contradiction to that which Marlow hears in the same room with her: a lie which Marlow is obliged to confirm as conscious cover-up of the continuing reverberation of Kurtz's last words: '"The horror! The horror!"' (pp. 112, 118, 123).

This is no doubt the point at issue: that Kurtz's final words answer so poorly to all of Marlow's insistence on summing-up as a moment of final articulation of wisdom, truth, and sincerity, as affirmation and as moral victory. Marlow affirms that it is Kurtz's ultimate capacity to judge, to use human language in its communicative and its normative dimensions to transmit an evaluation of his soul's adventures on this earth, that constitutes his victory: the victory of articulation itself. And yet '"The horror! The horror!"' is more accurately characterized when Marlow calls it a 'cry'. It comes about as close as articulated speech can come to the primal cry, to a blurted emotional reaction of uncertain reference and context. To present '"the horror!"' as articulation of that wisdom lying in wait at the end of the tale, at journey's end and life's end, is to make a mockery of storytelling and ethics, or to gull one's listeners – as Marlow himself seems to realize when he finds that he cannot repeat Kurtz's last words to the Intended, but must rather cover them up by a conventional ending: '"The last word he pronounced was – your name"' (p. 123). The contrast of this fictive act of naming – 'proper' naming – with Kurtz's actual cry may suggest how poorly Kurtz's summing-up fits Marlow's description of it. Indeed, his cry so resembles the 'word of careless contempt' that when we find this phrase in Marlow's account, we tend to take it as applying to Kurtz's last utterance, only to find that it is given as the very contrary thereof. Something is amiss.

We can concede to Marlow his reading of the ethical signified of Kurtz's last words, his 'judgement upon the adventures of his soul on this earth' (p. 112) – though we may find the reference of this signified somewhat ambiguous: is the horror within Kurtz or without? Is it experience or reaction to experience? But we have a problem conceiving the signifier as fulfilling the conditions of the wisdom-and-truth articulating function of the end. More than a masterful, summary, victorious articulation, '"The horror!"' appears as minimal language, language on the verge of reversion to savagery, on the verge of a fall from language. That Kurtz's experience in the heart of darkness should represent and be represented by a fall from language does not surprise us: this belongs to the very logic of the heart of darkness, which is consistently characterized as 'unspeakable'. There are the 'unspeakable rites' (p. 83) at which Kurtz presides, the 'unspeakable secrets' of his '"method"' (p. 101), and, at the very heart of the darkness – at the moment when Marlow pursues Kurtz into the jungle at night, to struggle with his soul and carry him back to the steamer – we have only this characterization of the dark ceremony unfolding by the campfire: '[i]t was very awful' (p. 106). Critics have most often been content to point to the moral signified of such phrases – or to criticize them, and Conrad, for a lack of referential or ethical specificity – but we should feel obliged to read them in their literal statement.[26] What stands at the heart of darkness – at the journey's end and at the core of this tale – is unsayable, extralinguistic.

It cannot be otherwise, for the heart of darkness – and Kurtz himself in the heart – is beyond the system of human social structure which makes language possible and is itself made possible by language: which is unthinkable except through and as language, as that which demarcates culture from nature.[27] ☐

Brooks's analysis demonstrates the value of a narratalogical approach that offers not only a formal account of levels and structures of narration but also acknowledges how the *ways* in which a story is told – as distinct from, though complemented by, *what* it tells – can engage us in nothing less than matters of life and death – and of guilt and complicity. In his own summing-up near the end of his analysis, Brooks says: 'one finally needs to read "Heart of Darkness" as act of narration even more than as narrative or as story. It shows this act to be far from innocent, indeed as based perhaps most of all on the need and the desire to implicate one's listeners in a taint one can't live with alone'.[28] To consider this 'taint' in relation to the colonial site of 'Heart of Darkness' might lead us once more to questions about imperialism, colonialism, racism and the representation of Africa – though this is not a road Brooks takes. In this respect, one might suggest a certain repression or evasion in his own analysis: there is, for example, in the extract just quoted, his statement that, when Marlow pursues Kurtz into the jungle at night, 'we have only this characterization of the dark ceremony unfolding by the campfire: "[i]t was very awful"'. But it is by no means clear that '[i]t was very awful' constitutes a 'characterization of the dark ceremony unfolding by the campfire'; it seems to apply more to the physical danger of the situation Marlow is in and to the spectacle of Kurtz's degradation; Marlow appears to have his back to the fires at the time of which he is speaking. Moreover, almost immediately afterwards, when Marlow does glance back to the fires, we do have an image of the 'dark ceremony' (this phrase is Brooks's own) unmentioned by Brooks. This is the 'black figure' with horns who stands up and strides across the glow from the fire 'on long black legs, waving long black arms' – precisely the description that Achebe singled out as an example of Conrad's 'fixation on blackness' (see p. 81).[29] Brooks's own compelling act of narration, his powerful retelling of 'Heart of Darkness', has its own shadows that obscure Africa more deeply than Conrad's tale.

The relationship of 'Heart of Darkness' to representations of Africa was, however, taken up again in the year following Brooks's book, in Christopher L. Miller's *Blank Darkness: Africanist Discourse in French* (1985). As indicated earlier in this chapter (p. 116), Miller's study follows on from Edward W. Said's influential book *Orientalism*, in which Said aimed to analyse the ways in which conceptions of the Orient were constructed in language, in discourse. Said himself had been influenced by the work of the French writer Michel Foucault, who had analysed the way in which discourses produced 'knowledges' – of criminals, for example, or of sexuality – that were also modes of power, ways of exercising control over those classified as criminal or sexually deviant. Similarly, for Said, the ways in which the Orient was written about in the West – the Western discourses of Orientalism – produced 'knowledges' of the Orient that were also means of exercising control over it. Christopher L. Miller's study, as his title suggests, applies and develops that approach in relation to what he calls 'Africanist' discourse, with a specific focus on French literature. Miller stresses that 'discourse' is an ambiguous term: '"[d]iscourse" is not a category equal or opposable to "language", "speech", "writing", "thought", or "idea". It participates in all of these but is not reducible to any of them. There is no "discourse" in the sense that there is a classical system of tropes known as "rhetoric"; there are only *discourses*, forming themselves according to the shape of their objects'.[30]

There is, for Miller, another key ambiguity in relation to the notion of discourse: discourse emerges between perception and thought, between a sensory immediacy that could not be represented, and abstraction wholly divorced from intentions, desires and emotions. Discourse is like dream in Freud's account. Miller puts it in the following way, with some help from a text that, like 'Heart of Darkness', first appeared around the turn of the century – Freud's *The Interpretation of Dreams* (1899; 1900).

■ Africanist discourse resembles dream in Freud's description. Both are made possible by a condition of blankness – of distance and ignorance, of sleep. Within that frame, a discourse unfolds having the singular capacity to appear real, to break the frame and fill the universe: a dream is not a dream unless the dreamer cannot distinguish it from reality. Similarly, Africanist fantasies come armed with measurements in centimetres, eyewitness accounts, and every appearance of accurate perception. But like the figure of 'Africa', dream is felt to be 'something alien, arising from another world and contrasting it with the remaining contents of the mind', 'extraneous to our minds'.[31] Yet, paradoxically, dreams can only be a result of 'the arbitrary decision of the mind'. They are the closest object to the mind and the furthest from it.[32] □

In the Freudian account, dreams offer apparent but strange realities that seem to come from the mind in that they fulfil wishes, but that also appear alien and threatening to the mind.

It is possible to see how these apparently paradoxical combinations of accurate perception and alienness, of apparent realities that are both intimately gratifying and threateningly other, might apply to 'Heart of Darkness', in which Marlow's tale seems to its supposed narrator like an attempt 'to tell you a dream' (p. 50). But why does Conrad's text figure in a discussion of Africanist discourse in *French*? As Miller points out, '[t]here is no "Heart of Darkness" in French literature – no text with such

a singularity of influence, producing so many rewritings and interpretations'.[33] He contends, however, that 'Heart of Darkness' is 'the strongest
of all Africanist texts', a text which perhaps offers the perspective that
makes the 'initial perception of a discourse as "Africanist"' possible:[34] it 'is a
seminal text within French and all European Africanist discourse not
because of its immediate influence on living writers but for what it
teaches us now about how to read the figure of Africa: for the light it
sheds – so to speak – on the discursive practice of European writers of
whatever language'.[35] Here, then, is a strong claim for the importance of
'Heart of Darkness' that rests not primarily on its literary quality or its
place within modernism but on its capacity to illuminate a whole range of
Western discourses that construct 'Africa'. This is not to say that Miller
denies Conrad's text literary quality; and he alludes to its modernism
when he describes it as 'a self-conscious meditation on misunderstanding'
that, because of its self-consciousness, is located 'at a highly significant
crossroads'. In contrast to Peter Brooks, however, Miller identifies this
crossroads as sited, not between nineteenth-century and modernist
fiction, but 'between an old and a new mode of Africanist expression,
between the projection of a corrupt and ignoble Africa and the later
critique of that projection and its political outgrowth, colonialism'. It is
because 'Heart of Darkness' stands at this crossroads that it arouses such
ambivalent responses in critics today: 'it is neither colonialistic enough to
be damnable nor ironic enough to be completely untainted by "colonialistic bias"'.[36] The 'net effect' of this 'is a subversion of Africanist discourse
from within'.[37]

Here is 'Narrating Backwards', a key section of Miller's analysis. He
begins by quoting what is, as he acknowledges, a frequently cited passage
from 'Heart of Darkness' – so frequently cited that the critic who quotes it
again sets himself the challenge of saying something new about it.

■ Going up that river was like travelling back to the *earliest beginnings
of the world*, when vegetation rioted on the earth and the big trees
were kings. An empty stream, a great silence, an impenetrable forest.
The air was warm, thick, heavy, sluggish. There was no joy in the
brilliance of sunshine . . . The broadening waters flowed through a
mob of wooded islands; you lost your way on that river as you
would in a desert, and butted all day long against shoals, trying to
find the channel, till you thought yourself bewitched and cut off for
ever from everything you had known once – somewhere – far away
– in another existence perhaps. There were moments when *one's past
came back to one*, as it will sometimes when you have not a moment to
spare to yourself; but it came in the shape of an unrestful and noisy
dream, remembered with wonder amongst the overwhelming realities of this strange world of plants, and water, and silence. And this

stillness did not in the least resemble a peace. It was the stillness of an implacable force brooding over an inscrutable intention. It looked at you with a vengeful aspect. I got used to it afterwards; I did not see it any more; I had no time. I had to keep guessing at the channel; I *had to discern, mostly by inspiration, the signs of hidden banks* ... When you have to attend to things of that sort, to the mere incidents of the surface, the reality – the reality, I tell you – fades. The inner truth is hidden – luckily, luckily (pp. 59–60 [Miller's italics]).

This often-quoted passage and its most basic armature – the phrase 'travelling back' – are a paradigm of Africanist narration [An 'armature' is a support and/or a driving force; a paradigm is a pattern or model]. Whereas the pre-anthropologists (such as [Charles] de Brosses) and the 'ethnologists' (such as [Joseph Arthur de] Gobineau) [writers whom Miller has discussed earlier in his book[38]] depicted the primitive world as static and isolated, the project of narration as seen in this passage will be to reach back to that frozen past and make it real in writing. Travelling back means bringing the primitive world forward, or, more accurately, projecting the primitive world as an anteriority [an earlier state and/or process] that can be reached geographically: 'we were travelling in the night of first ages' (p. 62). The temporal and the spatial are conflated in such a way that physical travel will take one 'back to the earliest beginnings of the world'. Narration, which would normally be the recounting of sequential events (a model from which it can never wholly escape if only because one word, one paragraph, must follow another), is here literally a 'backwards' process. As V. S. Naipaul writes in *A Bend in the River* (1979), the strongest Africanist narration since 'Heart of Darkness': 'I am going in the wrong direction'.[39]

But the immediate corollary of that backwards narration is the loss of directionality itself, for the primitive world into which one penetrates is a place where 'backwards' and 'forwards' have no more meaning. There is only a litany of negativity: 'an empty stream, a great silence, an impenetrable forest'. The stream is 'empty', one supposes, in the sense that there is no one there, it is devoid of life; yet the narrator is there to bear witness to its emptiness. The silence is impenetrable in its meaning because it has no form to be interpreted. The forest, and later the desert, are two principal Africanist figures for the loss of directionality. Penetration into this world is a process of 'discerning, mostly by inspiration', because the referents by which one could determine direction (*sens*, 'meaning' [or 'direction'] in French) keep slipping away: '[s]ometimes I would pick out a tree a little way ahead to measure our progress towards Kurtz by, but I lost it invariably before we got abreast' (p. 66). Africa is represented as dismantling European concepts of measure and progress. The forward movement of the steamship,

progressing towards Kurtz, is all but cancelled out by the vast emptiness on which the traveller can make no impression nor find his way:
'leaving hardly a sign – and no memories' (p. 62). The ability to make
distinctions between past and present, this and that – which is the
ability to narrate – is crippled in a world without substance: 'The rest of
the world was nowhere, as far as our eyes and ears were concerned . . .
swept off without leaving a whisper or a shadow behind' (p. 68). In
this context, it is no mere lapse into deconstructionist doggerel to assert
that what is being narrated is the impossibility of narration.

The referent of 'Heart of Darkness' is so commonly understood to be
Africa, and specifically the Congo Free State at the time of King
Leopold II's reign of terror and profit at the end of the nineteenth century, that it may come as a surprise to learn that 'Africa' is never
specifically named as its referent. The fact that a referential interpretation works so perfectly, as a 'slightly fictionalized record' of Conrad's
own experience in the Congo,[40] makes it all the more interesting to read
this passage, in which Marlow first describes his image of Africa. Here
the referent is named, then almost immediately repressed:

> Now when I was a little chap I had a passion for maps. I would look
> for hours at South America, or Africa, or Australia, and lose myself
> in all the glories of exploration. *At that time there were many blank
> spaces on the earth*, and when I saw one that looked particularly invit-
> ing on a map (but they all look that) I would put my finger on it and
> say, When I grow up I will go there. The North Pole was one of
> these places, I remember. Well, I haven't been there yet, and shall
> not try now. The glamour's off. Other places were scattered about
> the Equator, and in every sort of latitude all over the two hemi-
> spheres. I have been in some of them, and . . . well, we won't talk
> about that [Conrad's ellipsis]. But there was one yet – *the biggest, the
> most blank, so to speak* – that I had a hankering after.
>
> True, by this time it was not a blank space any more. It had got
> filled since my boyhood with rivers and lakes and *names. It had
> ceased to be a blank space* of delightful mystery – *a white patch* for a boy
> to dream gloriously over. *It had become a place of darkness* (pp. 21–22
> [Miller's italics]).

Everything Africanist is there except 'Africa' itself, which is mentioned
as one among 'many blank spaces'. Here, then, is Conrad's description
of the empty space in narrative (in Marlow's tale) that Africa can come
to 'fill'. But the fashion in which Africa is inserted in that space is
highly perverse. The description fits Africa perfectly: the boyhood fantasies produced by nineteenth-century adventure stories,[41] the
exchange of white (the North Pole) with black through the word

'blank', a felicity that French does not permit. But when the moment comes to name the object of his hankering, Marlow says only 'one . . . the biggest, the most blank'. That principal blank space is most definitely not identified as 'Africa'. The point at which the link is made between 'Heart of Darkness' and its supposed referent is the point where the question is begged; nowhere in the rest of the novel is 'Africa' mentioned after this.[42] Concern for propriety of course accounts to some extent for this 'repression of the referent': so that 'Heart of Darkness' would not become a mere political tract (perhaps banned in Belgium), Africa becomes the 'heart of darkness' and Brussels becomes 'a city that always makes me think of a whited sepulchre' (p. 24). The silence and the void of Africa that 'Heart of Darkness' is claimed to depict are thus reflected in the literal absence of the word 'Africa', which absence is in turn an appropriate reflection of a continent and a state never seen by its sole outright owner, Leopold II.[43] Just as the referential tree is lost by Marlow each time he tries to establish his position, so is the reader – teased into thinking he is reading a book 'about' Africa – led into a void that in fact has no name but 'heart of darkness'.

Several changes between the original handwritten version of 'Heart of Darkness' and the final version reveal a consistent effort to replace direct references with hints, allusions, and intimations. Ian Watt points out the suppressed references to 'some third-rate king', too readily identifiable as Leopold of the Belgians.[44] Further checking of the manuscript reveals that Conrad had originally included certain references to Africa – place-names – which he later took out. For example, when Marlow has set off from Europe, the manuscript reads: 'I left in a French steamer, and *beginning with Dakar* she called in every blamed port they have out there' [Miller's italics].[45] The final version reads: 'I left in a French steamer, and she called in every blamed port' (p. 29). Similarly, the manuscript shows: 'we passed various places: Gran'Bassam, Little Popo, names out/names that seemed to belong'; the final version: 'we passed various places – trading places – *with names like* Gran'Bassam, Little Popo, names that seemed to belong to some sordid farce' (p. 30 [Miller's italics]). The only African place-names left in 'Heart of Darkness' after Marlow's description of the 'blank space' are thus transformed from fact to simile, from places with names to places with names 'like' these – perhaps these names themselves, perhaps not.

Is Africa thus 'repressed' in anything but name? The word is practically synonymous with absence in Western discourse . . . Now in a text where every detail points to Africa, 'Africa' alone is missing, encoded in a new phrase, 'heart of darkness'. That phrase can never be wholly identified as either a repressed, encoded real referent or a fictive pseudo-referent, independent of the real world. 'Heart of Darkness' is in fact deeply engaged in both projects at once.

Kurtz, like 'Africa', is only a name for an absence, having substance only to the extent that he *discourses* (a word that Conrad uses [twice – 'discoursed' (p. 110); 'discoursing' (p. 79) – see also Miller below]). Kurtz cannot be a fixed goal or object for the text, even though that is the role he is assigned.

> There was a sense of extreme disappointment, as though I had found out I had been striving after something altogether without a substance. I couldn't have been more disgusted if I had travelled all this way for the sole purpose of talking with Mr Kurtz. Talking with . . . [Conrad's ellipsis] I flung one shoe overboard, and became aware that that was exactly what I had been looking forward to – a talk with Kurtz. I made the strange discovery that I had never imagined him as doing, you know, but as *discoursing* . . . The man presented himself as a *voice* (pp. 78–79 [Miller's italics]).

A great ambivalence lies in Conrad's use of the word 'voice': '[h]e was very little more than a voice'; yet '[t]he privilege was waiting for me' (p. 80).[46] When [Kurtz] finally speaks, a stream of dark gibberish is all that emerges, which it is no privilege to hear: '"Save me! – save the ivory, you mean. Don't tell me. Save *me*! Why, I've had to save you"' (p. 100). At the centre of the story, one action takes place: 'Kurtz *discoursed*. A voice! a voice! It rang deep to the very last. It survived his strength to hide in the magnificent folds of eloquence the barren darkness of his heart' (p. 110 [Miller's italics]). 'Discoursing' is the heart of the matter – a detached, empty spewing of words in which emptiness ('barren') and plenitude ('heart') cross. If the continent the young Marlow looked at was blank – white and then black – Kurtz's discourse is the central agency by which black and white cross and interchange: '[a]ll Europe' made him (p. 83), yet his was an 'impenetrable darkness', most un-European (p. 111); his only product, the only way to know he exists upriver, is the 'precious trickle of ivory' (p. 37), a stream of white; yet the 'powers of darkness claimed him for their own' (p. 81); he is an 'apparition *shining darkly*' (p. 97 [Miller's italics]), in a perfect Africanist oxymoron [an oxymoron is a trope or figure of speech that brings two contradictory ideas together, for example 'bitter-sweet' – or 'shining darkness'].[47] □

Christopher L. Miller's analysis demonstrates the fruitfulness of an approach that does not take 'Heart of Darkness' as an isolated literary text but sets it within a wider set of discourses about Africa. It is a valuable way of developing the debate about the 'racism' of Conrad's tale and also, perhaps, of achieving a broader understanding of how racist attitudes are constructed and promoted in discourse. But in the 1980s, another aspect of 'Heart of Darkness' started to come under scrutiny; not its possible racism, but its possible sexism: its construction of a male world that appears to exclude or marginalise women. The most powerful and influential essay on this topic is Nina Pelikan Straus's 'The Exclusion of the Intended from Secret Sharing in Conrad's "Heart of Darkness"', which first appeared in the Winter 1987 issue of the journal *Novel*. Straus finds in the mostly male mainstream criticism of Conrad's tale a covert identification 'with the heroic consciousness that Conrad presents'.[48] 'No matter how the meaning of "Heart of Darkness" is defined – as a quest within, as a journey to a mythic underworld, as apocalypse, as a critique of imperialism or of Western civilisation – the standard commentary centres upon the secret sharings of male characters whose isolation from female language or experience evokes (if not sanctions) the dream of a homocentric universe.' This 'secret sharing' extends to the critics themselves: '[t]he inhabitants of this universe are not confined to fictional characters or their authors; they include the commentator writing in the masculinist tradition'.[49] Feminist readers are 'apt to be more sceptical about and alienated from this masculinist tradition',[50] and to find access to the text in such masculinist terms more difficult – and not especially desirable.

What, Straus asks, can feminist readers 'do' with Conrad's text? One answer might be to deny it the status of high art because it is sexist: this response would be akin to Achebe's argument that 'Heart of Darkness' cannot be great art because it is racist. Straus rejects, however, what she calls 'the practice of feminist terrorism that mistakenly argues that sexist high art is not high art because it is sexist'.[51] She opts instead for 'a radical feminist criticism of high art [that] would remove the mask [of male critical objectivity] to disclose the particular delusions intrinsic to a particular literary work'.[52] Taking this approach, refusing the masculinist terms that, in her view, 'Heart of Darkness' and most of its critics offer, and drawing upon feminist and psychoanalytic perspectives, Straus provides, in the extract below, a new interpretation and evaluation of two much-discussed aspects of Conrad's novel – Marlow's lie to the Intended, and his relationship with Kurtz.

■ Although Marlow is often presented as one who, after Kurtz's death, comes back to Brussels heroically carrying the psychic load (if not dead body) of his secret sharer in order to somehow deliver its remains to the Intended, the thing the woman reader can 'do' is to note how contingent Marlow's mental state is upon the decision he makes to lie to the Intended, to decide that the truth about Kurtz is 'too dark' (p.123) to reveal to her, and to harbour within himself a mystery he will reveal much later only to those 'man' enough (p.63) to take it.

Mourning for Kurtz, nearly driven 'mad' by his revelations in the Congo, Marlow's self-reproaches are oddly passionate and each one of them is connected to Kurtz:

> And then they very nearly buried me.
> However, as you see, I did not go to join Kurtz there and then. . . . I remained to dream the nightmare out to the end, and to show my loyalty to Kurtz once more. Destiny. My destiny! Droll thing life is – that mysterious arrangement of merciless logic for a futile purpose. The most you can hope from it is some knowledge of yourself – that comes too late – a crop of unextinguishable regrets . . . (pp. 112–13)

Speaking of his near death, Marlow tells his hearers that 'I was within a hair's-breadth of the last opportunity for pronouncement, and I found with humiliation that probably I would have nothing to say. This is the reason why I affirm that Kurtz was a remarkable man . . . He had summed up – he had judged. "The horror!" He was a remarkable man . . . he had stepped over the edge, while I had been permitted to draw back my hesitating foot (p. 113) . . . Better his cry . . . ' (p. 114).

Better than what? Marlow never tells. Better than Marlow's 'having nothing to say', and obviously better than the Intended's hysterical '"I want – something . . . . . . I loved him – I loved him!"' (p. 123). But the point is that Marlow's self-disgust colours all he sees: the 'intruders' in the 'sepulchral city' whose 'bearing, which was simply the bearing of commonplace individuals going about their business in the assurance of perfect safety, was offensive to me like the outrageous flauntings of folly in the face of a danger it is unable to comprehend'. Marlow 'totter[s]' (p. 114) about the streets, finds the official who comes for Kurtz's papers 'darkly menacing' (p. 115), has a vision of Kurtz on the 'stretcher, opening his mouth voraciously, as if to devour all the earth with all its mankind' (p. 117). And in these images of being devoured, in the sense that Marlow is set apart with Kurtz from the 'commonplace' (p. 114), a glimpse of Marlow's narcissistic dream emerges. Censored and distorted by the language of romantic agony, Marlow's language is nonetheless immersed in what Freud calls '"narcissistic identification"' where 'the object' (Kurtz) 'has been set up in the ego itself':[53]

> He lived then before me; he lived as much as he had ever lived – a shadow insatiable of splendid appearances, of frightful realities; a shadow darker than the shadow of the night, and draped nobly in the folds of a gorgeous eloquence. The vision seemed to enter the house with me – the stretcher, the phantom-bearers, the wild crowd

of obedient worshippers, the gloom of the forests, the glitter of the reach between the murky bends, the beat of the drum, regular and muffled like the beating of a heart – the heart of a conquering darkness. It was a moment of triumph for the wilderness, an invading and vengeful rush which, it seemed to me, I would have to keep back alone for the salvation of another soul. (pp. 117–18)

Freud argues that in narcissistic identification, which is closer to homosexual object-choice than to the heterosexual kind, the self-reproaches and regrets are in the service of 'repelling an undesirably strong homosexual impulse[54] ... ... [The subject] strikes with a single blow at his own ego and at the loved and hated object'.[55]

Marlow's language, intertwining descriptions of Kurtz's 'abject pleading' (p. 118) with his 'gorgeous eloquence' (p. 117) and with Marlow's own 'humiliation' (p. 113) and suspicion that 'perhaps ... all truth, and all sincerity, are just compressed into that inappreciable moment of time in which we step over the threshold of the invisible' (pp. 113–14) – suggests what Freud calls narcissistic 'ambivalence'.[56] For it is clear that Marlow's identification with Kurtz is of a violently passionate kind; it leads to self-loathing, to the shadowing of self called depression, to an urge to escape from this state itself – an urge Marlow articulates in his '[t]here remained only his memory and his Intended – and I wanted to give that up too' (p. 117). There are glimpses in the text's imagery of Marlow's wish to be swallowed by Kurtz, to 'join' him in death (p. 112), and finally to be 'rush[ed]' and invaded by the wilderness which Kurtz embodies. Finally, in the passage quoted above, a particular movement of psychic energy is dramatized: a vision of Kurtz appears to Marlow, intensifies ('enter[ed] the house with me') and blossoms into savage rites for a dying god. In images which compound terror with desire (sexual energy with violence, if you will), the climactic moment is described in terms of the 'beating of a heart' (p. 117). It is at that climactic and visionary moment of excitement when Marlow's identification with Kurtz is most intense that Marlow decides to 'keep back' (p. 118) what he knows, the depth of what he feels, from the Intended.

Marlow's rationalization comes quickly, is perhaps hardly noticeable to the reader who accepts as heroic Marlow's decision to lie. The morality of 'salvation of another soul' is intrinsic to the conventions of high art from the story of Jesus through Joyce's *Ulysses* (1922). But whom does such morality save here? Does not Marlow save himself, at this crucial moment of memory, hate and desire, from the disclosure of a knowledge that is 'too dark' (p. 123) for him to bear? 'Not the least of the ironies of "Heart of Darkness"', suggests David Thorburn in his *Conrad's Romanticism* (1974), 'is Marlow's blindness to the fact that his comments about Kurtz's harlequin exactly describe his own responses to Kurtz and to the task of telling about him. His evasive account, as Guerard has shown,[57] approaches Kurtz only reluctantly, postponing the climactic encounter with obsessive ingenuity. Like the harlequin, Marlow, his life filled with Kurtz, is yet "jealous of sharing with any one the peculiar blackness of that experience" (p. 105)'.[58] Having gone this far in explaining the nature of Marlow's relation to Kurtz, both Thorburn and Guerard stop. The connection between Marlow's 'blindness' and his final encounter with the Intended does not interest these critics, for the Intended is not considered as in any way part of the text's problem. Whether Marlow is trustworthy or blinded, he is understood to heroically deliver the Intended from 'darkness', and his capacity to deliver insinuates his link to a more traditional heroism.

It is clear that Marlow prefers Kurtz's cry of '"the horror"' (pp. 112, 113, 118, 123) to the Intended's cry of '"I loved him"' (p. 123). For 'horror' is the secret password in the brotherhood of men who 'know'. Frederick [R.] Karl comes close to acknowledging that there is less a moral question involved than an aesthetic one, one that has to do with the conventions of art *per se* [in themselves]. 'Kurtz: death: ivory: art are intermingled. He *is* ivory'.[59] To take this one step further . . . the woman reader might notice that 'Heart of Darkness' is *about* art's relation to horror – that the excitement and mystery of horror, the 'fascination of the abomination' (p. 20) is the revelation that Marlow offers to his brotherhood of 'hearers' who constitute both his mates inside the text and his mates outside of it. If[,] for Conrad/Marlow, art is inextricably linked with a horror which only men can experience, it is finally this art-horror that Marlow must 'keep back alone' (p. 118) from the Intended who is woman.

If Marlow's sense of horror is unmasked to reveal his love for Kurtz, his love for Kurtz's 'cry' (pp. 112, 114, 118) which is his art, then the woman reader comes closer to understanding the motive for Marlow's behaviour with the Intended. So deeply impressed is Marlow with Kurtz's ability to 'cry' and 'say' something about the 'profound riddle of life' – that Marlow incorporates this riddle and these words of horror which embody it. He comes not only to possess these words but to jealously guard them; and finally, faced with the task of symbolically rendering Kurtz unto the Intended, Marlow cannot bear to share him with her.

. . . what the woman reader can 'do' is to recognize that in 'Heart of Darkness' women are used to deny, distort, and censor men's passionate love for on[e] another. Projecting his own love on to the form of the Intended, Marlow is able to conceal from himself the dark complexity of his own love – a love that strikes him with horror – for Kurtz. This is not to claim that the conventions of high art are homosexual, but rather to suggest that Marlow's relation to Kurtz as his commentator is a paradigm of the male critic's relation to the Strong Poet. [Straus alludes here to Harold Bloom's theory that a poet is engaged, in his writing, in a battle with previous poets in rather the same way as the son is engaged in a battle with the father. The Strong Poet is the poet who is able to achieve his (masculine) creative autonomy.[60]] That a homocentric loyalty exists (a loyalty to the sexist nightmare of one's choice) is not surprising, for it confirms the relations of love between men who are each other's 'narcissistic objects'; or to put it another way, whose enterprise as readers and critics (hearers-speakers) affirms the greatness of the one and the possessive attempt to appropriate that greatness by the other.

The 'psychotherapeutic plenitude' of which [Gayatri] Spivak speaks[61] may therefore be a result of gender identification. This suggests that high art is in some way a confirmation of the one gender's access to certain secrets (in this case the secret conjunction of art and horror) which would be both deconstructed and demystified if the Intended had access to it. Could Marlow's truth be dramatized without the Intended's contrasting delusion? Would such notions as romantic agony and secret experience of 'inner truth' be able to be named if there were not a nameless one who is 'allott[ed]' (to use [Ian] Watt's word) to a world of merely outer or 'public rhetoric'?[62] The guarding of secret knowledge is thus the undisclosed theme of 'Heart of Darkness' which a woman reader can discover. Marlow's protectiveness is no longer seen in the service of woman's deluded desires, but serves the therapeutic end of keeping the woman/intended mute. The male hearers of Marlow's tale never hear the Intended's name. She remains in the stereotypically convenient world of 'she'. She lacks that one distinguishing feature of the beloved, which is that she is absolutely individual to the one who loves her. The Intended is thus thrice voided or erased: her name is never spoken by Kurtz, by Marlow, or by Conrad; and it is determined that it will never be spoken by Conrad's commentators.

The erasure of the Intended represents a final stage in the development of the brutally sexist conventions of high art.[63] Dante's Beatrice and Yeats's Maud have faces, voices, and names. But Conrad's Intended is no more than a 'pale head, floating towards me in the dusk' (p. 118). What this figure achieves, as perhaps few other female characters in fiction do, is what could nicely be called negative capability but which is psychologically symbolic of the male's need for an infinite receptivity and passivity ['negative capability' is a phrase used by the Romantic poet John Keats[64]]. Male heroism and plenitude depend on female cowardice and emptiness. Dante creates truth and embodies it; when Maud shrieks from the lectern, Yeats is unmanned. Because the female figure's psychic penury is so valuable in asserting the heroism of the Strong Poet and the Strong Poet's character, the male commentator (who serves both) is filled with pleasure – a pleasure so therapeutic that it subverts his capacity to discover *on what terms* Marlow is a hero or a coward.

Because the woman reader is not so 'filled', she is in the position to insist that Marlow's cowardice consists of his inability to face the dangerous self that is the form of his own masculinist vulnerability: his own complicity in the racist, sexist, imperialist, and finally libidinally satisfying world he has inhabited with Kurtz.[65] □

At the end of this extract, Straus brings together the charge of sexism, and the charges of racism and imperialism, to constitute a powerful indictment. If Achebe had put the racist issue emphatically on the agenda of 'Heart of Darkness' criticism in 1977, it was Straus's essay above all that put the sexist issue on the agenda in 1987. Both essays were forceful and uncompromising; and if Achebe's attack carried extra weight because of his standing as a novelist, Straus's attack gained added authority because of its skilled marshalling of modern critical theory. Benita Parry's observation that Achebe dispensed with the recognised language of critical discourse (see p. 115)[66] could not apply to Straus. Since her essay, a range of other analyses of Conrad's representation of women in 'Heart of Darkness' that take account of feminist concerns has appeared – for example, Hyland (1988); Sedlak (1989); Smith (1989); London (1990); Torgovnick (1990), Nadelhaft (1991); Showalter (1991); and Bode (1994) (see Bibliography for details). By the 1990s, the debate about the novel's sexism was well under way.

The critics discussed in this chapter opened up a number of key issues in the 1980s. There is the relationship, explored by Benita Parry, between the imperialist, colonialist and racist representations of 'Heart of Darkness', and its textual contradictions and complicities; there are the intricate narrative processes, analysed by Peter Brooks, of a multi-layered tale that seems to promise a final report but does not deliver; there are the ways in which 'Heart of Darkness', in Christopher L. Miller's perspective, both draws on and contributes to the broader field of Africanist discourse; and there are the gender bondings and exclusions of the novel that Nina Pelikan Straus examines. As a result of such readings, 'Heart of Darkness' entered the 1990s as both a richly complex classic that amply rewarded modern theoretical approaches and as a deeply controversial text that seemed to be crucial in current debates about racism, sexism and post-colonialism. The final chapter examines how it fared.

CHAPTER FIVE

Metonymy, Neo-imperialism and a Biscuit-tin: Fresh Paths in 'Heart of Darkness' Criticism in the 1990s

A S THE end of the twentieth century draws near, 'Heart of Darkness' continues to arouse intense and wide-ranging interest. The debates promoted by the attacks of Achebe and Straus have continued, but they have, inevitably, become rather more complicated than they might initially have seemed; and the *need* to attack is perhaps rather less strong, since the status of any canonical text – and certainly of 'Heart of Darkness' – is now much more widely open to question than it would have been in the 1950s and 1960s. In regard to 'Heart of Darkness', Achebe and Straus performed, in their respective but related ways, a necessary clearing of the air, and helped to bring about vital changes of emphasis; and those changes were part of a broader transformation that came about in and around literary studies in the UK and the USA in the 1980s and which involved, among other things, the development and application of post-colonial criticism, narrative theory and discourse analysis – changes whose significance for 'Heart of Darkness' was first demonstrated by the work of Benita Parry, Peter Brooks and Christopher L. Miller, which was discussed in the previous chapter of this Guide. In the last decade of the century, the rich possibilities of this transformation can be explored; a range of approaches and perspectives can be combined to yield new understandings of 'Heart of Darkness'.

A good example of this kind of exploration, which combines an alertness to the racist dimensions of Conrad's text with rhetorical analysis and post-colonial theory, appeared at the start of the decade in *The English Academy Review*: Gail Fincham's 'Living Under the Sign of Contradiction: Self and Other in Conrad's "Heart of Darkness"'. Although Fincham's claim that 'Marlow's narrative covertly perpetuates a racist mentality' might seem to reinforce Achebe's attack on Conrad's novel, she dissociates herself from Achebe discreetly but firmly in an endnote: '[m]y position in suggesting the implications of the inadvertent racism of Conrad's *narrator* in "Heart of Darkness" is very far from Chinua Achebe's attack on *Conrad's* Eurocentric prejudice'.[1] Fincham feels that Achebe's argument depends on the reductive and questionable assumption that Conrad can be directly identified with Marlow; as she says in another endnote, '[i]f the story illustrates the impossibility of the *narrator's* escaping his cultural limitations, there is in my view no clear evidence of the *author's* attempting to salvage the ideology of imperialism'.[2] From this position, she also takes issue with Benita Parry's view that 'Heart of Darkness', for all its contradictions, ultimately rescues imperialist ideology. But to say that the charges of racism and pro-imperialism against Conrad will not stick is not, for Fincham, to deny the racist and imperialist aspects of the text; her aim, however, is not merely to condemn these aspects, but also to analyse them.

In her analysis, Fincham draws on the kind of post-colonial theory and discourse analysis that contends that colonialism seeks to construct a cultural 'Other' in terms of polarised oppositions such as white/black, good/evil, civilisation/savagery; she also employs a term from classical rhetoric that has become widespread in modern literary and critical theory – the term 'metonymy'. As mentioned in the previous chapter of this Guide in reference to Benita Parry's analysis (see p. 107), a 'metonymy' is a figure of speech, or trope, in which the name of an attribute or adjunct of a thing is used to refer to that thing itself, for instance, crown for king, Downing Street for the British Government, or, in the case that Parry discusses, the wilderness for 'dangerous passions'. Another related, rhetorical term is synecdoche, a trope or figure of speech in which a part of something is used to refer to the whole thing, for instance 'keel' for ship (or, more rarely, in which a whole is used to refer to a part, for example 'the law' for 'police').[3] Some of Fincham's 'metonymies' could also, and perhaps more precisely, be called 'synecdoches'. But her identification of such rhetorical devices is not merely formal; rather, she is concerned to suggest how they function in colonial discourse, and to show how 'Heart of Darkness' both deploys and deconstructs that discourse. Fincham addresses herself primarily to her fellow-teachers in South Africa, but her analysis clearly has worldwide application.

The extract begins at the point in Fincham's essay at which she probes to the heart of the fascination of Conrad's novel:

■ . . . the real fascination of 'Heart of Darkness' is not in the [cultural] stereotypes of the past that the tale overturns, but in the distortions which it creates. I refer to Marlow's unacknowledged projection onto Africa of what he fears, desires and suppresses in his own psyche: the attribution to the cultural Other of what cannot be tolerated in the Self

. . . . . . Since Marlow's narrative explores not 'the complexities of *African* cultures, but rather the "worldness" of the colonialist world',[4] it cannot ultimately disengage itself from that 'worldness'. A complicity in what it seeks to undermine – the fact that Marlow can ridicule and problematize, but never escape his own cultural heritage – makes 'Heart of Darkness' the richly revealing text that it remains a century after it was written.

In its repeated unconscious association of Africa with the instinctual and the libidinal, Marlow's narrative covertly perpetuates a racist mentality not very different from the imperialist mentality which it rejects. One explanation of this inadvertent racism is that the colonizer, unable to acknowledge the sexual guilt that is the inescapable legacy of Judaeo-Christian thinking, consistently represses this guilt and transfers it on to the colonized . . . . . . The first hints of Marlow's story of repressed ambivalence towards Africa surface in the early Edenic descriptions of the Congo. Marlow tells the frame auditors [that is, those listening to Marlow in the yawl, among them the first narrator, who form the 'frame' of Marlow's tale] that this part of the map of Africa has changed since his boyhood from 'a blank space of delightful mystery' to a space 'filled . . . with rivers and lakes and names'. No longer 'a white patch for a boy to dream gloriously over', it has now become 'a place of darkness'. Through this place of many names runs 'a mighty big river . . . resembling an immense snake uncoiled, with its head in the sea, its body at rest curving afar over a vast country, and its tail lost in the depths of the land'. The description ends portentously: 'And as I looked at the map of it in a shop-window, it fascinated me as a snake would a bird – a silly little bird' (p. 22).

Here, Marlow's project has become self-contradictory. He wants to dramatize the evils of imperialism that begin with the colonizers' act of naming and end by deforming what has been named – acts which turn an Eden into 'a place of darkness'. But his confusion about the *agency* of this negative transformation is captured in the archetypal image of the snake, which represents an evil that has lurked in Eden from the beginning, and whose chief victim is rather the alien colonizer than the native colonized. Implicit in the archetypal imagery of the map passage is a fundamental ambivalence towards 'precivilized' Africa. It is both mythologized as an Edenic wilderness to which Europeans make wistful secret pilgrimages in search of a lost plenitude, and negatively transformed into a chaotic postlapsarian jungle ['Postlapsarian' means 'after the Fall'; 'prelapsarian', used later by Fincham, means 'before the Fall']. Similarly, Africans either represent a vitality and wholeness of being lost to the West, or become the embodiment of psychosexual degeneration . . .

Deeply repressed fear of Africa as embodiment of all that the West attempts to censor and control is a recurring feature of Marlow's narrative. It is evident in the tale's multiple orchestrations of the motif of restraint, in its uneasy proclamations of the value of the Protestant work ethic to counter the demoralization of the jungle, and in the 'fascination of the abomination' (p. 20) exerted by the wilderness upon the weakened and disoriented colonizer. Equally revealing are Marlow's revelations of his 'remote kinship with this wild and passionate uproar' (p. 63) of the 'night of first ages' (p. 62), his scornful rhetorical boast to the frame auditors that 'I didn't go ashore for a howl and a dance' (p. 63), and the descriptions of Kurtz's depravities, which may suggest not only his megalomania but also sexual excesses learnt from an uncensored Africa.

As Marlow's narrative swings between desire for and recoil from Africa as psychic freedom, so his encounters with blacks reflect a curious combination of valorizing and degrading stereotypes. It is significant that he relies increasingly upon a metonymic mode which draws attention to the fleeting, the cryptic and the fragmentary. Such use of metonymy suggests that Africa, whether conceptualized as Edenic or demonic, cannot be decoded steadily or whole by the Western protagonist. Consider his depiction of the first Africans he meets *en route* to the Congo, the black oarsmen whose vitality and purposiveness he finds exhilarating:

> Now and then a boat from the shore gave one a momentary contact with reality. It was paddled by black fellows. You could see from afar the white of their eyeballs glistening. They shouted, sang; their bodies streamed with perspiration; they had faces like grotesque masks – these chaps; but they had bone, muscle, a wild vitality, an intense energy of movement, that was as natural and true as the surf along their coast. They wanted no excuse for being there. They were a great comfort to look at. (p. 30)

Here Marlow's perception of the black oarsmen nostalgically foregrounds attributes of health, physical mastery and connection with the natural world. This nostalgia for an unproblematic identity compatible with both physical vigour and social cohesion accounts perhaps for Marlow's euphoria in his initial encounter with blacks. The African 'reality' that is valorized is conceptualized as physical and organic, as opposed to a European 'reality' which is cerebral and fragmented. It is ironic, however, that the physical integrity which the African oarsmen are taken to embody can only be apprehended in the context of psychic inscrutability. Parts of bodies, moments of activity, are intensely glimpsed, while faces and minds remain occluded. Even in this representation of prelapsarian plenitude, a postlapsarian awareness of division intrudes itself. Marlow's thinking seems here to reflect a biblical equation of consciousness with guilt; in the Genesis story the moment of Adam's loss of innocence is the moment that he speaks his knowledge of his nakedness. For Marlow, therefore, the energy and vitality of 'the noble savage' can only be represented as purely corporeal, and can only be posited in isolation from consciousness.

The Grove of Death sequence which constitutes Marlow's second significant encounter with the Other of Africa equally registers the narrator's fragmented vision. Here the metonymy works to dissolve personality and volition. The horror of genocide is registered in the Company's reduction of 'enemies' (pp. 31, 33, 35, 96), 'rebels' (p. 96) and 'criminals' (pp. 33, 34, 35, 96) to inert vacancy:

> These moribund shapes were free as air – and nearly as thin. I began to distinguish the gleam of eyes under the trees. Then, glancing down, I saw a face near my hand. The black bones reclined at full length with one shoulder against the tree, and slowly the eyelids rose and the sunken eyes looked up at me, enormous and vacant, a kind of blind, white flicker in the depths of the orbs, which died out slowly. The man seemed young – almost a boy – but you know with them it's hard to tell. (p. 35)

For all his courage at the inhumanity of the colonizers' treatment of the Congolese, Marlow's perception of the dying slave as a dissolving fragment is curiously bereft of humanity.[5] Unable to confront the full enormity of this extermination in which he as Company employee is complicit, Marlow reverts to the distancing mechanism of racial differentiation. The specific agony of a particular individual dying before his eyes is transmuted into an insidiously vague generalization about the agelessness of blacks. Marlow's crypto-imperialist narrative at this point reflects the racism discussed by [Albert] Memmi in *The Colonizer and the Colonized* (1969): 'Another sign of the colonized's depersonalization is what one might call the mark of the plural. The colonized is never characterized in an individual manner; he is entitled only to drown in an anonymous collectivity ("They are this". "They are all the same")'.[6]

Throughout Marlow's narrative, metonymic description oddly conflates the impersonality or 'anonymous collectivity' of the Grove of Death epiphany with a meticulous registration of detail. A further instance of this drive to metonymy, a way of seeing that reflects the narrator's radical disorientation, occurs in the attack on the steamboat. Marlow, bemused at the suddenness of the offensive, initially fails to recognize that the '[s]ticks, little sticks . . . flying about – thick . . . whizzing before my nose, dropping below me, striking behind me against my pilot-house' (p. 75) are arrows. When, seconds later, he registers his danger, his perception of the attackers on shore is, once again, of human fragments, no longer moribund as in the Grove of Death but now frantically animated: '. . . I saw a face amongst the leaves on the level with my own, looking at me very fierce and steady; and then suddenly, as though a veil had been removed from my eyes, I made out, deep in the tangled gloom, naked breasts, arms, legs, glaring eyes, – the bush was swarming with human limbs in movement, glistening, of bronze colour' (p. 76). As in the Edenic depiction of the oarsmen or the horrific depiction of the Grove of Death, what is omitted from this episode is any account of the thought processes, the motives, or the feelings of the protagonists whose activities are recorded.

The same is true of Marlow's narrative when it deals with the death of the black helmsman and with Kurtz's African mistress. The metonymies become increasingly surreal, with the result that the narrative dwells more insistently on what has been omitted. The helmsman, whose 'lustrous and inquiring glance' had initially led Marlow to expect that 'he would presently put to us some question in an understandable language', dies suddenly, 'without uttering a sound, without moving a limb, without twitching a muscle'. A demonic African version of the genial inscrutability of the Cheshire Cat, the helmsman is reduced at last to only a frown. The fact that this disembodied frown is read as a final 'response to some sign we could not see, to some whisper we could not hear' (p. 78), makes it more rather than less ominous, a signifier that is intuited as meaningful although it refers to no shared signified.

The combination of detailed metonymic description with inflated rhetoric is nowhere more apparent than in Marlow's attempt to describe Kurtz's African mistress:

> She walked with measured steps, draped in striped and fringed cloths, treading the earth proudly, with a slight jingle and flash of barbarous ornaments. She carried her head high; her hair was done in the shape of a helmet; she had brass leggings to the knee, brass wire gauntlets to the elbow, a crimson spot on her tawny cheek, innumerable necklaces of glass beads on her neck; bizarre things, charms, gifts of witch-men, that hung about her, glittered and trembled at every step. She must have had the value of several elephant tusks upon her. She was savage and superb, wild-eyed and magnificent; there was something ominous and stately in her deliberate progress. And in the hush that had fallen suddenly upon the whole sorrowful land, the immense wilderness, the colossal body of the fecund and mysterious life seemed to look at her, pensive, as though it had been looking at the image of its own tenebrous and passionate soul. (p. 99)

In this passage, the disjunction between the physical and the psychic has become so extreme as to be comic. The only bridge between an atomistic catalogue of non-essential ornamentation in the first half of the passage and the grandiose essentialist claims of the second half is the naively mercantile: '[s]he must have had the value of several elephant tusks upon her'. Given that Marlow conceptualizes Kurtz's mistress as an embodiment of primal energy, the notes of commercialism, reification and instrumentalization introduced in the reference to elephant tusks are revealing in their incongruity. In the depiction of this woman who represents for Marlow a quintessence of the instinctual, a significant conflation of stereotypes has taken place. The Edenic overtones in the second half are unmistakable: as female representative of 'the noble savage', Kurtz's black mistress not only manifests the vitality Marlow eulogized in the oarsmen, but also shares a potential for maternity with 'the colossal body of the fecund and mysterious' African wilderness.

Yet these qualities of vitality, fecundity and organic connection are undercut by the fact that it is not the woman's body, nor her movements, nor her actions, but the clothes and ornaments with which she is adorned, that are principally described. In this passage, Kurtz's black mistress is simultaneously conceptualized in Edenic terms as Earth Mother and in postlapsarian terms as denatured object of exchange, her brass ornaments recalling for the reader the degenerate Company practice of paying for the labour of the cannibal crew on board Marlow's steamer with the weekly 'currency' of 'three pieces of brass wire, each about nine inches long' (p. 70).[7] □

Fincham concludes that, for students in Africa – and, indeed, elsewhere – '"Heart of Darkness" remains a seminal text . . . because it illustrates that the construction of Self in terms of a racially polarized Other is neither neutral [n]or natural, but has destructive consequences for both colonizer and colonized. Only when we think beyond difference can we escape "living under the sign of contradiction" which hangs over Conrad's Marlow'.[8] Her essay demonstrates how a combination of post-colonial theory, discourse analysis and close attention to rhetorical detail can produce an interpretation of 'Heart of Darkness' that provides new insights into Conrad's text and which has relevance to a world still working through the aftermath of colonialism and imperialism.

It is that world that Edward W. Said addresses in his major study *Culture and Imperialism*, which came out in 1993. By that time, Said had become well-known as the author of *Orientalism* (1978), his analysis of the way in which the West constructed versions of the Orient through discourse; this book was discussed in the previous chapter of this Guide in relation to Christopher L. Miller's account of 'Heart of Darkness' (pp. 116,

127–28). In *Orientalism* itself, Said makes only a few mentions of Conrad – although, significantly, he uses Marlow's famous observations in 'Heart of Darkness' about the conquest of the earth and 'the idea' as one of the epigraphs to his section on 'Orientalism Now'.[9] But Conrad had played a large part in Said's development; Conrad's own complex, cosmopolitan life seemed to echo some aspects of Said's own, as he acknowledged in an interview published in 1987: 'I felt, first coming across Conrad when I was a teenager, that in a certain sense I was reading, not so much my own story, but a story written out of bits of my life and put together in a haunting and fantastically obsessive way. I've been hooked on it ever since'.[10] Said's doctoral dissertation at Harvard studied Conrad's letters in relation to his fiction and later became his first published book, *Joseph Conrad and the Fiction of Autobiography* (1966). Here, Said interprets 'Heart of Darkness' in terms of binary oppositions, as one of the works that continues 'Conrad's examination of the encounter between truth and image, abstraction and concreteness, darkness and illumination'.[11] Said's emphasis is mainly metaphysical, though colonialism is mentioned briefly – 'Kurtz's spirit of adventure and colonialism has taken him to the centre of things, and this is where Marlow hopes to find him'.[12] Said returned to Conrad in *Beginnings* (1975), but his discussion of Conrad in that book focuses mainly on *Nostromo*. In 1986, he came back to 'Heart of Darkness' once more – but this time as the well-known author of *Orientalism* and a controversial spokesman on post-colonial matters. In his essay 'Intellectuals in the Post-Colonial World', he takes the 'narrative form' of 'Heart of Darkness' as the 'paradigm'[13] of the kind of post-colonial discourse that seeks to efface 'the ravages to the colonial people',[14] 'the immensely detailed and violent history of colonial intervention'.[15] It is this analysis that he incorporates and develops in *Culture and Imperialism*.

In *Culture and Imperialism*, Said is concerned to recover the imperialist traces in the products of Western culture, to mark the counterpoint between culture and imperialism. He does not want to engage in what he calls 'the rhetoric of blame'[16] that attacks writers and artists 'retrospectively, for being white, privileged, insensitive, complicit',[17] or to denigrate artistic achievement: his method 'is to focus as much as possible on individual works, to read them first as great products of the creative or interpretative imagination, and then to show them as part of the relationship between culture and empire'.[18] One of the works on which he focuses is 'Heart of Darkness'. As in his 1986 essay, he identifies a present-day discourse that seeks, retrospectively, to vindicate imperialism by effacing the 'immensely detailed, violent history of colonial intervention' and counterposing the civilised West to a Third World that has reverted to the oppression, brutality and corruption from which imperialism had briefly rescued it. Said contends that what we should notice about 'this kind of contemporary discourse, which assumes the primacy and even the complete centrality of the West, is how totalizing is its form, how all-enveloping its attitudes and gestures, how much it shuts out even as it includes, compresses, and consolidates. We suddenly find ourselves transported backward in time to the late nineteenth century'.[19] This is where 'Heart of Darkness' comes in.

■ This imperial attitude is, I believe, beautifully captured in the complicated and rich narrative form of Conrad's great novella 'Heart of Darkness', written between 1898 and 1899. On the one hand, the narrator Marlow acknowledges the tragic predicament of all speech – that 'it is impossible to convey the life-sensation of any given epoch of one's existence, – that which makes its truth, its meaning – its subtle and penetrating essence . . . We live, as we dream – alone' (p. 50) – yet still manages to convey the enormous power of Kurtz's African experience through his own overmastering narrative of his voyage into the African interior towards Kurtz. This narrative in turn is connected directly with the redemptive force, as well as the waste and horror, of Europe's mission in the dark world. Whatever is lost or elided or even simply made up in Marlow's immensely compelling recitation is compensated for in the narrative's sheer historical momentum, the temporal forward movement – with digressions, descriptions, exciting encounters, and all. Within the narrative of how he journeyed to Kurtz's Inner Station, whose source and authority he now becomes, Marlow moves backward and forward materially in small and large spirals, very much the way episodes in the course of his journey up-river are then incorporated by the principal forward trajectory into what he renders as 'the heart of Africa'.

Thus Marlow's encounter with the improbably white-suited clerk in the middle of the jungle furnishes him with several digressive paragraphs, as does his meeting later with the semi-crazed, harlequin-like Russian who has been so affected by Kurtz's gifts. Yet underlying Marlow's inconclusiveness, his evasions, his arabesque meditations on his feelings and ideas, is the unrelenting course of the journey itself, which, despite all the many obstacles, is sustained through the jungle, through time, through hardship, to the heart of it all, Kurtz's ivory-trading empire. Conrad wants us to see how Kurtz's great looting adventure, Marlow's journey up the river, and the narrative itself all share a common theme: Europeans performing acts of imperial mastery and will in (or about) Africa.

What makes Conrad different from the other colonial writers who were his contemporaries is that, for reasons having partly to do with the colonialism that turned him, a Polish expatriate, into an employee of the imperial system, he was so self-conscious about what he did. Like most of his other tales, therefore, 'Heart of Darkness' cannot just be a straightforward recital of Marlow's adventures: it is also a dramatization of Marlow himself, the former wanderer in colonial regions, telling his story to a group of British listeners at a particular time and in a specific place. That this group of people is drawn largely from the business world is Conrad's way of emphasizing the fact that during the 1890s the business of empire, once an adventurous and often individualistic enterprise, had become the empire of business . . . Although the almost oppressive force of Marlow's narrative leaves us with a quite accurate sense that there is no way out of the sovereign historical force of imperialism, and that it has the power of a system representing as well as speaking for everything within its dominion, Conrad shows us that what Marlow does is contingent, acted out for a set of like-minded British hearers, and limited to that situation.

Yet neither Conrad nor Marlow gives us a full view of what is *outside* the world-conquering attitudes embodied by Kurtz, Marlow, the circle of listeners on the deck of the *Nellie,* and Conrad. By that I mean that 'Heart of Darkness' works so effectively because its politics and aesthetics are, so to speak, imperialist, which in the closing years of the nineteenth century seemed to be at the same time an aesthetic, politics, and even [an] epistemology [that was] inevitable and unavoidable. For if we cannot truly understand someone else's experience and if we must therefore depend upon the assertive authority of the sort of power that Kurtz wields as a white man in the jungle or that Marlow, another white man, wields as narrator, there is no use looking for other, non-imperialist alternatives; the system has simply eliminated them and made them unthinkable. The circularity, the perfect closure of the whole thing is not only aesthetically but also mentally unassailable.

Conrad is so self-conscious about situating Marlow's tale in a narrative moment that he allows us simultaneously to realize after all that imperialism, far from swallowing up its own history, was taking place in and was circumscribed by a larger history, one just outside the tightly inclusive circle of Europeans on the deck of the *Nellie.* As yet, however, no one seemed to inhabit that region, and so Conrad left it empty.

Conrad could probably never have used Marlow to present anything other than an imperialist world-view, given what was available for either Conrad or Marlow to see of the non-European at the time. Independence was for whites and Europeans; the lesser or subject peoples were to be ruled; science, learning, history emanated from the West. True, Conrad scrupulously recorded the differences between the disgraces of Belgian and British colonial attitudes, but he could only imagine the world carved up into one or another Western sphere of dominion. But because Conrad also had an extraordinarily persistent residual sense of his own exilic marginality, he quite carefully (some would say maddeningly) qualified Marlow's narrative with the provisionality that came from standing at the very juncture of this world with another, unspecified but different . . . Conrad's realization is that if, like narrative, imperialism has monopolized the entire system of representation – which in the case of 'Heart of Darkness' allowed it to speak for Africans as well as for Kurtz and the other adventurers, including Marlow and his audience – your self-consciousness as an outsider can allow you actively to comprehend how the machine works, given that you and it are fundamentally not in perfect synchrony or correspondence. Never the wholly incorporated and fully acculturated Englishman, Conrad therefore preserved an ironic distance in each of his works.

The form of Conrad's narrative has thus made it possible to derive two possible arguments, two visions, in the post-colonial world that succeeded his. One argument allows the old imperial enterprise full scope to play itself out conventionally, to render the world as official European or Western imperialism saw it, and to consolidate itself after World War Two. Westerners may have left their old colonies in Africa and Asia, but they retained them not only as markets but as locales on the ideological map over which they continued to rule morally and intellectually . . . . . . The second argument is considerably less objectionable. It sees itself as Conrad saw his own narratives, local to a time and place, neither unconditionally true nor unqualifiedly certain. As I have said, Conrad does not give us the sense that he could imagine a fully realized alternative to imperialism: the natives he wrote about in Africa, Asia, or America were incapable of independence, and because he seemed to imagine that European tutelage was a given, he could not foresee what would take place when it came to an end. But come to an end it would, if only because – like all human effort, like speech itself – it would have its moment, then it would have to pass. Since Conrad *dates* imperialism, shows its contingency, records its illusions and tremendous violence and waste (as in *Nostromo*), he permits his later readers to imagine something other than an Africa carved up into dozens of European colonies, even if, for his own part, he had little notion of what that Africa might be . . . . . .

. . . Conrad's Africans . . . come from a huge library of *Africanism*, so to speak, as well as from Conrad's personal experience. There is no such thing as a *direct* experience, or reflection, of the world in the language of a text. Conrad's impressions of Africa were inevitably influenced by lore and writing about Africa, which he alludes to in *A Personal Record*; what he supplies in 'Heart of Darkness' is the result of his impressions of those texts interacting creatively, together with the requirements and conventions of narrative and his own special genius and history. To say of this extraordinarily rich mix that it 'reflects' Africa, or even that it reflects an experience of Africa, is somewhat pusillanimous and surely misleading. What we have in 'Heart of Darkness' – a work of immense influence, having provoked many readings and images – is a politicized, ideologically saturated Africa which to some intents and purposes was the imperialized place, with those many interests and ideas furiously at work in it, not just a photographic literary 'reflection' of it.

This is, perhaps, to overstate the matter, but I want to make the point that far from 'Heart of Darkness' and its image of Africa being 'only' literature, the work is extraordinarily caught up in, is indeed an organic part of, the 'scramble for Africa' that was contemporary with Conrad's composition. True, Conrad's audience was small, and, true also, he was very critical of Belgian colonialism. But to most Europeans, reading a rather rarefied text like 'Heart of Darkness' was often as close as they came to Africa, and in that limited sense it was part of the European effort to hold on to, think about, plan for Africa. To represent Africa is to enter the battle over Africa, inevitably connected to later resistance, decolonization, and so forth.[20] □

Said's emphases on both the textual complexity and the inevitable worldliness of 'Heart of Darkness' find echoes in Valentine Cunningham's vivid discussion of Conrad's novel in his extended and exciting quarrel with deconstruction, *In the Reading Gaol: Postmodernity, Texts, and History* (1984) – a title that puns on 'reading' as an activity and on 'Reading' (pronounced 'Redding') as the name of an English town. Like Said, Cunningham rejects the ultra-deconstructionist notion that there is nothing outside the text, and indeed argues that to embrace such a notion is to risk ending up behind bars – in the case of the proto-deconstructionist Oscar Wilde, the all-too-literal bars of Reading Gaol. As Cunningham puts it, 'Wilde was in Reading Gaol precisely because he foolishly imagined (or so he said) that a letter, an epistle, a piece of private reading matter, could be just that, a piece of art, or text, merely for art's, for text's sake. Misplaced faith in the prison-house of language, the reading gaol, landed Wilde in the Reading Gaol'.[21] Reading Gaol may seem a long way from Conrad's Congo, but there is an unexpected link. In 'Heart of Darkness', Marlow describes clambering on board his salvaged steamboat as it awaits the rivets needed for its repair and says that '[s]he rang under my feet like an empty Huntley & Palmer [*sic*] biscuit-tin kicked along a gutter' (p. 52). The Huntley & Palmers biscuit-tin, as Cunningham points out, was 'a piece of merchandise manufactured in the great sprawl of buildings adjacent to Wilde's Reading Gaol'.[22] This tin is empty, and in that sense it could function as a metaphor of the deconstructionist text, hollow inside, without contents. But it is also a tin that links the text to its context, to the material and metaphorical world of imperialism. In these respects, it is a metaphor for 'Heart of Darkness' itself, for an exemplary deconstructionist text that also breaks through the textual walls and resounds against reality with a clang whose reverberations spread outwards. It is this interplay between words and world in 'Heart of Darkness' to which Cunningham's reading, conducted with great *brio*, is constantly alert, as the following extract, which culminates in the matter of the biscuit-tin, demonstrates:

■ This so textualizing text isn't bounded only by textuality. This text whose material presses so insistently towards the establishment of heuristic vagueness, this hard-working set of self-emptying epistemological and hermeneutic scenarios, this group of narratives that so impressively inducts the reader into what Tzvetan Todorov has labelled the 'connaissance du vide'[23] – knowledge of the void – is by no means just a matter of an exemplary self-reflexive textual self-doubting. ['Heuristic' means 'performing the function of finding out or discovering'; 'epistemological' means 'concerned with ways of establishing knowledge and/or with the foundations of knowledge' – it is derived from the noun 'epistemology', which was defined in chapter three (p. 86); and 'hermeneutic' means 'concerned with interpretation'. Thus, 'Heart of Darkness' can be seen, and has been seen, as a text that dramatises a number of interrelated quests for definite knowledge and correct interpretation that never achieve their goals but always dissolve into vagueness and emptiness. As Cunningham goes on to argue, however, this vagueness and emptiness is not the whole story.] . . . . . . the fiction's episodes are historically and politically particular enough. The absurdity, the farce, are theatres of cruelty in which black lives are wasted. The frustration at the narrative and narratological levels is matched by anger at the political and moral levels. The pilgrims are on an exemplary literary journey, an intertextual engagement with Dante, one that inverts the Dantesque tradition of happy endings and heavenly comic conclusions. They are also trigger-happy nigger-killers. Those emblematic textual holes are also bullet holes. The network of erasures, the figures of meaning's traces, are also demolished homes, communities, lives. And Marlow carefully unites the bullet holes and the erased roadways in a single sarcastic instance. He comes across a drunken, uniformed white man guarded by armed Zanzibaris: 'Was looking after the upkeep of the road, he declared. Can't say I saw any road or any upkeep, unless the body of a middle-aged negro, with a bullet-hole in the forehead, upon which I absolutely stumbled three miles farther on, may be considered as a permanent improvement' (p. 39).

The *vides* of this text are full of political and moral accusation [*vides* is French for empty spaces, gaps, blanks, emptinesses]. The hollowness at the heart of 'Heart of Darkness' is by no means limited to a process of narrative self-emptying. The metatextual writing subject is also a colonial one. The astonishing bookkeeper is the agent of a colonialist

Russian devotee. The annotations prove not to be in cipher at all, but in Russian. And hatred of Russians was in Polish Conrad's blood. In fact, the terror at the heart of this fiction's darkness is like an archetypal Polish nightmare, concocted by a man with a German name [Kurtz] and a Russian friend, harsh reminders of the two enemies traditionally given to squeezing Poland in their unfriendly pincer embrace. 'Il y aura des Russes. Impossible!' [There will be Russians there. Impossible!], Conrad replied to Cunninghame Graham's invitation to sit on an international peace-meeting platform. He felt no fraternity with Russians.[25] The Russian reader of the 'Inquiry' is one with the likes of Vladimir, the nasty stirrer-up of trouble from the Russian Embassy in *The Secret Agent*, or the whole crew of Russians, especially Russian exiles, in *Under Western Eyes* (1911). Particularly offensive to Conrad about Russians was their proneness to happiness abroad. His Russians tend to be people with internationalist politics, like Laspara in *Under Western Eyes*, the Russian Jewish anarchist exiled to Geneva, where he edits a subversive journal ironically titled *The Living Word*. '"We'll have it translated,"' he assures Razumov of the article he wants him to write. In great contrast, Conrad was an unhappy exile whose foreign accent was reported to have worsened the longer he stayed in England. His fictions sank ever deeper into gloom about the livingness of the word, the possibility of translation, the nature of exile. Laspara's cheerfully *déraciné* politics and linguistics must have been designed to smell offensively rank. And Kurtz is another such internationalist. 'All Europe contributed to the making of Kurtz' (p. 83). And from the look of his patched rig-out, you'd think the whole map of the world had contributed to the making of Kurtz's Russian admirer. If anything, this man's rootless internationalism is even more pronounced than Kurtz's. And yet, staggeringly, this vagabond owns, reads, and admires Towson-Towser. Kurtz tells Marlow that 'his [Kurtz's] sympathies were in the right place' (p. 83) – namely, with the English, and with the England where he went to school. This claim is clearly treated by Marlow with a pinch of salt. There's no getting away, however, from the shock of learning who actually owns the 'Inquiry'. The book's power to *amaze* climaxes in what is for Marlow a terrible piece of knowledge.

Now That's Brotherly [Cunningham's section title]

What price, after this information, the bruited rightness of the British naval way of working if it may so enthral Kurtz's man? The luminosity of that moral professionalism abruptly darkens. It had already dimmed a lot when the Russian rubbed in other affinities with Marlow. He laid claim to a brotherhood of the sea that Marlow was not only helpless to system that makes money the supreme value, whose fetish is successful accountancy, spruce book-keeping. Kurtz's writing is done at the behest of a colonial agency. At the centre of the labyrinth of the Belgian head offices squats 'a heavy writing-desk' (p. 25). Colonizing means writing, and writing – whatever else it might mean – spells colonizing. The ink-stains on the Belgian clerk's jacket sleeves come to look like proleptic [anticipatory] emblems of the whole enterprise's moral stains that Marlow would soon encounter out in the field. And much of the consternation buzzing about Marlow's encounter with Towson-Towser's 'Inquiry' clearly has to do with its being an emphatically British piece of writing. One comes to feel that it stands at the centre of a piece of guilty self-accusation, a moral despair on the part of the narrator intimately connected with his criticism of imperialist enterprises, including British ones.

Marlow can scarcely stop himself reading the 'Inquiry'. 'I assure you to leave off reading was like tearing myself away from the shelter of an old and solid friendship' (p. 66). Approving adjectives, especially high moral terms, stud Marlow's account of this arresting text – it's dull, but also sound and good:

Not a very enthralling book; but at the first glance you could see there a singleness of intention, an honest concern for the right way of going to work, which made these humble pages, thought out so many years ago, luminous with another than a professional light. The simple old sailor, with his talk of chains and purchases, made me forget the jungle and the pilgrims in a delicious sensation of having come upon something unmistakably real. (p. 65)

What Marlow is evidently feeling is what the text's opening narrator calls 'the bond of the sea' (p. 15), and it's clearly a powerful moral affinity.

The values centred for Conrad in the British Merchant Marine – a shining professional work ethic that made 'Polish Joe' so keen to acquire his British merchant officer certificates, a moral touchstone of all his writing as the so-called Prose Laureate of the British Merchant Navy – could not be much clearer: *singleness, honest, right, work, luminous, real.* The tone of this readerly response to the 'Inquiry' chimes in with Marlow's reflections in Brussels on the 'vast amount of red' on the map, the overseas possessions of Britain: 'good to see at any time, because one knows that some real work is done in there' (p. 25). Towson-Towser was a 'Master in his Majesty's Navy' (p. 65). Marlow is also a British master mariner. So, since November 1886, had Conrad been. 'Possède certificat anglais de Cap^{ne} marin': it was one of the 'avantages' that this 'Polish nobleman, cased in British tar' boasted of.[24]

And the trouble is that the 'Inquiry' turns out to belong to Kurtz's rebuff but sealed with a gift of tobacco: '"Brother sailor . . . honour . . . pleasure . . . delight . . . introduce myself . . . Russian . . . son of an arch-priest . . . Government of Tambov . . . What? Tobacco! English tobacco; the excellent English tobacco! Now, that's brotherly. Smoke? Where's a sailor that does not smoke?"' (p. 88 [Conrad's ellipses]). When they part, he helps himself to another handful of Marlow's tobacco – '"Between sailors – you know – good English tobacco"' (p. 103) – and cadges a pair of Marlow's old shoes. He also begs a few cartridges for his Martini-Henry rifle. And he goes off with his copy of Towson in one pocket (dark blue), and another pocket bulging with cartridges. The pocket with the ammunition in it is bright red. So much for the 'real work done in there' (p. 25). The complicity of Marlow and the British Empire he represents and admires with the savage imperialism that comes from the barrel of an internationalist gun (the Martini-Henry combined the Swiss-made breech action invented by the Hungarian-born Frederick Martini with the American barrel developed by Tyler Henry), the complicity with Kurtz, with his sidekick, with what's going on in this heart of darkness, could not have been made clearer. And central to this complicity is a book.

The gift of the shoes is as arresting as the shared interest in the 'Inquiry'. The Russian will henceforth walk in Marlow's shoes. In a measure, Marlow has already been shown to stand in the Russian's shoes. The gift of shoes seals the connection in the same way as the loan of pajamas seals the bond between the neophyte [novice] ship's captain and the alleged murderer in Conrad's story 'The Secret Sharer'. By such exchanges do you recognize your Double, your *Doppelgänger* [wraith of living person – German for 'double-goer'], your mirror-self, in Conrad's fiction. This writing is commonly built on the widespread nineteenth-century trope of the *Doppelgänger* . . . The *Doppelgänger* fiction is a great moral leveller. And so it is in this passage between Marlow and the Russian. Marlow's central position as moral arbiter, proud Englishman, incorruptible British merchant mariner, is deeply shaken. And Marlow's decrease is the Russian's increase. It's rebuking enough to Marlow to have his instinctive assumption that Towson belonged to an Englishman ('"He must be English"' (p. 66)) overturned. It's even more sobering when this non-Englishman cheerfully assumes the right to teach Marlow a thing or two about keeping a tight ship ('"My faith, your pilot-house wants a clean-up!"' (p. 88)) and when Marlow, in-extricably locked into this new and estranging fraternalism, expresses envy and admiration for the person who is on the face of it an obnox-ious wanderer: 'seduced into something like admiration – like envy' (p. 90).

And this extravagant 'phenomenon' (p. 103) of a man is only the prelude or threshold to the even more momentous individual, Kurtz himself. The Russian isn't moved only by Towson, but by Kurtz. Whenever the Russian pockets, as it were, Towson, the approval is accompanied by an endorsement of Kurtz. At the end of chapter two, when Marlow returns the book and is nearly kissed in gratitude, the Russian, the 'Inquiry''s devoted annotator, instantly declares that '"this man"' – Kurtz – '"has enlarged my mind"' (p. 90). When he leaves Marlow, Towson and the bullets carefully pocketed, he enthuses about Kurtz's poetry: '"You ought to have heard him recite poetry – his own too it was, he told me. Poetry!"' And again: '"Oh, he enlarged my mind!"' (p. 103). These are his last words.

Marlow's own last words, at least to Kurtz's Intended, were his lie about Kurtz's last word, a lie about naming. '"The last word he pronounced was – your name"' (p. 123). Our narrator has thus got himself locked into a *Doppelgänger* relationship even more morally rebuking and upsetting than the one with the Russian. 'It is strange how I accepted this unforeseen partnership' (p. 110). This particular moral chiasmus [reversal] is particularly stunning. Kurtz, the hollow man, the person intimately associated with the unspeakability of Africa, with the unspeakable rituals conducted there by both Blacks and Whites, the man whose very name is a lie, is nonetheless a voice, a word-monger whose word not only persists but has a degree of affirmation that Marlow seeks and signally fails to achieve. Marlow has to be content with knowing life only as a 'riddle'. 'I was within a hair's-breadth of the last opportunity for pronouncement, and I found with humiliation that probably I would have nothing to say. This is the reason why I affirm that Kurtz was a remarkable man. He had something to say. He said it'. Kurtz's ghastly revelation is a summation, a 'sort of belief'. It has 'candour' and 'conviction': 'it had the appalling face of a glimpsed truth' (p. 113). What Marlow has to say is, by contrast, inconclusive, 'futile' (p. 112), tepidly sceptical, 'a vision of greyness' (p. 113). Kurtz has the positive assurance of the believing damned, Marlow the luke-warm Laodiceanism of the troubled agnostic ['Laodiceanism' means 'lukewarmness or indifference in religion, politics, etc.' It derives from the Bible, where the church of the Laodiceans, in the Roman province of Asia, was reproached for being 'lukewarm, and neither cold nor hot' in its Christian commitment (Revelations, 3:16)]. Not surprisingly, his story peters out in hesitations, a lie, and the allowing of lies, in the scene with the Intended that might be a pastiche of scenes in the later Henry James – *What Maisie Knew* (1897), say, or *The Golden Bowl* (1904) – a farcical dance of dubious and finally quite false claims to knowledge, a grim comedy in which the fiancée supplies the desirable but self-deluding words that Marlow cannot. '"It was impossible not to – " . . . . . . "Love him," she finished eagerly, silencing me into an appalled dumbness. "How true! how true!"' (p. 120). And as Marlow concludes his miserable confession, the darkness that he thought to avert by endorsing untruths ('I could not tell her. It would have been too dark . . . altogether' (p. 123)) descends anyway as the frame-narrator's thoughts lead away, under an overcast sky, to 'the uttermost ends of the earth', 'into the heart of an immense darkness' (p. 124).

Everything has collapsed for Marlow through meeting Kurtz and the Russian who acts as preface or *hors-texte* to Kurtz [*hors-texte*, as used here, means something that is 'outside' the text, as the Russian is 'outside' the 'text' of Kurtz]. Most notably damaged is Marlow's rhetorical confidence; and that's momentous because it was that confidence which sustained the ancient self-righteous tradition of seafaring Britain. This awful collapse eventuates in the texture of narrative hesitancy that comprises our prime experience here as readers. It's the thing we immediately encounter and learn most forcibly, perhaps, from this fiction. It's an experience of the failure of language and language stuff – the spoken, the written, narrative, rhetoric, story – that arises within a striking series of language encounters, a clash of voices, a war of rhetorics, a business of discourses, words, writings, books, bookishness. But this textual affair could and would not exist were it not for the historical, moral, and political; in short, the ideological experience that engenders it, first for Conrad, then for Marlow. It's Africa, the colonial scene, the imperial endurance test, the nineteenth-century business of foreign trade, that are, in the end, responsible for generating this famous display of narrative and rhetorical powerlessness, this decline in story-teller's confidence.

As with all of modernism's exemplary engagements with despair – its devoted revulsion from narrative, detective-style success – the rhetorical, hermeneutic, narrative issues never arise *in vacuo* [in a vacuum]. There is always, whether for Browning or James, for Joyce or Conrad, some experience or sense of moral, theological, political, social loss that is also significantly, and I would argue fundamentally, in play. No Kurtz, no Russian, no Towson, no African horrors: and no Marlow, no 'Heart of Darkness'. And if the rhetorical collapse so prominent in this fiction cannot be considered separately from the experience it registers and reflects of a collapsed confidence in the value of white imperialism, especially the rightness and righteousness embodied in Towson's 'Inquiry', in Marlow's own moralizing seafaring craft, then neither does the reader have a choice in deciding which aspect of this so modernist text to emphasize. The historical and the rhetorical, the contextual and the textual, are no more separable than Kurtz the ivory-trader is separable from Kurtz the poet, or the Russian as adventurer from the Russian as reader.

What 'Heart of Darkness' is doing is unpicking a tradition of the English novel in which writing and colonizing have gone intimately together. Robinson Crusoe, founding father of the English Novel, was a man with a pen in one hand and a gun in the other. The Russian with cartridges in one pocket and a book in the other, Kurtz the ivory-trading poet, are Crusoe's updated analogues. They are also a focus of the modernist cavilling at the tradition of Defoe, the undoing of Crusoe's certainties. And the cavilling is aimed not just at the tradition's textual features, the writing confidences, the faith in reading and writing that got into the tradition from Defoe's puritan background, but also at that tradition's sustaining moral and political assumptions, its belief in the God-given right to plunder and enslave. Targeting both is merely logical. These things hung together in their eighteenth-century ascendancy, and now they were inseparable in their late nineteenth-century downfall.

The notorious problem of yarns and yarning in 'Heart of Darkness' is also a problem with yarn. The text's famous difficulties with textual stuff are inextricable from the questions it's asking about literal stuff, *Stoff*, cloth. Textual problems converge upon, are intricately woven into, problems with textiles – especially the trade in textiles between Europe and Africa. And where do they come from, the 'confounded spotted cotton handkerchiefs', the 'ghastly glazed calico' trade goods (p. 51), the torn twill curtain, the bit of white worsted around the neck of the dying Negro, the stuff the tattered flag is made of? Why, assuredly, from England. Lancashire was where the world's cotton goods were processed. Yorkshire was where the world's worsted woollen things were produced. Of course, the story's Martini-Henry rifles call the whole violent culture of white Western man into question. The railway boiler 'wallowing in the grass' (p. 32), the upturned railway truck, the stack of rusty rails, doubtless came, like the energetically farcical railway engineers, pointlessly blasting away at a cliff, from Belgium. But the colonialist cloth, the yarns so carefully woven into the *tissu* of this Conradian yarn, are English.

And thus the *Doppelgänger* relationship arranged between Marlow and Kurtz and the Russian is extended, subversively, even secretively, to a Double relationship between nations, Belgium and England. Conrad's satiric anger over the imperialist despoliation of Africa is intense. The 'vilest scramble for loot that ever disfigured the history of human conscience and geographical exploration', he called it, famously, in his late essay 'Geography and Some Explorers'.[26] And imperial Britain, Towson's home, Conrad's and Marlow's ground of assurance and of righteous feelings, turns out also to be on trial in this satire. We are compelled in the end by Marlow's progress to recognize the allegedly benign British Empire as the fraternal double of the obviously terrible Belgian enterprise of King Leopold. 'And this also,' said Marlow suddenly, 'has been one of the dark places of the earth'

(p. 18). Marlow's slow realization, and ours, is that it is still dark even at the end of the civilized nineteenth century, and that the 'dreams of men, the seed of commonwealths, the germs of empires' (p. 17) do not enjoy a simple 'greatness' just because it's our Commonwealth, our Empire that's in question.

An Empty Huntley & Palmers Biscuit Tin [Cunningham's title]

And if all the yarn in this story is critically exemplary for this story of empires, both global empires and narrative empires, forcing us to read this material, this *Stoff*, as emblematic of what's going amiss with yarns of the narrative sort and also as representative of what's up with Britain's huge colonial export trade not least in cloth; even more exemplary, I'd say, in both of these directions, is the sudden arrival on the Congo river and in our text of a Huntley & Palmers biscuit-tin. The tin arrives with a consoling clatter of English reassurance amidst the annoying absence of rivets, the dumbness of the jungle, and after the jabber of the hook-nosed agent, the 'papier-mâché Mephistopheles' (p. 48) of the Central Station, the man who makes bricks without straw:

> It was a great comfort to turn from that chap to my influential friend, the battered, twisted, ruined, tin-pot steamboat. I clambered on board. She rang under my feet like an empty Huntley & Palmer [*sic*] biscuit-tin kicked along a gutter; she was nothing so solid in make, and rather less pretty in shape, but I had expended enough hard work on her to make me love her. No influential friend would have served me better. (p. 52)

Why a biscuit-tin? Why this particular brand of biscuit-tin? [What follows is from Cunningham's next section, 'Empire Biscuits'] . . . . . . This tin is empty. It exists for us as metaphor, the essence of rhetoricism. Furthermore, it is a metaphor of emptiness. But attractive, and even highly plausible, though this reading might be, the precision in the naming of the biscuit-tin seems to require some further interpretative response. This is not just any old biscuit-tin, but one supplied by Huntley & Palmers. Thus named, it has a quite specific identity and origin. And the specificity of this thing takes it way beyond the very suggestively British material stuff, the cottons and worsted wool, that so clamantly [noisily, insistently, urgently] indict themselves as part and parcel of the European colonial enterprise.

For what Huntley & Palmers stood for was one of the most extraordinary and far-flung triumphs of colonialist marketing and propaganda that Victorian Britain knew. Huntley & Palmers biscuits, well-preserved in their tins, went simply everywhere. They were with

Scott on his 1910–12 journey to the South Pole: British foodstuffs that encapsulated the spirit of the Empire and the British class system all at once. In Scott's hut at Cape Evans, a wall of Huntley & Palmers biscuit-tins made the boundary between officers and men: the ward-room of Scott and his fellow officers and the scientists on one side of the metal hedge, the mess-deck for ordinary seamen on the other. (Thomas Kenneally, the Australian novelist of *inter alia* colonial adventurism, has a fossilized piece of Huntley & Palmers biscuit from Scott's last expedition hanging on his study wall.) Henry – 'Dr. Livingstone[,] I presume' – Stanley once pacified a war-like tribe in Suna (now Central Tanzania) with Huntley & Palmers biscuit-tins. Ugandan Christians kept Bibles and Prayer Books in theirs – good for warding off ants and such. When a Royal Navy landing party went ashore on the Pacific island of Juan Fernandez off the coast of Chile – one of the candidates for Robinson Crusoe's island – they found only a few goats and an empty Huntley & Palmers biscuit-tin. These biscuits were sold 'By Appointment to the King of the Belgians'. Their various names revealed the company's colonialist ambition and success – Traveller, Camp, Cabin, African, Cape, Colonial, Empire, Prince, Queen, and so on. Their highly ornamental tins (extremely 'pretty in shape' (p. 52), as Marlow puts it) also proclaimed the imperialist association. There were, for example, tins labelled Indian, Arctic, Orient, Ivory, Arabian (brought out in 1891, this one had boat scenes on it from around the world, including the Congo). When in 1896 Prince Henry of Battenberg, husband of Victoria's youngest daughter, caught a fever fighting the Ashanti in West Africa and died on the boat journey home, his body was preserved in rum in a casket hammered together from Huntley & Palmers biscuit-tins. The municipal museum at Reading owns two swords taken as trophies from the battlefield of Omdurman where, in 1898, the year before 'Heart of Darkness' was published, General Kitchener defeated the Sudanese Mahdi and finally avenged the death of General Gordon. Their scabbards are bound together with bits of tin. The name *Huntley & Palmers* is clearly legible, stamped into these metal straps. Once again the Reading biscuit-tin had proved its versatility in the colonial effort. The Reading museum also holds a photograph taken by a Reverend R.D. Darby of a Conrad-style Belgian trading steamer on the Upper Congo river. A large Huntley & Palmers tin is clearly visible on the roof of the vessel. The photo is captioned 'Huntley & Palmers Biscuits foremost again'.[27]

When Conrad put such a biscuit-container into a metaphor on the Congo river in his intensely anti-colonial fiction, he knew the inference that his British readers would draw. Once again, British trade is being implicated, clearly and by name, in the Belgian horrors.[28] What's more, we are invited to contemplate an empty biscuit-tin. Someone, in the metaphor, has eaten the sweet contents. Huntley & Palmers's African and Empire biscuits were advertised at the time of Conrad's tale as 'slightly sweetened'. The suggestion of sweetness, even of slight sweetness, is, in the context of Conrad's tale, most ironic.

It will take more than the sweet exports of Biscuit City to sweeten the horrors Marlow has discovered, just as it will need more than the Swedish ship's biscuit that Marlow felt compelled to give the dying Black with the bit of white worsted round his neck to halt his death by malnutrition – 'The fingers closed slowly on it and held – there was no other movement and no other glance' (p. 35). As an opium of the people, biscuits are of little avail. They represent a failure of nutrition, though, that the metaphor-as-meaning does not share. The biscuit-tin in question is empty of biscuits but not of point. In fact, the metaphor fills up very busily with bleakly unconsoling meanings: political, ideological messages from Reading to supplement whatever self-referential message of bookish, textual emptiness, the abysmality of reading, which this trope might also be construed as conveying.[29] □

Cunningham's reading brilliantly brings out the creative tension between rhetoric and reality in 'Heart of Darkness', and demonstrates that it is still possible to find something new to say about this much-discussed text. It is approaching its hundredth anniversary, and there is no sign of impending silence. Critical celebrations are on the cards, and look set to continue into the next century. But there will also be spectres at the feast – the ghosts of the insulted and excluded raised by critics like Straus and Achebe. How far will Conrad's tale survive their scrutiny? In an essay published in 1996, the British scholar and critic Cedric Watts, a Conrad enthusiast who was one of the first to rise to his defence against Achebe, allows himself to entertain the possibility that 'Heart of Darkness' could fall from favour: its reputation 'is now a matter of controversy, and its standing may decline'. He also affirms, however, that 'its complexity guarantees that it will prove fruitful to many readers for a long time yet'.[30] This promise of future fruitfulness should be fulfilled. As long as the world still has to work through the global consequences of imperialism, 'Heart of Darkness' will remain a key text; as long as stories are told, there are likely to be readers who choose to hear, who cannot choose but hear, the darkly enlightening tale of Marlow's strange journey.

NOTES

INTRODUCTION

1 Joseph Conrad, *Notes on Life and Letters* (London: Dent, 1921), p.168.

2 Joseph Conrad, *Tales of Hearsay and Last Essays* (London: Dent, 1928; Harmondsworth: Penguin, 1944), p.110.

3 Conrad (1944), p.113.

4 Karl, Frederick R. and Davies, Laurence, eds, *The Collected Letters of Joseph Conrad:* vol. 1: 1861–1897 (Cambridge: Cambridge University Press, 1983), p.62.

5 Karl and Davies (1983), p.61.

6 Conrad (1944), p.113.

7 Karl and Davies (1983), p.61.

8 Karl, Frederick R. and Davies, Laurence, eds, *The Collected Letters of Joseph Conrad:* vol. 2: 1898–1902 (Cambridge: Cambridge University Press, 1986), p.139.

9 Karl and Davies (1986), pp.139–40.

10 Karl and Davies (1986), p.153.

11 Karl and Davies (1986), p.157.

12 Karl and Davies (1986), pp.157–58.

13 Karl and Davies (1986), p.158.

14 Karl and Davies (1986), p.175.

15 Karl and Davies (1986), p.375.

16 Karl and Davies (1986), p.407. This is a translation of a letter originally written in French, where the passage reads: 'Histoire farouche d'un journaliste qui devient chef de station à l'intérieur et se fait adorer par une tribu de sauvages. Ainsi décrit le sujet a l'air rigolo, mais il ne l'est pas' (Karl and Davies (1986), p.406).

17 Karl and Davies (1986), p.417.

CHAPTER ONE

1 Norman Sherry, ed., *Conrad: The Critical Heritage*, The Critical Heritage series (London: Routledge and Kegan Paul, 1973), p.131.

2 Hugh Clifford, 'The Art of Mr. Joseph Conrad', *The Spectator*, 89 (29 November 1902), pp.827–28; reprinted in *Living Age*, 236 (10 January 1903), pp.120–23; Leonard F. Dean, ed., *Joseph Conrad's*

'Heart of Darkness': Backgrounds and Criticisms (Englewood Cliffs, New Jersey: Prentice-Hall, 1960), pp.144–45. This quotation Clifford (1902), p.828.

3 Clifford (1902), p.828.

4 Edward Garnett, 'Mr. Conrad's New Book', *The Academy and Literature*, 63 (6 December 1902), pp.606–07. Reprinted Sherry (1973), pp.131–33. Future Garnett page references to Garnett (1902). These quotations, Garnett (1902), p.606.

5 Garnett (1902), pp.132, 133. Garnett twice uses the phrase 'the high-water mark of the author's talent'.

6 Garnett (1902), p.607.

7 Garnett (1902), p.606.

8 Garnett (1902), p.606.

9 Karl and Davies (1986), pp.467–68, and p.468, note 2. For Henry James's 'The Figure in the Carpet', see Peter Rawlings, ed., *Henry James' Shorter Masterpieces*, vol. 2 (Brighton, Sussex: Harvester, 1984), pp.46–88.

10 Karl and Davies (1986), p.468.

11 Sherry (1973), p.135.

12 *Times Literary Supplement* (12 December 1902), p.372. Reprinted in Sherry (1973), pp.136–37.

13 Anon., the *Athenaeum*, 2 (20 December 1902), p.824. Reprinted in Sherry (1973), pp.137–39. Theodore G. Ehrsam's *A Bibliography of Joseph Conrad* (Metuchen, New Jersey: Scarecrow, 1969), p.326, attributes this review to A.J. Dawson.

14 John Masefield, 'Deep Sea Yarns', *The Speaker*, 7 (31 January 1903), p.442. Reprinted in Dean (1960), pp.148–49.

15 See Ehrsam (1969), p.327.

16 Anon., 'Five Novels', *The Nation*, 76:1980 (11 June 1903), p.478.

17 Frederic Taber Cooper, 'The Sustained Effort and Some Recent Novels', *The Bookman*, New York, 18 (November 1903), pp.310–11.

18 Cooper (1903), p.311.

19 T.S. Eliot, *The Complete Poems and Plays of T.S. Eliot* (London: Faber and Faber, 1969), p.81.

20 F.R. Leavis, *The Great Tradition: George*

Eliot; Henry James; Joseph Conrad (London: Chatto and Windus, 1948; Harmondsworth: Penguin Books in association with Chatto and Windus, 1972), p. 201.

21 Lionel Trilling, 'On the Modern Element in Modern Literature', *Partisan Review* (January–February 1961), pp. 9–35; reprinted with slight revisions as 'On the Teaching of Modern Literature' in Trilling, *Beyond Culture: Essays on Literature and Learning* (Harmondsworth: Penguin Books in association with Secker and Warburg, 1967), pp. 19–41. This quotation, Trilling (1967), p. 32.

22 J. H. Stape, ed., *The Cambridge Companion to Joseph Conrad*, Cambridge Companions to Literature series (Cambridge: Cambridge University Press, 1996), p. 248.

23 Edward Crankshaw, *Joseph Conrad: Some Aspects of the Art of the Novel* (London: Bodley Head, 1936; reissued Russell and Russell, 1963; second edn, Macmillan, 1976), p. vii.

24 M. C. Bradbrook, *Joseph Conrad: Józef Teodor Konrad Nałęcz Korzeniowski: Poland's English Genius* (Cambridge: Cambridge University Press, 1941), p. 27.

25 Joseph Conrad, 'Author's Note' to *Youth, a Narrative and Two Other Stories* reprinted in Robert Hampson ed., 'Heart of Darkness' *with* 'The Congo Diary' (London: Penguin, 1995), p. 11.

26 Bradbrook (1941), p. 28.

27 Bradbrook (1941), pp. 30–31.

28 Leavis (1972), p. 201.

29 T. S. Eliot, 'Hamlet' (1919) in *Selected Essays*, 2nd edition (London: Faber and Faber, 1934), p. 145.

30 Conrad (1995), p. 11.

31 Leavis (1972), pp. 201–02, 202, 203, 204–05, 206, 208, 209.

32 Raymond Williams, *Reading and Criticism*, Man and Society series (London: Frederick Muller, 1950). Note facing title page.

33 Williams (1950), p. 1.

34 Williams (1950), p. ix.

35 Joseph Conrad, 'Preface' to *The Nigger of the 'Narcissus': A Tale of the Sea*,

Everyman's Library series no. 980 (London: J. M. Dent, 1945), p. 5.

36 D. H. Lawrence, 'Morality and the Novel', *Calendar of Modern Letters* (December 1925), reprinted in Edward D. McDonald, ed., *Phoenix: The Posthumous Papers of D. H. Lawrence* (New York: Viking, 1936; Viking Compass series, 1972), pp. 527–32. On p. 528, Lawrence says: 'Morality in the novel is the trembling instability of the balance. When the novelist puts his thumb in the scale, to pull down the balance to his own predilection, that is immorality'. Williams's allusion to Lawrence here is a further index of the influence of Leavisian aesthetics.

37 Conrad (1945), p. 5. Williams himself renders 'My task is' as 'My object is' (Williams (1950), p. 79), but gives no source for this version.

38 Leavis (1972), pp. 206–07, quotes a passage that includes the phrases cited here by Williams, and offers that passage as evidence on which Conrad must 'stand convicted of borrowing the arts of the magazine-writer'.

39 Williams (1950), pp. 75–85. In the original, the quotations are in italics rather than between quotation marks and short quotations of one or two lines are set off and indented as separate paragraphs. In the extract in this Guide, the quotations have been put between quotation marks and the paragraph breaks before and after short quotations have been omitted, without indicating this by six dots.

40 Williams (1950), p. 86.

41 Williams (1950), p. 85.

42 Raymond Williams, *The English Novel from Dickens to Lawrence* (London: Chatto and Windus, 1970), p. 145. In Williams's original text, 'Heart of Darkness' is referred to as *The Heart of Darkness* in this passage.

43 Chinua Achebe, 'The Song of Ourselves', *New Statesman and Society*, 3:87 (9 February 1990), p. 32.

44 Jerome Thale, 'Marlow's Quest', *University of Toronto Quarterly* (July 1955), pp. 351–58. Reprinted in Dean (1960),

pp. 159–166; Robert Kimbrough, ed., *Joseph Conrad: 'Heart of Darkness': An Authoritative Text; Backgrounds and Sources; Criticism*, 1st edn (New York: Norton, 1963), pp. 180–86; 2nd edn (1971), pp. 176–81; Keith Carabine, ed., *Joseph Conrad: Critical Assessments*, vol. 2 (Robertsbridge, East Sussex: Helm Information, 1992), pp. 318–25. Thale references that follow to Dean (1960). These quotations, Dean (1960), p. 159.

45 Dean (1960), p. 166.

46 Dean (1960), p. 162.

47 Robert Burden, 'Heart of Darkness': *An Introduction to the Variety of Criticism*, The Critics Debate series (London: Macmillan, 1991), p. 13.

48 Thomas Moser, *Joseph Conrad: Achievement and Decline* (Cambridge, Massachusetts: Harvard University Press, 1957), p. 50.

49 Moser (1957), pp. 78–81.

50 Albert J. Guerard, *Conrad the Novelist* (Cambridge, Massachusetts: Harvard University Press, 1958), p. 33.

51 Guerard (1958), p. 34.

52 Guerard (1958), p. 35.

53 Guerard (1958), p. 36.

54 Guerard (1958), p. 37.

55 Leavis (1972), p. 211.

56 [*Guerard's Note*:] Lilian Feder finds a number of parallels with the sixth book of [Virgil's] *Aeneid* in 'Marlow's Descent into Hell', *Nineteenth-Century Fiction*, 9 (March 1955), pp. 280–92 [reprinted Kimbrough (1963), pp. 186–89; (1971), pp. 181–84]; Robert O. Evans finds chiefly the influence of Dante's *Inferno* in 'Conrad's Underworld', *Modern Fiction Studies*, 2 (May 1956), pp. 56–62 [reprinted Kimbrough (1963), pp. 189–95; (1971), pp. 218–23]. My views on literary influence differ from those of Miss Feder and Mr. Evans. But echoes and overtones may exist. We may apply to *Heart of Darkness* Thomas Mann's words on 'Death in Venice' (1912): a little work of 'inexhaustible allusiveness'.

57 [*Guerard's Note*:] The analogy of unspeakable Kurtz and enchanted princess may well be an intended irony.

But there may be some significance in the fact that this once [that is, in this one instance] the double is imagined as an entranced feminine figure.

58 [*Guerard's Note*:] Like any obscure human act, this one invites several interpretations, beginning with the simple washing away of guilt. The fear of the blood may be, however, a fear of the primitive towards which Marlow is moving. To throw the shoes overboard would then mean a token rejection of the savage, not the civilized-rational. In any event it seems plausible to have blood at this stage of a true initiation story.

59 Leavis (1972), p. 206.

60 Guerard (1958), pp. 38–43.

CHAPTER TWO

1 Jocelyn Baines, *Joseph Conrad: A Critical Biography* (London: Weidenfeld and Nicolson, 1960; 1969), p. 224.

2 Baines (1969), p. 225.

3 Baines (1969), p. 229.

4 Trilling (1967), p. 37.

5 Trilling (1967), p. 39.

6 Trilling (1967), p. 19.

7 Trilling (1967), p. 40.

8 Trilling (1967), p. 32.

9 Trilling (1967), p. 36.

10 Trilling (1967), pp. 32–33.

11 Eloise Knapp Hay, *The Political Novels of Joseph Conrad: A Critical Study* (Chicago: University of Chicago Press, 1963), p. 112.

12 Hay (1963), p. 113.

13 [*Hay's Note*:] The general manager is made an archetype of bad government. His one hold over his subordinates is his power to inspire uneasiness. His managerial genius is seen in the round table he has had made to end quarrels over precedence at meals. In tacit contrast to King Arthur, '[w]here [the manager] sat was the first place – the rest were nowhere' (p. 42).

14 [*Hay's Note*:] The book ['An Inquiry into some Points of Seamanship'] is obviously suggested by Alfred Henry Alston's manual of seamanship, which Conrad kept from his own training days and is still

saved by his son John as one of Conrad's favourite books ... [*Editor's Note:*] Hampson (1995), p.136, note 89, refers to J.A. Arnold's suggestion that the book is linked both to J.T. Towson, who published two books of navigation tables (1848 and 1849) but not a handbook on points of seamanship, and to Nicholas Tinmouth, whose *An Inquiry Relative to Various Important Points of Seamanship, Considered as a Branch of Practical Science* came out in 1845. See J.A. Arnold, 'The Young Russian's Book in Conrad's "Heart of Darkness"', *Conradiana: A Journal of Joseph Conrad Studies*, 7:2 (1976), pp.121–26.

15 Mario D'Avanzo, 'Conrad's Motley as an Organizing Metaphor', *College Language Association Journal*, 9 (March 1966), pp.289–91; reprinted Kimbrough (1971), pp.251–53.

16 Conrad (1944), p.112.

17 [*Hay's Note:*] Something of the Russian sycophant's relationship to Kurtz may have been put in Conrad's mind by Sir Henry Stanley's 'prosaic newspaper "stunt"' [(Conrad (1944), p.113)] in trailing David Livingstone – who, like Kurtz, was a 'restless wanderer refusing to go home any more' [(Conrad (1944), p.112)] (Conrad's description of Stanley's discovery and of Livingstone is in 'Geography and Some Explorers' [Conrad (1944), pp.112–13]). The Russian would of course be a more ingenuous Stanley, and Kurtz a Livingstone wanting in all the sympathetic qualities Conrad recognizes in the essay . . . Guerard has suggested Stanley as a model not for the Russian but for Kurtz, being 'no mean example of a man who could gloss over the extermination of savages with pious moralisms which were very possibly "sincere"' (Guerard (1958), p.34).

If I have urged that Rhodes was a likelier model for Kurtz than Livingstone or the real agent Conrad met in the Congo, the Belgian Georges Antoine Klein (whose name appears instead of Kurtz through much of the Yale manuscript), it is partly because I think too

much stress has been laid on these two elsewhere. Livingstone and Klein may have loomed large in Conrad's mind in 1890 when he went to the Congo, but Rhodes and other British imperialists must have troubled him more eight years later when he came to write the story. [Gérard] Jean-Aubry describes the autobiographical background of 'Heart of Darkness' in *Joseph Conrad: Life and Letters*, vol. 1 (New York: Doubleday Page, 1927), pp.119–43; in *The Sea Dreamer* (London: George Allen and Unwin, 1957), pp.152–76.

18 Jean-Aubry (1927), vol. I, p.141.

19 Guerard (1958), p.38.

20 Guerard (1958), p.34.

21 Moser (1957), p.80.

22 [*Editor's Note:*] See Hay (1963), pp.115–16. As part of his expansionist ambitions in Africa, Rhodes had created the conditions that made it possible for Dr. Leander Starr Jameson to launch 'the Jameson Raid' – a celebrated, or notorious, imperialist incident late in 1896 in which Jameson had entered Boer territory and set off for Johannesburg, ostensibly to rescue British immigrants there, but possibly to encourage insurrection. The Boers forced Jameson into a humiliating surrender. Joseph Chamberlain, Colonial Secretary in Lord Salisbury's government, denounced the raid but did not insist that Rhodes disclose the full story to Parliament.

23 [*Hay's Note*:] Henry Steele Commager, Jr., has remarked on this. [See 'The Problem of Evil in "Heart of Darkness"', Bowdoin Prize Essay, Harvard University, 1972.]

24 [*Hay's Note:*] Marlow's refusal to admit that Kurtz's atrocious successes had anything to do with commerce and finance is an obvious evasion which amounts to a lie . . .

25 Morton Dauwen Zabel, 'Introduction', Joseph Conrad, *Youth* (New York: Doubleday Anchor, 1959), p.21.

26 Hay (1963), pp.133–34, 135–36, 137, 138–40, 143–51, 152, 153–54.

27 J. Hillis Miller, *Poets of Reality: Six*

Twentieth-Century Writers (Cambridge, Massachusetts: The Belknap Press of Harvard University Press, 1966), p. 6.

28 Miller (1965), p. 5.

29 Miller (1965), p. 6.

30 Miller (1965), pp. 6–7

31 Conrad (1945), p. 5.

32 Joseph Conrad, *The Secret Agent: A Simple Tale*, Penguin Popular Classics Series (London: Penguin/Godfrey Cave, 1994), p. 223.

33 [*Miller's Note*:] See Moser (1957), pp. 53, 54.

34 [*Miller's Note*:] See, for example, Robert Penn Warren, 'Nostromo', *Sewanee Review*, 59:3 (1951), pp. 377, 378.

35 [*Miller's Note*:] See Seymour Gross, 'A Further Note on the Function of the Frame in "Heart of Darkness"', *Modern Fiction Studies*, 3:2 (1957), pp. 167–70. [Reprinted Kimbrough (1963), pp. 199–202; (1971), pp. 227–29.]

36 *Lord Jim* (Edinburgh and London: Blackwood, 1900; Penguin Popular Classics series: London: Penguin; 1994), p. 29.

37 Miller (1965), pp. 13–14, 15–17, 18–20, 23–24, 26–27, 29–31, 34–35, 36–37, 38–39.

38 Stanton de Voren Hoffman, *Comedy and Form in the Fiction of Joseph Conrad*, Studies in English Literature series, vol. 49 (The Hague: Mouton, 1969), p. 16.

39 Hoffman (1969), p. 51.

40 [*Hoffman's Note*:] This third use needs amplification. There are two literary analogues which illustrate what is possibly being done in the case of this third use and function of comedy or burlesque in 'Heart of Darkness'. The medieval morality play with its allegorizations of spiritual and moral states, its vices, had an element of low comedy or burlesque in its midst. Satan's helpers could often be buffoons. And this buffoonery is kin to a certain kind of evil. Yet there also must be dangers in bringing together evil and comedy. It can become difficult to regard the pilgrims or what they represent as real and serious threats, and here again one seems to return to something that Marlow as character is trying to do. This threatens to transfer itself to auditor [listener] and reader. A second literary analogue might show that there is and can be a recognition of the importance of a certain kind of comedy to a certain kind of evil and disorder. In the wastelands of 'Heart of Darkness', activity is meaningless and futile – this is proper, for the disordered person's activity will be meaningless, or rather, part of his disorder is that he can bring his actions into no kind of relationship to ends and consequences. The devils of this novel are a bit like those of [Milton's] *Paradise Lost* (1667), especially in the second book. There they too engage in restless and aimless and undirected activity, in a landscape of doom, of extremes in climate and topography. In 'Heart of Darkness', in a landscape of ravines and hills, of crevices and rocks, with a fire and the extinguishing of it, with a road and its upkeep, the shooting at the hippo, the talk of futures and careers, with starched collars, detonations, and the building of a railroad, there is a similar sense of restless and useless activity. It is a comedy of reasoning about all things and becoming lost in wandering mazes.

41 Hoffman (1969), pp. 43–45.

42 Hoffman (1969), pp. 48–49.

43 Hoffman (1969), p. 50.

44 Hoffman (1969), pp. 50–51.

45 Chris Baldick, *The Concise Oxford Dictionary of Literary Terms* (Oxford: Oxford University Press, 1990; 1991), p. 15.

CHAPTER THREE

1 The image of the 'cultural bomb' is taken from Ngũgĩ wa Thiong'o, *Decolonizing the Mind: The Politics of Language in African Literature* (London: James Currey, 1986), p. 3. Ngũgĩ sees the 'cultural bomb' as 'the biggest weapon wielded and actually daily unleashed by imperialism against [the] collective defiance' of the 'oppressed and exploited of the earth'. But as the writings of Achebe and of Ngũgĩ himself demonstrate, there are 'cultural bombs' that can be used to

strengthen that 'collective defiance'.

2 Chinua Achebe, 'An Image of Africa', *Massachusetts Review*, 18:4 (Winter, 1977), pp. 782–94. This quotation, p. 788. The revised version of this lecture, under the title 'An Image of Africa: Racism in Conrad's "Heart of Darkness"' is in Achebe, *Hopes and Impediments: Selected Essays 1965–1987* (London: Heinemann, 1988), pp. 1–13; Kimbrough (1988), pp. 251–62; Carabine (1992), vol. 2, pp. 393–404. As Cedric Watts, in Stape (1996), p. 60, note 15, points out, Carabine prints the revised version, though wrongly giving his source as the 1977 *Massachusetts Review*.

3 C. B. Cox, *Joseph Conrad: The Modern Imagination* (London: J. M. Dent, 1974), p. 16.

4 Cox (1974), p. 18.

5 Joseph Conrad, *Lord Jim: A Tale*, Penguin Popular Classics series (London: Penguin/Godfrey Cave, 1994), p. 164.

6 Cox (1974), pp. 45–46.

7 Cox is not specific about which comments of Forster he is alluding to here, but presumably he means those made in 'Joseph Conrad: A Note' (1926; collected in Forster's *Abinger Harvest* (London: Edward Arnold, 1936)). Cox discusses these remarks later in *Joseph Conrad: The Modern Imagination* (pp. 171–72), and had previously considered them in his 'Introduction' to the 'Casebook' on Conrad he had edited (*Conrad: 'Heart of Darkness'; Nostromo; Under Western Eyes*, Macmillan Casebook series (London: Macmillan, 1981), pp. 15–16). As Cox points out in that Introduction, Leavis quotes a passage from Forster's piece near the start of his discussion of Conrad in *The Great Tradition* (Leavis (1972), p. 200), and it is possibly this passage to which Cox is referring in *Joseph Conrad: The Modern Imagination*. Forster was not, however, as Cox implies, specifically criticising Conrad's treatment of 'the wilderness' – he was, rather, reviewing and criticising Conrad's *Notes on Life and Letters* (1921), although his comments could clearly be taken to apply more generally to Conrad's

writing. For, in the passages partly quoted by Leavis, Forster says: 'What is so elusive about him is that he is always promising to make some general philosophic statement about the universe, and then refraining with a gruff disclaimer. Dealing, even in the slightest of these essays, with vast and eternal issues, he won't say whether such issues lead or don't lead to a goal . . . . . . And the disclaimers continue each time a general point is raised. He never gives himself away. Our impertinence is rebuked; sentence after sentence discharges its smoke screen into our abashed eyes, yet the problem isn't settled really. Is there not also a central obscurity, something noble, heroic, beautiful, inspiring half a dozen great books; but obscure, obscure? While reading the half-dozen books one doesn't or shouldn't ask such a question, but it occurs, not improperly, when the author professes to be personal, and to take us into that confidence of his. These essays do suggest that he is misty in the middle as well as at the edges, that the secret casket of his genius contains a vapour rather than a jewel; and that we need not try to write him down philosophically because there is, in this particular direction, nothing to write. No creed, in fact. Only opinions, and the right to throw them overboard when facts make them look absurd. Opinions held under the semblance of eternity, girt with the sea, crowned with the stars, and therefore easily mistaken for a creed'. *Abinger Harvest and England's Pleasant Land*, Elizabeth Heine, ed., The Abinger Edition of E. M. Forster, vol. 10 (London: André Deutsch, 1996), pp. 131–32. According to the Abinger Edition, p. 421, 'Joseph Conrad: A Note' first appeared under the title 'The Pride of Mr. Conrad' in the *Nation and Athenaeum* (19 March 1921).

8 Cox (1974), pp. 46–47.

9 Cedric Watts, '"Heart of Darkness"' in Stape (1996), p. 60, note 15. See also Watts, *Joseph Conrad*, Writers and Their Work series (Plymouth, Devon: Northcote House in association with The

British Council, 1994), pp. 51–52.

10 Compare Achebe (1977), pp. 788–89 and Achebe (1988), p. 9, Kimbrough (1988), p. 257, Carabine (1992), vol. 2, p. 399. In the 1977 version, the following passage occurs after 'No, it cannot', and runs to the end of the paragraph: 'I would not call that man an artist, for example, who composes an eloquent instigation to one people to fall upon another and destroy them. No matter how striking his imagery or how beautiful his cadences fall such a man is no more a great artist than another may be called a priest who reads the mass backwards or a physician who poisons his patients. All those men in Nazi Germany who lent their talent to the service of virulent racism whether in science, philosophy or the arts have generally and rightly been condemned for their perversions. The time is long overdue for taking a hard look at the work of creative artists who apply their talents, alas often considerable as in the case of Conrad, to set people against people. This, I take it, is what Yevtushenko is after when he tells us that a poet cannot be a slave trader at the same time, and gives the striking example of Arthur Rimbaud who was fortunately honest enough to give up any pretences to poetry when he opted for slave trading. For poetry surely can only be on the side of man's deliverance and not his enslavement; for the brotherhood and unity of all mankind and against the doctrines of Hitler's master race or Conrad's "rudimentary souls"' (p. 84). The next paragraph then begins, in the 1977 version, 'Last year was the 50th anniversary of Conrad's death. He . . .', and, in the 1988 version, 'Conrad . . .'. The text that then follows, 'was born in 1857', etc., is the same in both versions.

11 Achebe (1988), p. 2.

12 Guerard (1950), p. 9.

13 Leavis (1972), p. 204.

14 [*Editor's Note*:] For example, James Cameron, in a hostile account of a visit to Schweitzer's hospital at Lambarene, quotes Schweitzer as saying, in regard to his attitude to Africans: 'You know the formula – I coined it – "I am your brother, that is true, but I am your elder brother"'. Cameron, *Point of Departure: Experiment in Biography* (London: Grafton, 1969), pp. 166–67.

15 Conrad, quoted in Jonah Raskin, *The Mythology of Imperialism: Rudyard Kipling; Joseph Conrad; E. M. Forster; D. H. Lawrence and Joyce Cary* (New York: Random House, 1971), p. 143.

16 Conrad, quoted in Bernard C. Meyer, MD, *Joseph Conrad: A Psychoanalytic Biography* (Princeton: Princeton University Press, 1967), p. 30.

17 [*Editor's Note*:] See Frantz Fanon, *Peau Noire, Masques Blancs* (Paris: Seuil, 1952); translated by Charles Lam Markmann as *Black Skin, White Masks* (New York: Grove Press, 1967; London: Pluto Press, 1986); *Les Damnés de la Terre* (Paris: Maspero, 1961); translated by Constance Farrington as *The Wretched of the Earth* (New York: Grove Press, 1965; London: MacGibbon and Kee, 1965; Harmondsworth: Penguin Books, 1967), especially chapter five.

18 Meyer (1967), p. 30.

19 Frank Willett, *African Art: An Introduction* (London: Thames and Hudson, 1971), pp. 35, 36.

20 Achebe (1988), pp. 2–11, 12, 13.

21 C. P. Sarvan, 'Racism and the "Heart of Darkness"', *The International Fiction Review*, 7 (1980), pp. 6–10; reprinted in Kimbrough (1988), pp. 280–85. This quotation, Sarvan (1980), p. 6, note 3.

22 Achebe (1988), pp. ix–x. In his 'Preface', Achebe twice refers, on p. ix, to his '1974' lecture. A footnote in the *Massachusetts Review* states, however, that '[t]his paper was given as a Chancellor's Lecture at the University of Massachusetts, Amherst, February 18, 1975' (Achebe (1977), p. 782, unnumbered note).

23 Frances B. Singh, 'The Colonialistic Bias of "Heart of Darkness"', *Conradiana: A Journal of Joseph Conrad Studies*, 10 (1978), pp. 41–54. Reprinted in Kimbrough (1988), pp. 268–80. This quotation, Singh (1978), p. 52.

24 For example, Cedric Watts, although an early dissenter from Achebe's judgement (see Watts (1983)), acknowledges in his essay on 'Heart of Darkness' in the recent *Cambridge Companion to Joseph Conrad* that 'Achebe's lecture had a powerful impact, and its text was repeatedly reprinted and widely discussed' (Stape (1996), p. 53). On the other hand, Martin Ray's *Joseph Conrad*, Modern Fiction series (London: Edward Arnold, 1993), does not mention Achebe in his discussion of 'Heart of Darkness' on pp. 19–31.

25 Stephen A. Reid, 'The "Unspeakable Rites" in "Heart of Darkness"', *Modern Fiction Studies*, 9:4 (Winter 1963–4), pp. 347–56. This quotation, p. 351. Reprinted in Marvin Mudrick, ed., *Conrad: A Collection of Critical Essays* (Englewood Cliffs, New Jersey: Prentice-Hall, 1966), pp. 45–54.

26 Leo Gurko, *Joseph Conrad: Giant in Exile* (London: Frederick Muller, 1965), p. 171.

27 Guerard (1958), p. 36.

28 [*Meisel's Note:*] See Claude Lévi-Strauss, *La Penseé Sauvage* (Paris: Plon, 1962); translated as *The Savage Mind* (no translator named), The Nature of Human Society series (London: Weidenfeld and Nicolson, Press, 1966).

29 Guerard (1958), p. 36.

30 Guerard (1958), p. 39.

31 Guerard, (1958), p. 41.

32 Guerard (1958), p. 39.

33 Guerard (1958), p. 41.

34 Ferdinand de Saussure, *Course in General Linguistics*, revised edn (London: Fontana/Collins, 1974), Charles Bally and Albert Sechehaye eds., in collaboration with Albert Reidlinger, translated by Wade Baskin, p. 120.

35 [*Meisel's Note:*] James Guetti has also shown that Marlow 'admits that it is impossible' to 'look beneath the surface', although his reasons for why 'language . . . fails to discover the meaning of Kurtz and of experience' are simply that 'the reality of experience lies beyond language' and that 'the essentials of experience remain . . . alinguistic'; see

'"Heart of Darkness" and the Failure of the Imagination', *Sewanee Review* (Summer 1965), pp. 498, 500, 501, 502.

36 See Jacques Derrida, 'Structure, Sign, and Play in the Discourse of the Human Sciences', in Richard Macksey and Eugenio Donato, eds., *The Structuralist Controversy* (Baltimore: Johns Hopkins University Press, 1972), pp. 247–65.

37 [*Meisel's Note:*] Mario D'Avanzo has also noticed the similarity between the harlequin's motley and the map in Brussels, but finds in both only a recurrent 'symbol' for 'disorder'; see [Kimbrough (1971) p. 252].

38 Guerard (1958), p. 40.

39 See Guetti (1965), p. 62; (1967), p. 62.

40 Meisel (1978), pp. 20–26, 27.

41 Meisel (1978), p. 26.

42 Ian Watt, *Conrad in the Nineteenth Century* (Berkeley: University of California Press, 1979; London: Chatto and Windus, 1980), p. 214.

43 Watt (1980), p. 159.

44 Watt (1980), p. 160.

45 [*Watt's Note:*] [Max] Beerbohm hit off Conrad's use of delayed decoding for the climax of his story. The protagonist is 'silenced by sight of what seemed to be a young sapling sprung up from the ground within a yard of him – a young sapling tremulous, with a root of steel' (*A Christmas Garland*, London[: Heinemann, 1921, p. 130; Kimbrough (1963), p. 161; Carabine (1992), vol. 1, p. 510]). The closest analogy seems to be this passage, although Jocelyn Baines says that 'Max Beerbohm based his witty parody of Conrad in *A Christmas Garland*' on 'Karain' and 'The Lagoon' (Baines (1969), p. 190) and Addison C. Bross argues, in 'Beerbohm's "The Feast" and Conrad's Early Fiction' (*Nineteenth-Century Fiction*, 26:3 (December 1971), pp. 329–36, for 'An Outpost of Progress' as a closer source. [*Editor's Note:*] Watt does not mention an earlier example of the 'delayed decoding' of the flight of a spear that occurs, not in Conrad, but in H. Rider Haggard's *King Solomon's Mines* (1885; Dennis Butts, ed., Oxford World's

Classics series (Oxford: Oxford University Press, 1989), pp. 110–11: 'At last [Good] succeeded in getting the worst of the scrub off the right side of his face and chin, when suddenly I, who was watching, became aware of a flash of light that passed just by his head . . . . . . Good sprang up with a profane exclamation . . . and so did I, without the exclamation, and this was what I saw. Standing there, not more than twenty paces from where I was, and ten from Good, were a group of men . . . In front of them stood a youth of about seventeen, his hand still raised and his body bent forward in the attitude of a Grecian statue of a spear thrower. Evidently the flash of light had been a weapon, and he had thrown it'.

46 Watt (1980), pp. 176–79.

47 Evans (1956), pp. 59, 60.

48 [*Watt's Note*:] The phrase, 'gespentische Gegenständlichkeit' ['spectral objectivity'] is that of Georg Lukács, *Existentialismus oder Marxismus?* (Berlin [no publisher given], 1951), p. 41, summarising one aspect of Marx's view of reification.

49 Max Weber, *The Theory of Social and Economic Organization*, translated by A. M. Henderson and Talcott Parsons (New York: Free Press, 1964), p. 340.

50 Conrad (1945), p. 5.

51 Watt (1980), pp. 189–96.

CHAPTER FOUR

1 See Nicolas Tredell, *The Critical Decade: Culture in Crisis* (Manchester: Carcanet, 1993) for a discussion of the critical revolution of the 1980s. See also Tredell, *Conversations with Critics* (Manchester: Carcanet, 1994) for interviews with some of the leading figures in that revolution.

2 The term 'Conradophiles' is used by Allen Carey-Webb in the essay '"Heart of Darkness", *Tarzan*, and the "Third World": Canons and Encounters in World Literature, English 109', *College Literature*, 19/20: 3/1 (1992), p. 126. Carey-Webb says: 'We may want to ask about why "Heart of Darkness" in particular has such

a revered place, and what it signifies, that to accuse it of racism should bring a covey of Conradophiles down on your head'.

3 [*Parry's Note*:] In '"Gnawed Bones" and "Artless Tales" – Eating and Narrative in Conrad', Tony Tanner writes of 'Heart of Darkness': 'This is a study of a certain kind of white imperial consciousness which, as it were, wants to engorge the world and transform it into self'. See Norman Sherry, ed., *Joseph Conrad: A Commemoration: Papers from the 1974 International Conference on Conrad* (London: Macmillan, 1976), p. 32.

4 [*Parry's Note*:] In *The Savage in Literature: Representations of 'Primitive' Society in English Fiction 1858–1920*, International Library of Anthropology series (London: Routledge and Kegan Paul, 1975), Brian V. Street shows that many of the stereotypes about 'primitive' life had hardened even before the scramble for Africa and that 'imperialists tended to use theories already worked out by scientists and which lent themselves to political manipulation' (p. 5). Street gives a telling summary of the image devised in anthropological studies: '"Primitive" peoples are considered to be the slaves of custom and thus to be unable to break the despotism of their own "collective conscience". Any custom "discovered" among a "primitive" people is assumed to dominate their whole lives; they are unconscious of it and will never change it themselves. This provides the basis for the analysis of many customs being reported back to nineteenth-century England by the growing number of travellers' (p. 6).

5 [*Parry's Note*:] [Compare] K. K. Ruthven, 'The Savage God: Conrad and Lawrence', *Critical Quarterly*, 10:1/2 (Spring/Summer 1968), pp. 41–46 [Extract in Cox (1981), pp. 78–84], who appears to concur with the construction devised by the *'fin de siècle* Decadent Movement' about savage primitivism possessing a 'pre-logical consciousness' and fostering the 'whole man' repressed and dismembered by civilisation.

6 [*Parry's Note*:] It is Ruthven's argument

(Ruthven (1968)) that, concealed behind Marlow's overt disapproval is a cautious and evasive case for Kurtz, a strategic celebration of his achievement in transcending civilisation's restraints and repressions.

7 [*Parry's Note*:] In Marlow's perceptions of Africa, the 'primitive' is associated with some postulated 'prehuman' condition that is lawless and irrational. Although there is evidence that Conrad shared this view, the fiction opens up such assumptions to question, and present-day critics who continue to ascribe the dislocation of white protagonists to the unconscious, mindless and uncaring immensity of the Non-European cosmos, are uncritically perpetuating that ethnic solipsism which Conrad's fictions register but interrogate.

8 [*Parry's Note*:] [Compare] John A. McClure, 'The Rhetoric of Restraint in "Heart of Darkness"', *Nineteenth-Century Fiction*, 32:3 (1977), pp. 310–26, who contrasts the passion for domination reflected in Kurtz's speech with Marlow's restrained and probing manner of address, which he sees as 'a symbolic manifestation of his ethos of self-restraint' (p. 313). The argument in the present discussion is that Marlow and Kurtz represent variations within one consciousness, against which is posed the consciousness of the other hemisphere.

9 [*Parry's Note*:] In the manuscript version, the sentence 'It could only be obtained by conquest – or by surrender', follows 'We were cut off from the comprehension of our surroundings' (p. 62). See Kimbrough (1963 [1971]), p. 36, [(1988), p. 37].

10 [*Parry's Note*:] The converging crowds carrying spears, bows and shields, casting wild glances, making savage movements and uttering weird cries, the dark shapes in fantastic headdresses and spotted skins, standing warlike and still in statuesque repose, are amongst the many clichés used by Conrad and later adopted by popular 'epic' films set in Africa.

11 [*Parry's Note*:] In his reading of the fiction, Jeremy Hawthorn . . . contrasts

Conrad's suspicion of eloquence with his trust in technical language as a register of truth and reality. [See Hawthorn, *Joseph Conrad: Language and Fictional Self-Consciousness* (London: Edward Arnold, 1979), especially pp. 7–11.]

12 Benita Parry, *Conrad and Imperialism: Ideological Boundaries and Visionary Frontiers* (London: Macmillan, 1983), pp. 28–39.

13 Parry (1983), p. 138, note 40.

14 An earlier version, 'Un Rapport Illisible: "Coeur des Ténèbres"' appeared in a French translation by Vincent Giroud in *Poétique: Revue de Théorie et D'Analyse*, 11:44 (1980), pp. 472–89.

15 See Nicolas Tredell, ed., *Charles Dickens: 'Great Expectations'*, Icon Critical Guides series (Cambridge: Icon, 1998).

16 Brooks (1992), pp. xiii–xiv.

17 Brooks (1992), p. 13.

18 See Baldick (1991) for useful definitions of *fabula* (p. 80), *sjužet* (p. 206), *histoire* (p. 99), *récit* (p. 186), and *discours* (p. 59).

19 Brooks (1992), p. 328, note 18.

20 [*Brooks's Note*:] These 'narratological' questions have not been much discussed in the extensive critical literature on Conrad, and I shall thus not make much reference to other interpretations of 'Heart of Darkness'. Let me, however, acknowledge a debt to James Guetti's argument [Guetti (1967)], which has similarities to my own. Guetti is concerned with the failure of Marlow's search for a meaning postulated as at the end of the journey and in the heart of darkness. But Guetti conceives this failure as essentially linguistic – the failure of metaphor – rather than as a problem in narrative. Another study touching on some of the same issues as mine is the fine essay by Garrett Stewart, 'Lying as Dying in "Heart of Darkness"', *PMLA*, 95:3 (1980), pp. 319–31 [reprinted Kimbrough (1988), pp. 358–74] – an essay published at nearly the same time as a first version of the present chapter, in an interesting convergence of perspectives. I have also learnt from Tzvetan Todorov, '"Coeur des

Ténèbres"' in *Les Genres du Discours* (Paris: Seuil, 1978) [pp.172–83]; and [Guerard (1958)]. [Todorov's analysis of 'Heart of Darkness' was originally published as 'Connaissance du vide', *Nouvelle Revue de Psychanalyse*, 11 (Spring 1975), pp.145–54; translation by Walter C. Putnam III, as 'Knowledge in the Void: "Heart of Darkness"', *Conradiana*, 21:3 (1989), pp.161–81. Translation reprinted in Carabine (1992), vol. 2, pp.364–74.]

21 [*Brooks's Note*:] . . . Properly, this quotation should be in double quotation marks, since everything said by Marlow is already presented in quotation marks, as a report by the first narrator, while everything cited by Marlow is already in double quotes, and ought properly to be in triple quotation marks in my text. For the sake of simplicity, I shall eliminate the first set of quotation marks when I cite Marlow. But it is not without pertinence to my subject that we are always made aware that Marlow is being cited by another.

22 The French translation of Brooks's original essay renders 'The Company as ordering' as '*La Compagnie comme principe d'ordre*' [The Company as [a] principle of order], (Brooks (1980), p.474).

23 Brooks's slip goes uncorrected in Bloom (1987), p.109 and Jordan (1996), p.71.

24 See Walter Benjamin, 'The Storyteller: Reflections on the Work of Nikolai Leskov' (*Der Erzähler* (1936)), in Hannah Arendt, ed., *Illuminations*, translated by Harry Zohn (London: Fontana/Collins, 1973), pp.83–109. 'Wisdom' is mentioned on p.94.

25 [*Brooks's Note*:] On the 'dialogic' and 'double-voicedness', see in particular Mikhail Bakhtin, 'Discourse in the Novel', in Michael Holquist ed., *The Dialogic Imagination*, translated by Holquist and Caryl Emerson (Austin: University of Texas Press, 1981), pp.259–422; and *Problems of Dostoevsky's Poetics*, translated by R.W. Rotsel (New York: Ardis, 1973).

26 [*Brooks's Note*:] F.R. Leavis succinctly states a common critical position when, in reference to another passage from 'Heart of Darkness', he says: 'He [Conrad] is intent on making a virtue out of not knowing what he means' [(Leavis (1972), p.207)]. Among other failures of perception, this remark fails to take account of the fact that it is Marlow, not Conrad, who is speaking. [*Editor's Note*:] The passage that Leavis is discussing is on pp.106–08 of 'Heart of Darkness', starting with 'I tried to break the spell . . .' and ending 'yet struggling blindly with itself', and his quotation from it has some interesting omissions, including a sentence which uses the term 'niggers'.

27 Brooks (1992), pp.238–44, 245, 246–51.

28 Brooks (1992), p.261.

29 Achebe (1988), p.9.

30 Christopher L. Miller, *Blank Darkness: Africanist Discourse in French* (Chicago: University of Chicago Press, 1985). Extracts in Jordan (1996), pp.87–102. This quotation, Miller (1985), p.61.

31 Sigmund Freud, *The Interpretation of Dreams* [1900] (New York: Basic Books, 1965), translated by James Strachey, pp.39, 80.

32 Miller (1985), p.62.

33 Miller (1985), p.182.

34 Miller (1985), p.170.

35 Miller (1985), p.182, note 19.

36 Singh (1978). [*Miller's Note*:] Todorov also refers to an alleged 'ethnocentric paternalism of Conrad's' (Todorov (1975), p.149). [*Editor's Note*:] See also Carabine (1992), vol. 2, p.369, where the phrase is rendered, in translation, as 'paternalistic ethnocentrism'. The French original reads: '. . . tout l'ethnocentrisme paternaliste de Conrad (qui pouvait passer pour anticolonialisme au XIXe) ne peut nous empêcher de voir que sa sympathie va aux habitants indigènes du continent noir; le Blanc est cruel et stupide' (Todorov (1978), p.177): '. . . all the paternalistic ethnocentrism of Conrad (which could pass for anti-colonialism in the nineteenth century) cannot prevent us from seeing that his sympathy goes to the indigenous inhabitants of the dark

continent; the White man is cruel and stupid' (Editor's translation).

37 Miller (1985), p.171.

38 See Miller (1985), pp. 43–47, 132–34, for discussions of De Brosses, and pp.16–19, 87-91, for discussions of Gobineau.

39 V.S. Naipaul, *A Bend in the River* (New York: Knopf, 1979), p.4.

40 [*Miller's Note:*] Guerard (1950), p.13. See also Norman Sherry, *Conrad's Western World* (Cambridge: Cambridge University Press, 1971), pp.9–125, and Jean-Aubry (1957), p.159: 'Marlow, who is Conrad himself'.

41 [*Miller's Note:*] The point at which Africa became the property of boys' adventure stories is a matter of some interest. Conrad tells of his own experience, in his short essay 'Geography and Some Explorers', about his youthful fascination with geography: 'And it was Africa, the continent out of which the Romans used to say some new thing was always coming, that got cleared of the dull imaginary wonders of the dark ages, which were replaced by exciting spaces of white paper. Regions unknown! My imagination could depict to itself there worthy, adventurous and devoted men, nibbling at the edges, attacking from north and south and east and west, conquering a bit of truth here and a bit of truth there, and sometimes swallowed up by the mystery their hearts were so persistently set on unveiling' (Conrad (1944), p.110).

42 [*Editor's Note:*] A point confirmed by Bender's *Concordance*, which records only one use of the name 'Africa', in the passage quoted by Miller. See Bender (1979), p.6.

43 [*Miller's Note:*] The political intertextuality of 'Heart of Darkness' is of course very rich, involving, as it does, the controversy that raged over the Congo Free State at the turn of the century. Leopold II, King of the Belgians, made himself not only the sovereign but also the sole owner of the Congo, saying, 'The Congo has been, and could have been, nothing

but a personal undertaking. There is no more legitimate or respectable right than that of an author over his own work, the fruit of his labour . . . My rights over the Congo are to be shared with none; they are the fruit of my own struggles and expenditure' (quoted in Ruth Slade, *King Leopold's Congo* (Oxford; New York: Oxford University Press, 1962), p.175). The most useful reading to complement 'Heart of Darkness' could be the 'Report of the Commission of Enquiry in the Congo Free State', translated by E.A . Huybers for the Federation of the Defence of the Belgian Interests Abroad' (Brussels: Hayez, 1905). The commissioners, sent into 'the heart of Africa', which was 'steeped in the lowest barbarism', where 'atrocious massacres were of constant occurrence', found that the system of forced labour then in place had its evils (those not providing their quota of rubber were alleged to have had their hands cut off; the quota became one of severed hands exacted out of the Force Publique rather than buckets of rubber out of the populace); but on a continent where the 'mutilation of dead bodies is an ancient native custom' (p.90), why should not a Kurtz do likewise? 'Native witnesses . . . saw seven sexual organs which had been removed from natives killed during the fight, and which were suspended to a cord tied to two sticks in front of the hut of a European' (p.89). [Compare] 'Heart of Darkness', p.94, when Marlow comes upon Kurtz's house: 'I had expected to see a knob of wood there, you know . . . and there it was, black, dried, sunken, with closed eyelids, – a head that seemed to sleep at the top of that pole'.

44 Watt (1980), p.158.

45 [*Miller's Note:*] [Joseph] Conrad, 'Heart of Darkness', autograph manuscript, Beinecke Rare Book Library. [See also Kimbrough (1963; 1971), p.13, (1988), p.16; Hampson (1995), p.132, note 48].

46 [*Miller's Note:*] The 'privilege of the voice' in Western metaphysics is the subject of Jacques Derrida's *La voix et le*

Phénomène (Paris: Presses Universitaires de France, 1967 [translated, with other essays, by David B. Allison as *Speech and Phenomena: And Other Essays on Husserl's Theory of Signs*, Northwestern University Studies in Phenomenology and Existential Philosophy series (Evanston: Northwestern University Press, 1973)]). [Derrida's] explication of that privilege could account to some extent for the insistence on 'loyalty' and 'faith' to the voice of Kurtz: its magical quality needs no outside determinant; it is purely autonomous and present.

47 Miller (1985), pp. 171-76.

48 Nina Pelikan Straus, 'The Exclusion of the Intended from Secret Sharing in "Heart of Darkness"', *Novel: A Forum on Fiction*, 20:2 (Winter 1987), p. 123.

49 Straus (1987), p. 126.

50 Straus (1987), p. 123.

51 Straus (1987), p. 124.

52 Straus (1987), p. 131.

53 Sigmund Freud, *Introductory Lectures on Psychoanalysis*, Pelican Freud Library, vol. 1 (Harmondsworth: Penguin, 1976), James Strachey and Angela Richards, eds., translated by James Strachey, p. 477.

54 Freud (1976), p. 476.

55 Freud (1976), p. 478.

56 Freud (1976), p. 478.

57 Guerard (1958), pp. 40–41.

58 David Thorburn, *Conrad's Romanticism* (New Haven: Yale University Press, 1974), p. 143.

59 Frederick R. Karl, *Joseph Conrad: The Three Lives: A Biography* (London: Faber, 1979), p. 459, unnumbered note.

60 [*Editor's Note*:] See Harold Bloom, *The Anxiety of Influence: A Theory of Poetry* (New York: Oxford University Press, 1973).

61 [*Editor's Note*:] See Gayatri Chakravorty Spivak, 'Finding Feminist Readings: Dante–Yeats' (1980) in Spivak, *In Other Worlds: Essays in Cultural Politics* (New York: Methuen, 1987), p. 18.

62 See Watt (1980), pp. 244–45.

63 [*Editor's Note*:] The phrase 'the brutally sexist conventions of high art' adapts Spivak's question in 'Finding Feminist Readings: Dante–Yeats', cited by Straus

earlier in her essay (p. 123): '[w]hy are the traditions and conventions of art so brutally sexist?' (Spivak (1987), p. 26).

64 Keats used the phrase 'negative capability' in a letter of 21 December 1817 to George and Thomas Keats: '*Negative Capability*, that is when man is capable of being in uncertainties, Mysteries, doubts, without any irritable reaching after fact & reason'. Robert Gittings, ed., *Selected Poems and Letters of John Keats*, The Poetry Bookshelf series (London: Heinemann, 1966), pp. 40–41.

65 Straus (1987), pp. 131–35.

66 Parry (1984), p. 138, note 40.

CHAPTER FIVE

1 Gail Fincham, 'Living under the Sign of Contradiction: Self and Other in Conrad's "Heart of Darkness"', *The English Academy Review*, 7 (1990), p. 10, note 3.

2 Fincham (1990), p. 11, note 8.

3 See Baldick (1991), p. 135 for 'metonymy', p. 221 for 'synecdoche'.

4 Abdul R. JanMahomed, *Manichean Aesthetics: The Politics of Literature in Colonial Africa* (Amherst: University of Massachusetts Press, 1983), p. 48.

5 [*Editor's Note*:] It is interesting to compare Fincham's analysis of this description with Raymond Williams's praise, in chapter one of this Guide, of its 'magnificent particularity' (see p. 27): 'magnificent' seems an odd adjective to use in this context, as if Williams's response had been displaced from the human suffering that was being represented to the artistic achievement of the representation – a displacement that, in a sense, undermines his high evaluation of the passage since it could indicate that Conrad has failed artistically, insofar as his aim was to convey a powerful image of human suffering. Williams's displacement was possibly prompted by the metonymic fragmentation that Fincham observes: Conrad at this point is perhaps too particular, so that a sense of the suffering whole is lost in the display of Marlow's disorientated, fragmented perception.

6 Albert Memmi, *The Colonizer and the Colonized* (Boston: Beacon, 1969), p.85, translated by Howard Greenfield from *Portrait du Colonisé Précédé de Portrait du Colonisateur* (Paris: Editions Buchet/Chastel, Corêa, 1957).

7 Fincham (1990), pp.2, 3–7.

8 Fincham (1990), p.10.

9 Edward W. Said, *Orientalism* (London: Routledge and Kegan Paul, 1978; Penguin, 1991), p.199.

10 Imre Salusinszky, *Criticism in Society: Interviews with Jacques Derrida, Northrop Frye, Harold Bloom, Geoffrey Hartman, Frank Kermode, Edward Said, Barbara Johnson, Frank Lentricchia, and J. Hillis Miller*. New Accents series (London: Methuen, 1987), p.133.

11 Edward W. Said, *Joseph Conrad and the Fiction of Autobiography* (Cambridge, Massachusetts: Harvard University Press, 1966), p.147.

12 Said (1966), pp.147–48.

13 Edward W. Said, 'Intellectuals in the Post-Colonial World', *Salmagundi*, 70–1 (1986), p.48.

14 Said (1986), p.47.

15 Said (1986), p.48.

16 Edward W. Said, *Culture and Imperialism* (London: Chatto and Windus, 1993), pp.19, 115.

17 Said (1993), p.115.

18 Said (1993), p.xxiv.

19 Said (1993), p.24.

20 Said (1993), pp.24–25, 26–27, 28, 79–80.

21 Valentine Cunningham, *In the Reading Gaol: Postmodernity, Texts, and History* (Oxford: Blackwell, 1994), p.2.

22 Cunningham (1994), p.3.

23 See Todorov (1975;1978).

24 Letter to Marguerite Poradowska, 1? February 1891, and to Karol Zagórski, 22 May 1890, Karl and Davies (1983), pp.67, 52.

25 Karl and Davies (1986), p.158.

26 Conrad (1944), p.113.

27 [*Cunningham's Note:*] Information about Reading biscuits and tins from T.A.B. Corley, *Quaker Empire in Biscuits: Huntley & Palmers of Reading 1822–1972* (London: Hutchinson, 1972); M.J. Franklin, *British Biscuit Tins 1868–1939: An Aspect of Decorative Packaging* (London: New Cavendish, 1979); Ian Bradley, *Enlightened Entrepreneurs* (London: Weidenfeld and Nicolson, 1987), chapter on 'George Palmer (1818–1897)'; Paul Brown, 'Scott's Last Outpost, Frozen History', *Guardian* (15 February 1989), p.24; Tim Toni, 'My Style: Tom Kenneally', *Sydney Morning Herald* (26 September 1985).

28 [*Cunningham's Note:*] In other words, the direct involvement of Britain in the *nouvelle*'s critique of imperialism is far wider than Hunt Hawkins allows in 'Conrad's Critique of Imperialism in "Heart of Darkness"', *Publications of the Modern Language Association of North America*, 94:1 (1979), 286–99. And, of course, at no point does Conrad's text sustain the colonialist racism Chinua Achebe professes to detect in his curious misreading of it in the notorious 'An Image of Africa: Racism in Conrad's "Heart of Darkness"' (Achebe (1988)). For a more temperate discussion of the racism charge, see 'Epilogue: Kurtz's "Darkness" and Conrad's "Heart of Darkness"' in Patrick Brantlinger, *Rule of Darkness: British Literature and Imperialism 1830–1914* (Ithaca, NY: Cornell University Press, 1988), pp.255–74.

29 Cunningham (1994), pp.241–49, 252–54.

30 Stape (1996), p.58.

SELECT BIBLIOGRAPHY

Works by Conrad

This list gives the first British editions, followed by details of later editions where these have been cited in the text of this Guide. Details are also given of the edition of 'Heart of Darkness' used in this Guide.

Almayer's Folly. London: Fisher Unwin, 1895.

An Outcast of the Islands. London: Fisher Unwin, 1896.

The Nigger of the 'Narcissus'. London: Heinemann, 1897.

Tales of Unrest. London: Fisher Unwin, 1898. Contains 'Karain'; 'The Idiots'; 'An Outpost of Progress'; 'The Return'; 'The Lagoon'.

Lord Jim: A Tale. Edinburgh and London: Blackwood, 1900; Penguin Popular Classics series. London: Penguin/Godfrey Cave, 1994.

The Inheritors (with Ford Madox Hueffer). London: Heinemann, 1901.

Youth: A Narrative and Two Other Stories. Edinburgh and London: Blackwood, 1902. Contains 'Youth'; 'Heart of Darkness'; 'The End of the Tether'.

Typhoon and Other Stories. London: Heinemann, 1903. Contains 'Typhoon'; 'Amy Foster'; 'To-morrow'; 'Falk'.

Nostromo. London: Harper, 1904.

The Mirror of the Sea. London: Methuen, 1906.

The Secret Agent: A Simple Tale. London: Methuen, 1907; Penguin Popular Classics series. London: Penguin/Godfrey Cave, 1994.

A Set of Six. London: Methuen, 1908. Contains 'Gaspar Ruiz'; 'The Informer'; 'The Brute'; 'An Anarchist'; 'The Duel'; 'Il Conde'.

Under Western Eyes. London: Methuen, 1911.

Some Reminiscences. London: Nash, 1912. Published in the USA as *A Personal Record* and usually known today by this title.

Twixt Land and Sea. London: Dent, 1912. Contains 'A Smile of Fortune'; 'The Secret Sharer'; 'Freya of the Seven Isles'.

Chance. London: Methuen, 1914.

Within the Tides. London: Dent, 1915. Contains 'The Planter of Malata'; 'The Partner'; 'The Inn of the Two Witches'; 'Because of the Dollars'.

Victory. London: Methuen, 1915.

The Shadow-Line. London: Dent, 1917.

The Arrow of Gold. London: Fisher Unwin, 1919.

The Rescue. London: Dent, 1920.

Notes on Life and Letters. London: Dent, 1921.

The Rover. London: Fisher Unwin, 1923.

Suspense. London: Dent, 1925.

Tales of Hearsay. London: Fisher Unwin, 1925. Contains 'The Warrior's Soul'; 'Prince Roman'; 'The Tale'; 'The Black Mate'.

Last Essays. London: Dent, 1926.

Tales of Hearsay and Last Essays. London: Dent 1928; Harmondsworth:

Penguin, 1944. The essay 'Geography and Some Explorers', often cited in discussions of 'Heart of Darkness', is one of the *Last Essays*.
'Heart of Darkness' *with* 'The Congo Diary', ed. Robert Hampson. London: Penguin, 1995.

Letters

Blackburn, William, ed. *Joseph Conrad: Letters to William Blackwood and David S. Meldrum*. Durham, North Carolina: Duke University Press, 1958.
Jean-Aubry, Gerard, ed. *Twenty Letters to Joseph Conrad*. London: First Edition Club, 1926.
Karl, Frederick R. and Davies, Laurence, eds. *The Collected Letters of Joseph Conrad*. Cambridge: Cambridge University Press. Vol. 1: *1861–1897* (1983); vol. 2: *1898–1902*; vol. 3: *1903–1907* (1988); vol 4: *1908–1911* (1990); vol 5: *1912–1916* (1996); still in progress – projected 8-volume series.
Najder, Zdzislaw, ed. *Conrad's Polish Background: Letters to and From Polish Friends*. Translated Halin Carroll. Oxford: Oxford University Press, 1964.
Watts, C.T., ed. *Joseph Conrad's Letters to R.B. Cunninghame Graham*. Cambridge: Cambridge University Press, 1969.

Concordance

Bender, Todd K. *A Concordance to Conrad's 'Heart of Darkness'*. Garland Reference Library of the Humanities, vol. 135. New York: Garland, 1979.

Bibliographies

Ehrsam, Theodore G. *A Bibliography of Joseph Conrad*. Metuchen, New Jersey: Scarecrow, 1969.
The MLA (Modern Language Association) Database, which lists books and journal articles in literature, languages, linguistics and folklore, is an invaluable guide to more recent Conrad criticism, though it should not be regarded as comprehensive. It can be accessed through many university and college computer systems.

Journals

The Conradian: Journal of the Joseph Conrad Society (UK). Subscriptions from: The Honorary Secretary, The Joseph Conrad Society (United Kingdom), c/o The Polish Social and Cultural Association, 238–46 King Street, London W6 0RF, UK.
Conradiana: A Journal of Joseph Conrad Studies. Subscriptions from: Texas Tech Press, Sales Office, Texas Tech University, Lubbock, TX 79409-1037, USA.
L'Epoque Conradienne. Subscriptions from: Société Conradienne Française, Faculté des Lettres et des Sciences Humaines, Campus universitaire de Limoges-Vanteaux, 39E rue Camille-Guerin, 87036 Limoges, France.
Joseph Conrad Today: The Newsletter of the Joseph Conrad Society of America. Subscriptions from: The Joseph Conrad Society of America, c/o Department of Humanities, Drexel University, Philadelphia, PA 19104-2875, USA.

Biographies

Allen, Jerry. *The Sea Years of Joseph Conrad*. London: Methuen, 1967.

Baines, Jocelyn. *Joseph Conrad: A Critical Biography*. London: Weidenfeld and Nicolson, 1960; 1969.

Batchelor, John. *The Life of Joseph Conrad: A Critical Biography*. Oxford: Blackwell, 1994.

Jean-Aubry, Gérard. *Joseph Conrad: Life and Letters*. 2 vols. New York: Doubleday, Page, 1927.

Jean-Aubry, Gérard. *Vie de Conrad*. Paris: Gallimard, 1947. Translated by Helen Sebba as *The Sea Dreamer: A Definitive Biography of Joseph Conrad*. London: George Allen and Unwin, 1957.

Karl, Frederick R. *Joseph Conrad: The Three Lives: A Biography*. London: Faber, 1979.

Meyer, Bernard C., MD. *Joseph Conrad: A Psychoanalytic Biography*. Princeton: Princeton University Press, 1967.

Meyers, Jeffrey. *Joseph Conrad: A Biography*. London: John Murray, 1991.

Najder, Zdzisław. *Joseph Conrad: A Chronicle*. Translated by Halina Carroll-Najder. Cambridge: Cambridge University Press, 1983.

Sherry, Norman. *Conrad and His World*. London: Thames and Hudson, 1972. Republished under title of *Conrad*, Thames and Hudson Literary Lives series. London: Thames and Hudson, 1988.

Sherry, Norman. *Conrad's Eastern World*. Cambridge: Cambridge University Press, 1966.

Sherry, Norman. *Conrad's Western World*. Cambridge: Cambridge University Press, 1971. Extract in Kimbrough (1977), pp.25–32.

Tennant, Roger. *Joseph Conrad: A Biography*. London: Sheldon Press, 1981.

Watts, Cedric. *Joseph Conrad: A Literary Life*. Macmillan Literary Lives series. London: Macmillan, 1989.

Critical books

On Conrad in general

Bradbrook, M.C. *Joseph Conrad: Józef Teodor Konrad Nałęcz Korzeniowski: Poland's English Genius*. Cambridge: Cambridge University Press, 1941.

Cox, C.B. *Joseph Conrad: The Modern Imagination*. London: J.M. Dent, 1974. Extract on 'Heart of Darkness' in Bloom (1987), pp.29–43.

Crankshaw, Edward. *Joseph Conrad: Some Aspects of the Art of the Novel*. London: Bodley Head, 1936; reissued Russell and Russell, 1963; second edition, Macmillan, 1976.

Guerard, Albert J. *Conrad the Novelist*. Cambridge, Massachusetts: Harvard University Press, 1958. Extract on 'Heart of Darkness' in Kimbrough (1963), pp.122–24, 168–76; (1971), pp.122–24, 167–75; Bloom (1987), pp.5–28; Kimbrough (1988), pp.243–50; Bloom (1992), pp.17–20.

Gurko, Leo. *Joseph Conrad: Giant in Exile*. New York: Macmillan, 1962; London: Frederick Muller, 1965. Extract on 'Heart of Darkness' in Kimbrough (1963), pp.218–23; (1971), pp.196–200.

Hay, Eloise Knapp. *The Political Novels of Joseph Conrad: A Critical Study*. Chicago: University of Chicago Press, 1963.

Hoffman, Stanton de Voren. *Comedy and Form in the Fiction of Joseph Conrad*. Studies in English Literature series, vol. 49. The Hague: Mouton, 1969.

Moser, Thomas. *Joseph Conrad: Achievement and Decline*. Cambridge, Massachusetts: Harvard University Press, 1957.

Nadelhaft, Ruth L. *Joseph Conrad*. Feminist Readings series. Hemel Hempstead: Harvester Wheatsheaf, 1991.

Parry, Benita. *Conrad and Imperialism: Ideological Boundaries and Visionary Frontiers*. London: Macmillan, 1983.

Ray, Martin. *Joseph Conrad*. Modern Fiction series. London: Edward Arnold, 1993.

Said, Edward W. *Joseph Conrad and the Fiction of Autobiography*. Cambridge, Massachusetts: Harvard, 1966.

Spittles, Brian. *Joseph Conrad: Text and Context*. Writers in Their Time series. London: Macmillan, 1992.

Thorburn, David. *Conrad's Romanticism*. New Haven: Yale University Press, 1974.

Watt, Ian. *Conrad in the Nineteenth Century*. Berkeley: University of California Press, 1979; London: Chatto and Windus, 1980. Extracts under title 'Impressionism and Symbolism in "Heart of Darkness"' in Kimbrough (1988), pp. 311–36; extract of section 'Ideological Perspectives: Kurtz and the Fate of Victorian Progress' in Jordan (1996), pp. 32–47; section on 'Marlow and Henry James' in Bloom (1992), pp. 98–110.

Watts, Cedric. *Joseph Conrad*. Writers and Their Work series. Plymouth, Devon: Northcote House in association with The British Council, 1994.

On 'Heart of Darkness'

Burden, Robert. 'Heart of Darkness': *An Introduction to the Variety of Criticism*. The Critics Debate series. London: Macmillan, 1991.

Watts, Cedric. 'Heart of Darkness': *A Critical and Contextual Discussion*. Milan: Mursia, 1977.

Review/essay collections

On Conrad in general

Bloom, Harold, ed. *Marlow*. Major Literary Characters series. New York: Chelsea House, 1992.

Carabine, Keith, ed. *Joseph Conrad: Critical Assessments*. 4 vols. Robertsbridge, East Sussex: Helm Information, 1992.

Cox, C. B., ed. 'Heart of Darkness', *Nostromo* and *Under Western Eyes*: *A Casebook*. Macmillan Casebook series. London: Macmillan, 1981.

Jordan, Elaine, ed. *Joseph Conrad*. Macmillan New Casebooks series. London: Macmillan, 1996.

Mudrick, Marvin, ed. *Conrad: A Collection of Critical Essays*. Twentieth Century Views series. Englewood Cliffs, New Jersey: Prentice-Hall, 1966.

Murfin, Ross C., ed. *Conrad Revisited: Essays for the Eighties*. Alabama: University of Alabama Press, 1985, pp. 31–50.

Sherry, Norman, ed. *Conrad: The Critical Heritage*. The Critical Heritage series. London: Routledge and Kegan Paul, 1973.

Sherry, Norman, ed. *Joseph Conrad: A Commemoration: Papers from the 1974 International Conference on Conrad*. London: Macmillan, 1976.

Stallman, R.W., ed. *The Art of Joseph Conrad: A Critical Symposium*. Michigan: Michigan State University Press, 1960.

Stape, J.H., ed. *The Cambridge Companion to Joseph Conrad*. Cambridge Companions to Literature series. Cambridge: Cambridge University Press, 1996.

On 'Heart of Darkness'

Bloom, Harold, ed. *Joseph Conrad's 'Heart of Darkness'*. Modern Critical Interpretations series. New York: Chelsea House, 1987.

Dean, Leonard F., ed. *Joseph Conrad's 'Heart of Darkness': Backgrounds and Criticisms*. Englewood Cliffs, New Jersey: Prentice-Hall, 1960.

Kimbrough, Robert, ed. *Joseph Conrad: 'Heart of Darkness': An Authoritative Text, Background and Sources, Criticism*. Norton Critical Edition series. New York: Norton, 1988: 1st edn (1963); 2nd edn (1971); 3rd edn (1988).

Murfin, Ross C., ed. *Joseph Conrad: 'Heart of Darkness': A Case Study in Contemporary Criticism*. New York: Bedford Books of St. Martin's Press (1989).

Other books that discuss Conrad and 'Heart of Darkness'

Page references are given to the most extended discussions of 'Heart of Darkness' in the books below, but useful comments on Conrad's novel may be found on other pages of these books – use the book's index, where it has one, to check for further references.

Achebe, Chinua. *Hopes and Impediments: Selected Essays 1965–1987*. London: Heinemann, 1988, pp.1–13.

Brantlinger, Patrick. *Rule of Darkness: British Literature and Imperialism 1830–1914*. Ithaca, NY: Cornell University Press, 1988, pp.255–74.

Brooks, Peter. *Reading for the Plot: Design and Intention in Narrative*. Cambridge, Massachusetts: Harvard University Press, 1984; 1992. Extract on 'Heart of Darkness' in Bloom (1987), pp.105–27; Jordan (1996), pp.67–86.

Cunningham, Valentine. *In the Reading Gaol: Postmodernity, Texts, and History*. Oxford: Blackwell, 1994, pp.227–58.

Guetti, James. *The Limits of Metaphor: A Study of Melville, Conrad, and Faulkner*. Ithaca, NY: Columbia University Press, 1967, pp.46–68.

Hawthorn. Jeremy. *Joseph Conrad: Language and Fictional Self-Consciousness*. London: Edward Arnold, 1979, pp.7–36.

Leavis, F.R. *The Great Tradition: George Eliot; Henry James; Joseph Conrad*. London: Chatto and Windus, 1948; Harmondsworth: Penguin Books in association with Chatto and Windus, 1972, pp.200–10.

London, Bette. *The Appropriated Voice: Narrative Authority in Conrad, Forster, and Woolf*. Ann Arbor: University of Michigan Press, 1990, pp. 29–58.

Meisel, Perry. *The Myth of the Modern: A Study of British Literature and Criticism after 1850*. New Haven: Yale University Press, 1987, pp. 229–45.

Miller, Christopher L. *Blank Darkness: Africanist Discourse in French* (Chicago: University of Chicago Press, 1985), pp. 169–83. Extract under title 'The Discoursing Heart: Conrad's "Heart of Darkness"' in Jordan (1996), pp. 87–102.

Miller, J. Hillis. *Poets of Reality: Six Twentieth-Century Writers*. Cambridge, Massachusetts: The Belknap Press of Harvard University Press, 1966, pp. 6–8, 13–39.

Raskin, Jonah. *The Mythology of Imperialism: Rudyard Kipling; Joseph Conrad; E. M. Forster; D. H. Lawrence and Joyce Cary*. New York: Random House, 1971, pp. 172–83.

Said, Edward W. *Culture and Imperialism*. London: Chatto and Windus, 1993, pp. 24–29, 32–34, 79–82, 198–201.

Showalter, Elaine. *Sexual Anarchy: Gender and Culture at the Fin de Siècle*. London: Bloomsbury, 1991, pp. 95–104.

Todorov, Tzvetan. *Les Genres du Discours*. Paris: Seuil, 1978, pp. 172–83.

Torgovnick, Marianna. *Gone Primitive: Savage Intellects, Modern Lives*. Chicago: University of Chicago Press, 1990, pp. 141–58.

Trilling, Lionel. *Beyond Culture: Essays on Literature and Learning*. London: Secker and Warburg, 1966; Harmondsworth: Penguin in association with Secker and Warburg, 1967. Extract on 'Heart of Darkness', under title 'Kurtz, Hero of the Spirit', in Cox (1981), pp. 63–64.

Trilling, Lionel. *Sincerity and Authenticity: The Charles Eliot Norton Lectures 1969–1970*. London: Oxford University Press, 1972; with corrections, 1974, pp. 106–11. Extract on 'Heart of Darkness' in Carabine (1992), vol. 2, pp. 326–29.

Williams, Raymond. *Reading and Criticism*. Man and Society series. London: Frederick Muller, 1950, pp. 75–86.

Raymond Williams. *The English Novel from Dickens to Lawrence*. London: Chatto and Windus, 1970, pp. 144–47.

Reviews

Anon., the *Athenaeum*, 2 (20 December 1902), p. 824. Reprinted in Sherry (1973), pp. 137–39. Ehrsam (1969), p. 326, attributes this review to A. J. Dawson.

Anon., 'Five Novels', *The Nation*, 76:1980 (11 June 1903), pp. 477–79. Ehrsam (1969) attributes this review to Annie Logan.

Clifford, Hugh. 'The Art of Mr. Joseph Conrad'. *The Spectator*, 89 (29 November 1902), pp. 827–28; reprinted in *Living Age*, 236 (10 January 1903), pp. 120–23; extract in Dean (1960), pp. 144–45.

Cooper, Frederic Taber. 'The Sustained Effort and Some Recent Novels', *The Bookman*, New York, 18 (November 1903), pp. 309–14.

Garnett, Edward, 'Mr. Conrad's New Book', *The Academy and Literature*, 63 (6 December 1902), pp. 606–07. Reprinted in Sherry (1973), pp. 131–33.

Masefield, John. 'Deep Sea Yarns'. *The Speaker*, 7 (31 January 1903), p.442. Reprinted in Dean (1960), pp.148–49.

Essays in Journals and Books

General essays on Conrad

Humphries, Reynold. 'The Discourse of Colonialism: Its Meaning and Relevance for Conrad's Fiction'. *Conradiana: A Journal of Joseph Conrad Studies*. 21:2 (Summer 1989), pp.107–33.

Leavis, F.R. 'Revaluations (XIV): Joseph Conrad'. *Scrutiny: A Quarterly Review*, 10:1 (June and October 1941), pp.22–50, 157–81. Extract in Carabine (1992), vol. 1, pp.607–25. Slightly revised version in Leavis (1948; 1972), pp.200–57.

Tanner, Tony. '"Gnawed Bones" and "Artless Tales" – Eating and Narrative in Conrad'. Sherry (1976), pp.17–36.

Essays on 'Heart of Darkness'

Achebe, Chinua. 'An Image of Africa'. *Massachusetts Review*, 18:4 (Winter 1977), pp.782–94. Revised version, under title 'An Image of Africa: Racism in Conrad's 'Heart of Darkness" in Achebe (1988), pp.1–13; Kimbrough (1988), pp.251–62; Carabine (1992), vol. 2, pp.393–404.

Blake, Susan L. 'Racism and the Classics: Teaching "Heart of Darkness"'. *College Language Association Journal*, 25:4 (1982), pp.396–404.

Bode, Rita. '"They . . . Should Be Out of It": The Women of "Heart of Darkness"'. *Conradiana: A Journal of Joseph Conrad Studies*, 26:1 (1994), pp.20–34.

Brantlinger, Patrick. '"Heart of Darkness": Anti-Imperialism, Racism, or Impressionism?'. *Criticism*, 27:4 (Fall 1985), pp.363–85. Reprinted in Carabine (1992), vol. 2, pp.428–46; in revised form in Brantlinger (1988), pp.255–74.

Brooks, Peter, translated into French by Vincent Giroud. 'Un Rapport Illisible: "Coeur des Ténèbres"'. *Poétique: Revue de Théorie et D'Analyse*, 11:44 (1980). Revised version in Brooks (1992).

Burden, Robert. 'Conrad's "Heart of Darkness": the Critique of Imperialism and the Post-Colonial Reader', *L'Epoque Conradienne*, 18 (1992), pp.63–83.

Carey-Webb, Allen. '"Heart of Darkness", *Tarzan*, and the "Third World": Canons and Encounters in World Literature, English 109'. *College Literature*, 19/20:3/1, pp.121–41.

Commager, Henry Steele, Jr. 'The Problem of Evil in "Heart of Darkness", Bowdoin Prize Essay, Harvard University, 1972.

D'Avanzo, Mario. 'Conrad's Motley as an Organizing Metaphor', *College Language Association*, 9 (March 1966), pp.289–91. Reprinted in Kimbrough (1971), pp.251–53.

Evans, Robert O. 'Conrad's Underworld', *Modern Fiction Studies*, 2:2 (May 1956), pp.56–62. Reprinted in Kimbrough (1963), pp.189–95; (1971), pp.218–23.

Feder, Lilian. 'Marlow's Descent into Hell', *Nineteenth-Century Fiction*, 9:4

(March 1955), pp. 280–92. Reprinted in Kimbrough (1963), pp. 186–89; (1971), pp. 181–84.

Fincham, Gail. 'Living under the Sign of Contradiction: Self and Other in Conrad's "Heart of Darkness"', *The English Academy Review*, 7 (1990), pp. 1–12.

Gross, Seymour. 'A Further Note on the Function of the Frame in "Heart of Darkness"'. *Modern Fiction Studies*, 3 (1957), pp. 167–70. Reprinted in Kimbrough (1963), pp. 199–202; (1971), pp. 227–29.

Guetti, James. '"Heart of Darkness" and the Failure of The Imagination'. *Sewanee Review*, 73:3 (Summer 1965), pp. 488–502. Extract in Cox (1981), pp. 65–77; revised version in Guetti (1967), pp. 46–68.

Hamner, Robert. 'Colony, Nationhood and Beyond: Third World Writers and Critics Contend with Joseph Conrad'. *World Literature Written in English*, 23:1 (1984), pp.108–16. Reprinted in Carabine (1992), vol. 2, pp. 419–27.

Harris, Wilson. 'The Frontier on Which "Heart of Darkness" Stands'. *Research on African Literatures*, 12 (1981), pp. 86–92. Reprinted in Kimbrough (1988), pp. 262–68.

Hawkins, Hunt. 'Conrad's Critique of Imperialism in "Heart of Darkness"'. *PMLA: Publications of Modern Language Association of America* (1979), 94, pp. 286–99.

Hawkins, Hunt. 'The Issue of Racism in "Heart of Darkness"'. *Conradiana: A Journal of Joseph Conrad Studies*, 14:3 (1982), pp. 163–71.

Hoffman, Stanton de Voren. 'The Hole in the Bottom of the Pail: Comedy and Theme in "Heart of Darkness"'. *Studies in Short Fiction*, 2 (1965), pp. 113–23. Expanded version in Hoffman (1969), pp. 16–51.

Huggan, Graham. 'Anxieties of Influence: Conrad in the Caribbean'. *Commonwealth*, 11 (1988), pp.1–12. Reprinted in Carabine (1992), vol. 2, pp. 447–59.

Hyland, Peter. 'The Little Woman in "Heart of Darkness"'. *Conradiana: A Journal of Joseph Conrad Studies*, 20 (1988), pp. 1–11.

Joffe, Phil. 'Africa and Joseph Conrad's "Heart of Darkness"': The "Bloody Racist" (?) as Demystifier of Imperialism'. Carabine, Keith, Knowles, Owen, Krajka, Wieslaw, eds., *Conrad's Literary Career*. Conrad: Eastern and Western Perspectives, vol. 1; East European Monographs series no. 353. Lublin: Maria Curie-Skłodowska University, 1992, distributed by Columbia University Press, New York, pp. 75–90.

Kinkead-Weekes, Mark. '"Heart of Darkness" and the Third World Writer'. *Sewanee Review*, 98:1 (1990), pp. 31–49. Revised version in Carabine (1992), vol. 2, pp. 468–80.

Kuesgen, Reinhardt. 'Conrad and Achebe: Aspects of the Novel'. *World Literature Written in English*, 24:1 (1984), pp. 27–33.

McClure, John A. 'The Rhetoric of Restraint in "Heart of Darkness"'. *Nineteenth-Century Fiction*, 32:3 (1977), pp. 310–26.

Meisel, Perry. 'Decentring "Heart of Darkness"', *Modern Language Studies*, 8:3 (1978), p. 24. Revised version in Meisel (1987), pp. 235–46.

Miller, J. Hillis. '"Heart of Darkness" Revisited' in Murfin (1985), pp. 31–50.

Reid, Stephen A. 'The "Unspeakable Rites" in "Heart of Darkness"'. *Modern Fiction Studies*, 9:4 (Winter 1963–4), pp. 347–56. Reprinted in Mudrick (1966), pp. 45–54.

Robertson, P.J.M. '*Things Fall Apart* and "Heart of Darkness": A Creative Dialogue'. *International Fiction Review*, 7:2 (1980), pp. 106–11.

Sarvan, C.P. 'Racism and the "Heart of Darkness"'. *The International Fiction Review*, 7 (1980), pp. 6–10. Reprinted Kimbrough (1988), pp. 280–88.

Sedlak, Valerie M. '"A World of Their Own": Narrative Distortion and Fictive Exemplification in the Portrayal of Women in "Heart of Darkness"', *College Literature Association Journal*, 32:4 (June 1989), pp. 443–65.

Shetty, Sandya. '"Heart of Darkness": Out of Africa Some New Thing Never Comes'. *Journal of Modern Literature*, 15:4 (1989), pp. 461–74.

Singh, Frances B. 'The Colonialistic Bias of "Heart of Darkness"'. *Conradiana*, 10 (1978), pp. 41–54. Reprinted in Kimbrough (1988), pp. 268–80.

Smith, Johanna M. '"Too Beautiful Altogether": Patriarchal Ideology in "Heart of Darkness"' in Murfin (1989), pp. 179–95.

Stewart, Garrett. 'Lying as Dying in "Heart of Darkness"'. *PMLA: Publications of the Modern Language Association*, 95:3 (1980), pp. 319–31. Reprinted in Kimbrough (1988), pp. 358–74; Bloom (1992), pp. 111–27.

Straus, Nina Pelikan. 'The Exclusion of the Intended from Secret Sharing in "Heart of Darkness"'. *Novel: A Forum on Fiction*, 20:2 (Winter 1987), pp. 123–37. Reprinted in Carabine (1992), vol. 2, pp. 349–63; Jordan (1996), pp. 48–66.

Thale, Jerome. 'Marlow's Quest', *University of Toronto Quarterly*, 24 (July 1955), pp. 351–58. Reprinted in Dean (1960), pp. 159–66; Kimbrough (1963), pp. 180–86; (1971), pp. 176–81; Carabine (1992), vol. 2, pp. 318–25.

Todorov, Tzvetan. 'Connaissance du vide', *Nouvelle Revue de Psychanalyse*, 11 (Spring 1975), pp. 145–54. Reprinted in Todorov (1978), pp. 172–83; translation by Walter C. Putnam III, as 'Knowledge in the Void: "Heart of Darkness"'. *Conradiana*, 21:3 (1989), pp. 161–81. Translation in Carabine (1992), vol. 2, pp. 161–81.

Watt, Ian. 'Conrad's "Heart of Darkness" and the Critics'. *North Dakota Quarterly*, 57:3 (Summer 1989), pp. 5–15.

Watts, Cedric. '"A Bloody Racist": About Achebe's View of Conrad'. *Yearbook of English Studies*, 13 (1983), pp. 196–209. Reprinted in Carabine (1992), vol. 2, pp. 405–18.

Zhuwarara, R. '"Heart of Darkness" Revisited: The African Response'. *Kunapipi*, 16:3 (1994), pp. 21–37.

Essays on other topics that discuss 'Heart of Darkness'

Achebe, Chinua. 'Viewpoint'. *Times Literary Supplement*, 4010 (1 February 1980), p. 113.

Achebe, Chinua. 'The Song of Ourselves'. *New Statesman and Society*, 3:87 (9 February 1990), pp. 30–32. Also published as 'African Literature as Restoration of Celebration', *Kunapipi*, 12:2 (1990), pp. 1–10.

Ruthven, K.K. 'The Savage God: Conrad and Lawrence'. *Critical Quarterly*, 10:1/2 (Spring and Summer 1968), pp.41–46. Extract in Cox (1981), pp.78–84.

Said, Edward W. 'Intellectuals in the Post-Colonial World'. *Salmagundi*, 70-1 (1986), pp.44–64.

Trilling, Lionel. 'On the Modern Element in Modern Literature'. *Partisan Review*. 28 (January–February 1961), pp.9–35. Reprinted with slight revisions as 'On the Teaching of Modern Literature' in Trilling (1965), pp.19–41.

Introductions

Guerard, Albert J. 'Introduction', Joseph Conrad, 'Heart of Darkness' *and* 'The Secret Sharer'. New York: Signet, 1950.

Zabel, Morton Dauwen. 'Introduction', Joseph Conrad, *Youth*. New York: Doubleday Anchor, 1959.

Discussions of 'Heart of Darkness' and *Apocalypse Now*

Bogue, Ronald L. 'The Heartless Darkness of *Apocalypse Now*'. *The Georgia Review*, 35:3 (Fall 1981), pp.611–26.

Cahir, Linda Costanzo. 'Narratological Parallels in Joseph Conrad's "Heart of Darkness" and Francis Ford Coppola's *Apocalypse Now*'. *Literature/Film Quarterly*, 20:3 (1992), pp.181–87.

Costanzo, W.W. 'Conrad and Coppola'. *Joseph Conrad Today*, 5:1 (October 1979), pp.129–32.

Deltcheva, Roumiana. 'Destination Classified: On the Transformation of Spatial Forms in Applying the Narrative Text to Film (the Case of "Heart of Darkness" and *Apocalypse Now*)'. *Canadian Review of Comparative Literature/Revue Canadienne de Littérature Comparée*, 23:3 (September 1996), pp.753–64.

Dorall, E.N. 'Conrad and Coppola: Different Centres of Darkness'. *Southeast Asian Review of English*, 1:1 (December 1980), pp.19–27. Reprinted in Kimbrough (1988), pp.301–11.

Gillespie, Gerald. 'Savage Places Revisited: Conrad's "Heart of Darkness" and Coppola's *Apocalypse Now*'. *The Comparatist: Journal of the Southern Comparative Literature Association*, 9 (May 1985), pp.69–88.

Hagen, William M. '"Heart of Darkness" and the Process of *Apocalypse Now*'. *Conradiana: A Journal of Joseph Conrad Studies*, 13:1 (1981), pp.45–54. Reprinted in Kimbrough (1988), pp.293–301.

Hagen, William M. '*Apocalypse Now* (1979): Joseph Conrad and the Television War', in Rollins, Peter C., ed., *Hollywood as Historian: American Film in a Cultural Context*. Lexington: University of Kentucky Press, 1983, pp.230–45.

Jacobs, Diane. 'Coppola Films Conrad in Vietnam' in Michael Klein and Gillian Parker, eds., *The English Novel and the Movies*. New York: Ungar, 1981, pp.211–17.

Kutcha, Todd M. 'Framing "the Horror": Voice and Voice-Over in "Heart of Darkness" and *Apocalypse Now'*. *Studies in the Humanities*, 21:1 (June 1994), pp. 45–59.

LaBrasca, Robert. 'Two Visions of "The Horror"'. *Madison Press Connection*. (17 November 1979), no page numbers available. Revised version in Kimbrough (1988), pp. 288–93.

Laskowsky, Henry J. '"Heart of Darkness": A Primer for the Holocaust'. *Virginia Quarterly Review: A National Journal of Literature and Discussion*, 58:1 (Winter 1982), pp. 93–110.

London, Bette. *The Appropriated Voice: Narrative Authority in Conrad, Forster, and Woolf*. Ann Arbor: University of Michigan Press, 1990, pp. 16–18.

Lothe, Jakob. 'From Conrad to Coppola to Steiner'. *The Conradian*, 6:3 (September 1981), pp. 10–14.

Nixon, Rob. *London Calling*. Oxford: Oxford University Press, 1992, pp. 96–98.

Pinsker, Sanford. '"Heart of Darkness" through Contemporary Eyes, or What's Wrong with *Apocalypse Now?'*. *Conradiana: A Journal of Joseph Conrad Studies*, 13:1 (1981), pp. 55–58.

Showalter (1991), pp. 99–104.

Sivaramakrishnan, Arvind. '"Entre Deux Rivières": "Heart of Darkness", *Apocalpyse Now*, and an Indian Predicament', *Panjab University Research Bulletin (Arts)*, 24:1 (1993), pp. 1–12.

Stewart, Garrett. 'Coppola's Conrad: The Repetitions of Complicity'. *Critical Inquiry*, 7:3 (Spring 1981), pp. 455–74.

Sundelson, David. 'Dance Macabre'. *Conradiana: A Journal of Joseph Conrad Studies*, 13:1 (1981), pp. 41–44.

Watson, Wallace. 'Willard as Narrator: A Critique and a Modest Proposal', *Conradiana: A Journal of Joseph Conrad Studies*, 13:1 (1981), pp. 35–40.

Whaley, Preston. '"Heart of Darkness" and *Apocalypse Now*: Reflectors of a Precarious Social Knowledge' in Bonnie and Hans Braendlin, eds., *Authority and Transgression in Literature and Film*. Gainesville, Florida: University Press of Florida, 1996, pp. 111–26.

Wilmington, Mike. 'Worth the Wait: *Apocalypse Now'*. *Madison Press Connection* (19 October 1979), no page numbers available. Reprinted in Kimbrough (1988), pp. 285–88.

Worthy, Kim. 'Emissaries of Difference: Conrad, Coppola, and Hearts of Darkness'. *Women's Studies: An Interdisciplinary Journal*, 25:2 (January 1996), pp. 153–67.

Nicolas Roeg's film of 'Heart of Darkness', with John Malkovich as Kurtz and Tim Roth as Marlow, came out in 1994. For a review, see: Hassell, Graham. 'Drumming up the Dark Continent'. *Times Literary Supplement*, 4775, 7 October 1994, p. 27.

ACKNOWLEDGEMENTS

The editor and publishers wish to thank the following for their permission to reprint copyright material: Chatto and Windus (for material from *The Great Tradition: George Eliot; Henry James; Joseph Conrad* and *Conrad in the Nineteenth Century* and *Culture and Imperialism*); Harvard University Press (for material from *Conrad the Novelist* and *Poets of Reality: Six Twentieth-Century Writers* and *Reading for the Plot: Design and Intention in Narrative*); University of Chicago Press (for material from *The Political Novels of Joseph Conrad: A Critical Study* and *Blank Darkness: Africanist Discourse in French*); Heinemann (for material from 'An Image of Africa: Racism in Conrad's *Heart of Darkness*'); Macmillan (for material from *Conrad and Imperialism: Ideological Boundaries and Visionary Frontiers*); Blackwell (for material from *In the Reading Gaol: Postmodernity, Texts, and History*).

There are instances where we have been unable to trace or contact copyright holders before our printing deadline. If notified, the publisher will be pleased to acknowledge the use of copyright material.

The editor is most grateful to his wife, Angela Tredell, and to her colleagues in East Sussex Library Services, for their speed and efficiency in obtaining copies of the many books and essays consulted in the preparation of this Guide.

Nicolas Tredell teaches American and English literature, art history, and cultural and film studies for Sussex University. He has contributed widely to journals in the UK and the USA, and his recent books include *Uncancelled Challenge: The Work of Raymond Williams, The Critical Decade: Culture in Crisis, Conversations with Critics, Caute's Confrontations: The Novels of David Caute* and the Icon Critical Guides to *The Great Gatsby* and *Great Expectations*.

INDEX

Columbia Critical Guides Series